THE LEARNING GAME
Arguments for an Education Revolution

Michael Barber

VICTOR GOLLANCZ
LONDON

First published in Great Britain 1996
as a simultaneous hardback and paperback
by Victor Gollancz
An imprint of the Cassell Group
Wellington House, 125 Strand, London WC2R 0BB

A catalogue record for this book is
available from the British Library.

ISBN 0 575 06235 5 hb
ISBN 0 575 06364 5 pb

Typeset by Rowland Phototypesetting Ltd
Bury St Edmunds, Suffolk
Printed and bound in Great Britain by
Mackays of Chatham plc, Chatham, Kent

99 98 97 96   5 4 3 2 1

For Karen

Contents

Preface

I have set out in this book to create a new vision of education. The programme is intentionally an ambitious one: its twin goals are clear. Within the foreseeable future, Britain will need an education service which is capable of providing higher standards, to match those anywhere on earth, and which simultaneously promotes and supports a thriving, diverse, liberal democracy. Put another way, we want to match the Asian tiger economies in terms of performance while maintaining and renewing our liberal traditions.

In envisioning (to use an American term which says exactly what I want to say) an education system that might meet these goals, I have drawn on a wide range of research and analysis in education and related fields. I have also set out to question some of the basic assumptions which have underpinned education thinking in the twentieth century and which, in my view, have so often limited the search for policy solutions to our educational problems. In particular, I have consciously challenged much of both old-left and new-right thinking, since neither seems to me capable of matching up to the challenges ahead of us.

I have, in short, attempted to use my imagination. This may, to some traditionalists, seem unscholarly. In my view, it is essential for people in academic positions to link their knowledge of research, which in social science is always limited because it refers to the past, to imaginative thinking about the future. If academics, who have the privilege of freedom of thought and of not being held to account for their views, do not think boldly about the future, who will?

The reader will, of course, decide how far I have succeeded in achieving these objectives. Suffice to say here that, when faced with the choice, I have erred on the side of recklessness rather than caution in the hope that I can provoke debate and further radical thinking. Perhaps as a result of this approach I should describe *The Learning Game* – in Mark Twain's words about *Tom Sawyer* – as 'mostly a true book with some stretchers'.

There are many people I should thank. Ideas often emerge at the most unlikely moments following sometimes fleeting conversations. I have met and discussed education with literally thousands of people over the last five years or so and I am indebted to many of them for their inspiration and insight. I cannot thank them all personally, but a few stand out. David Pitt-Watson, a lifelong friend, does not work in the field of education, but has one of the most incisive and inventive minds I have ever come across. Every conversation I have had with him about my work has left me with new insights and new inspiration.

Conversations with Tim Brighouse, the Chief Education Officer of Birmingham, have had a similar effect on me. Tim has many friends in the education service and an incomparable record of achievement as an educational administrator. Here I want to pay tribute to his remarkable ability to generate new ideas and new ways of promoting the ideals to which he has devoted his career.

A number of others have made important contributions to my thinking on the themes in this book: Alan Evans, now of the School of Education in Cardiff, and my distinguished predecessor as Education Officer of the NUT; David Milliband, with whom I have debated some of the central ideas; Geoff Mulgan of DEMOS; Peter Mortimore, Director of the Institute of Education in London where I have the pleasure of working; Kate Myers, Pam Sammons and Louise Stoll, also colleagues at the Institute; and Tim Denning, Gerry Gough, Jim Graham and particularly Mike Johnson with whom I enjoyed a productive research partnership during my two years in Keele. Patricia Rowan, Editor, and Bob Doe, Deputy Editor, of the *Times Education Supplement* have enabled me through my monthly column to be in constant dialogue with educators across the country.

I also want to pay tribute to the many heads and teachers from whom I have taken inspiration. I try to visit a school, on average, at least once a week, and many of my visits have prompted thoughts and ideas. I would particularly pick out from those visits the inspiration I have gained from my association with Pat Collarbone, headteacher of Haggerston School in Hackney and three former members of her staff, each of whom have moved on to even greater things: Enda Cullen, Maggie Farrar and David Owen; from my meetings with Janet Warwick, the transformative headteacher of Rhyn Park School in Shropshire; from my association with Graeme Arnold and Ronnie Channer at Adams School, Wem; from the time spent in the three schools in the Two Towns Project in Stoke-on-Trent; and from discussions over the years with Cynthia Thumwood, head of Hanover Primary School in Islington, which my youngest daughter attended.

Three people have been closely involved in turning the book into a reality. Gina Pollinger, my agent, sprang the idea on me three years ago and since then has set standards which I can only strive to achieve; Sean Magee at Victor Gollancz has been supportive and encouraging throughout; and Tanya Kreisky has prepared the manuscript with her usual care and insight. We have now worked together on five books, and I am indebted to her for not only word-processing the text, but also correcting the many infelicities of style. Her sense of humour and a shared lack of respect for Arsenal football club have been the essential ingredients of our successful working partnership.

Needless to say, none of the people I have mentioned can be held culpable for any of the content of the book, for which I take full responsibility.

Finally, I owe an incalculable debt to my family – Karen, Naomi, Anja and Alys – who have put up with my overwork, bouts of irritability and occasional stubbornness. They, too, provide me with a source of inspiration.

Abbreviations

ATL	Association of Teachers and Lecturers
CPS	Centre for Policy Studies
DES	Department of Education and Science, now DfEE
DfE	Department for Education, since 1995 DfEE
DfEE	Department for Education and Employment
DTI	Department of Trade and Industry
ERA	Education Reform Act
GCSE	General Certificate of Secondary Education
GMS	Grant Maintained Status
GNVQ	General National Vocational Qualifications
ILEA	Inner London Education Authority
HMCI	Her Majesty's Chief Inspector
HMI	Her Majesty's Inspectors
LMS	Local Management of Schools
NAHT	National Association Head Teachers
NASUWT	National Association of Schoolmasters and Union of Women Teachers
NCC	National Curriculum Council
NCVQ	National Council for Vocational Qualifications
NUT	National Union of Teachers
OFSTED	Office for Standards in Education
PAT	Professional Association of Teachers
SCAA	School Curriculum and Assessment Authority
SCDC	School Curriculum and Development Committee
SEAC	School Examination and Assessment Council
SHA	Secondary Heads' Association
STRB	School Teachers' Review Body
TES	*Times Educational Supplement*
TGAT	Task Group on Assessment and Testing

PART ONE

The Challenge

1 · Crisis? What Crisis?

> We cannot face the 21st century inured in those values of
> the 20th century that failed to serve us well as a global
> neighbourhood; the values ... that will yet make this country
> remembered as both the best of times and the worst of times
> ... the best of times for a few, the worst of times for many.
>
> Sir Shridath Ramphal

An Awesome Destiny

The problems facing people, not only in this country but across the globe, on the edge of the new millennium are of a staggering magnitude. To the young people currently in schools will fall the task of solving them. The argument for a dramatic improvement in the performance of schools in this country is that simple – and that complicated.

Walk along the Strand in central London late at night, or early in the morning. There is Simpson's, the classically English restaurant where even a bowtie is considered too frivolous. There is the Savoy, with all its polished brass properly faded to show the age and tradition of the place, and its cool, marbled comfort. And in every shop doorway, even in the depths of winter, homeless people are huddled together trying to sleep. There is no escaping the fact that there are many more beggars on the streets of London now than there were a decade ago. They will not go away, however often John Major tells them to do so. Similar contrasts are evident on the ocean front in Santa Monica, California and in the squares of the Latin Quarter in Paris. It is increasingly apparent that in even the most prosperous societies on earth, there are growing numbers who are becoming alienated, and in some cases disaffected, in spite of the immense economic progress made in the late twentieth century. The homeless people in the shop doorways on the Strand are the most visible evidence of a society which is not only grotesquely inequitable but also dangerously unstable. The terrifying images of some of America's worst urban areas beckon.

The inequitable distribution of wealth within prosperous societies represents an immense challenge, yet compared to global inequalities it pales into insignificance. As the *Independent on Sunday* reported on 21 July 1996, 'There are now 447 dollar billionaires and their wealth exceeds the combined annual incomes of half the world's people.' To make matters worse we now have the dubious privilege of being able to sit drinking tea in a comfortable living room while watching television pictures of Rwandan bodies floating into Lake Victoria, and witnessing the inhabitants of refugee camps as populous as Birmingham fight over the paltry food aid that western countries have scraped together. Before the Rwandans it was the Kurds, the Sudanese, the Bangladeshis, the Ethiopians. When the Bosnians – at the heart of Europe – were added to that fearful catalogue, the same cruelty, starvation and destruction were happening right here, just beyond the other end of the Channel tunnel. European society was shocked to the core, but it was still unable to act effectively. Perhaps at last it has begun to dawn on us that the inequalities of wealth and power across the globe are not just a matter of conscience; they are a direct threat to the peace and prosperity of the otherwise triumphant western democracies. These problems are made immensely more complicated by the rapid growth of population in the world's most poverty-stricken regions, especially Africa, and by the fact that some of the poorest societies on earth possess nevertheless large stocks of the most effective instruments of destruction mankind has been able to devise.

This raises another apparently intractable problem that will face the successor generation. The new world order, heralded with such optimism by George Bush as recently as 1990, turns out to be a dangerous place. It poses problems to which as yet we simply do not have solutions. Take Bosnia for example: for four years the best diplomats in the western world made countless attempts to solve its complex puzzle, but each time returned home shaking their heads. The 'solution', meanwhile, to the Somalian problem turned out to be to pull out not only the American soldiers but also the television cameras. That way we could stop worrying about Somalia's slide into anarchy. Liberia, similarly anarchic, is now famous only for having exported the world's best footballer. The post-war system of managing conflict was forty years in the making. The next generation faces problems of even greater complexity and must solve them much more quickly if catastrophe is to be averted.

Meanwhile the revolutions in information technology, communications and management continue apace. While they have immense creative potential, they also bring problems. How will work be defined and organised once the information superhighway is in place? How will people find security, which is a universal human need, in a world of short-term jobs and bewilderingly rapid change? And if work is becoming something for the young – and there are talented, experienced people of forty-five who believe they may never work again – what will people do in the half of their lives after they retire? These questions too will need answers in the decades to come.

As if all of that were not sufficient, there is genuine concern about the survival of the planet as a home fit for human beings, never mind heroes. The present generation has perhaps begun to identify the problems of the global environment more clearly. It has identified the holes in the ozone layer, the destruction of rainforests and the sensitivity of the ecological balance. It has begun to inform the globe's inhabitants about them. It may even have begun to recognise that unfettered materialism is a juggernaut likely to career out of control. The next generation will inherit the task of bringing that juggernaut under control while managing the difficult social consequences of doing so. Compounding these problems is the consciousness that, in our endeavours to find solutions, we might fail. We, ourselves, might be responsible for our own destruction.

Taken together, these problems present a set of challenges more profound than any in human history. Of course in the past there were scourges of disease, famine and conflict, but until relatively recently these were often considered beyond the power of human solution: they were acts of God. No one until the mid-twentieth century believed, or even pretended, that mankind had the power to shape its destiny, or to destroy it. This generation and its successors cannot pass the buck. It is their destiny to inherit a unique combination of unparalleled power and terrible responsibility.

A well-balanced, thoughtful society would surely give the highest imaginable priority to ensuring that its young people were well prepared for this awesome destiny. It would examine the upbringing and education provided for its young, and ask whether the arrangements were equal to the task. If this society decided the present arrangements were inadequate, then it would surely promote creative thought about how they might be improved. In doing so, it would seek solutions not only in the past, but also in the farthest reaches of analysis and imagination. In choosing solutions, the need to take risks, to be radical and to invest time, money and energy even at the expense of present comfort would be recognised because everyone would be conscious that the risk of doing nothing would be infinitely greater.

This is the justification for a radical programme of education reform. Perhaps it ought also to be the justification for a much wider agenda of social reform including an examination of the role of the family, the Church and other social institutions of late-twentieth-century society, though much of that lies outside the scope of this book. It was H. G. Wells who said that 'human history becomes more and more a race between education and catastrophe'. It would appear that now, three-quarters of a century later, that race is entering its final furlong.

Moral Panic or Moral Indifference?

On 25 November 1993, the United Kingdom was gripped by one of its periodic bouts of moral panic. Anxiety about the state of the nation's youth, though never far from the surface, ebbs and flows. That day it flowed with a vengeance. The tabloids were in their own hypocritical element. Even the *Guardian*, steeped in liberalism and conscious of the need to avoid cheap populism, devoted a leading article, three whole inside pages and an editorial to the outcome of one court case in Preston, Lancashire. The *Independent* and *The Times* gave the story similar priority. One American magazine headlined its article on the case 'A Monster Society'.

Jon Venables and Robert Thompson, both then aged eleven, had been convicted of the abduction and murder of James Bulger. They had led the innocent three-year-old away from a Merseyside shopping centre in full view, as it later turned out, of the centre's closed-circuit cameras. They had dragged the screaming boy over two miles, past dozens of adults, none of whom saw fit to intervene, and then on to a railtrack at Walton where they had beaten him to death with bricks and an iron bar.

The judge, Mr Justice Morland, described the murder as a cunning and wicked act of 'unparalleled evil and barbarity'. The *Guardian* in its front-page article described the moment that the jury's verdict was handed down:

> Court No. 1 was hushed as the jury delivered its verdicts. As the Foreman said 'guilty' to the count of murder, Susan Venables, Jon's mother, cried and his father, Neil, buried his head in his hands. Jon looked at the jury wide-eyed while Robert Thompson sat impassively. His mother, Anne, was not in court ... Outside the court, a crowd of about 200 people had gathered by 6.20 pm when separate police vans drove Thompson and Venables away. There were shouts of 'Kill them' and 'Hang them' but no violence.

Sergeant Phil Roberts, one of the detectives on the case commented: 'These two are freaks who just found each other. You should not compare these two boys with other boys ... They were evil.' Possibly Sergeant Roberts was right but, on 25 November 1993, there was barely an adult in the country who felt that way. There were so many perspectives on the nightmare of the Bulger murder that virtually no adult could remain indifferent to the tragedy. First, and most obviously, there was enormous sympathy for the parents of the toddler. All parents have experienced those moments when, in a public place, their child is suddenly out of sight: the anxiety, the beating of the heart, the desperate search. Almost every parent knows the overwhelming sense of relief when the child is found. The outpouring of love as the child is swept up into the parent's arms is so strong that it almost eclipses the panic of a few moments before. The thought that the Bulger parents experienced the panic and then, instead of that outpouring, a descent into hell is unbearable.

Secondly, it was tempting to condemn the people who saw the distraught child being led away and did nothing to intervene. But, given the nature of late-twentieth-century society, how many people would have done differently? The pressures to walk on past scenes like that are immense. It can be passed off as a sibling quarrel or 'bloody kids'; it can be ignored altogether because the pressures of late-twentieth-century life often induce a numb insensitivity. Being there is one thing; feeling a sense of belonging or responsibility is another matter altogether.

Thirdly, and most terrifying of all, many parents must surely have asked themselves this question: could my child be capable of that appalling brutality? Perhaps Sergeant Roberts, and all those writers from Jean Jacques Rousseau through to A. A. Milne, were wrong. Perhaps those demons that caused Jon Venables and Robert Thompson to kill James Bulger are indeed there inside every child. As Superintendent Albert Kirby told the *Independent* on 25 November 1993: 'When their backgrounds are analysed, nothing marks them out from other boys . . . nothing identifies a potential to murder.' Perhaps even if one made every parenting decision correctly – and no one ever does – perhaps even then there would be some children over whom sooner or later the demons would gain control.

In addition to these broad human perspectives there are the professional ones: the police, social workers, teachers, priests . . . In short, on the morning of 25 November 1993 there was no escape.

Drawing out the meaning of the appalling tragedy is less straightforward. The *Guardian* argued, in its editorial that day, that the Bulger murder had triggered a national debate on 'isolation, alienation and indifference in modern Britain'. It continued:

The best memorial to Jamie would be a more serious debate about crime . . . Both sides, the structuralists (crime is caused by poverty, poor housing, etc.) and the pathologists (crime is caused by individual deviancy, irresponsibility, etc.) need to recognise that both play a part

. . . Informal social controls (family, school, church) have always been more successful than formal controls (police, courts, prison) in maintaining law and order.

The *Guardian*'s assertion notwithstanding, the crime debate that followed was overwhelmed by the shallow hysteria surrounding John Major's misguided policy thrust, 'Back to Basics', and the political response to it. Various Conservatives flailed at the informal social controls. John Patten, Secretary of State for Education from 1992 to 1994, repeatedly accused schools of being 'value-free zones'. Certain types of family – and especially single mothers – found themselves in the firing line of right-wing ministers like Peter Lilley and Michael Portillo. And the Church was under attack within hours of the Bulger judgement. On 26 November the *Guardian*'s front-page headline was 'BULGER TAUNT ANGERS CHURCH'. The article began:

> Senior churchmen last night clashed with the criminal justice Minister David Maclean, calling him 'bizarre' and 'ill-informed' after he accused the Church of remaining strangely silent for the past decade on the importance of teaching children the difference between right and wrong.

This latter accusation was consistent with John Patten's attack on schools and with the views of Nick Tate, Chief Executive of the School Curriculum and Assessment Authority who, in 1996, called for a new emphasis on teaching right and wrong and a modern Ten Commandments. Knowing the difference between right and wrong is of course important, but it is not enough. There is surely no doubt that Jon Venables and Robert Thompson knew that what they were doing was wrong. The central issue is why they chose to do what they knew was wrong. 'They were', in the words of Jonathan Foster writing in the *Independent*, 'two bored truants when they met James, sagging off [sic] school because they were no good at lessons, bored because the excitement of shoplifting soon diminishes.' Chillingly, the *Independent* concluded its description of the two boys by saying that they had 'nothing in common except a pact in underachievement'.

However, in this country at least, moral panic is rapidly followed by moral indifference. Once the torrent of outrage has passed, British society reverts to its favourite pastime of looking the other way. In the first section of this chapter the case was made for a balanced and thoughtful society to rethink the upbringing and education of young people. It has not happened yet because British society appears too often to be neither balanced nor thoughtful. Recently, I overheard a conversation in an Islington café which seemed to sum up the new indifference. The subject was shopping and a woman said to her companion: 'I prefer to shop at Tesco. You don't get children there – only normal people.'

As if to compound my anxiety, within a few weeks I had a conversation with a senior official in a teachers' organisation who responded to my case for an urgent improvement in standards of education by saying: 'Look, education is a lottery, it always will be.' This seemed to me to represent a combination of complacency and fatalism which transgressed the borders of responsibility. In August 1994, the *Independent on Sunday* described a dispute in a rural corner of Buckinghamshire which seemed to sum up the desire of the comfortable to cut themselves off from the growing social crisis in urban Britain:

Alistair Horne, military historian, biographer of Harold Macmillan and the relatively new owner of a £100,000 home, has taken no chances. Four rows of young trees, 20 yards apart, have been planted in the extensive grounds of his Old Vicarage in the Chiltern village of Turville. They shut off his garden from what was once the village school.

The shield was needed because, if the energetic vicar who lives next door had his way, poor children from the East End of London would come for summer holidays to the school. Mr Horne did not want to see them. Indeed, he and some of his fellow villagers went to great lengths to try and ensure that the children never got to Turville.

First there was a genteel demonstration, in which placards were waved in front of the Bishop of Oxford. Then Mr Horne wrote an article for the *Daily Mail* in which the vicar, the Rev. Paul Nicholson, appeared as a 'fervent Marxist clergyman', who was largely responsible for the malaise in idyllic Turville by disturbing its 'boring peace' with his plan to extend the school and create a 'possible eyesore in a corner of such rare and serene beauty'.

With all the fuss it is easy to forget how modest the vicar's proposals were. The red-brick school had been closed in the early 1980s, despite protests from the villagers. There were plans to turn it into a field centre or nursery, but they came to nothing. Mr Nicholson's 'Marxist' plot is to use the building as a private Montessori school for the children of local commuters and charge their parents £10,000 a year. Profits would be used to bring children from London for holidays in the six-week summer break. 'It's the Robin Hood principle, which I thoroughly approve of,' he said. 'That's what the Church is here for. We're knee deep in millionaires round here. If you can't present the gospel as helping the poor to them, what's the point of carrying on?' The summer residents would not be juvenile delinquents, crack addicts or joyriders. They would be chosen by the Children's Country Holiday Fund, a London-based charity, which had never seen anything like the outrage in Turville in all its history. 'Not in my backyard' has become a well known cry in the last generation, and the determination of communities to protect their way of life is by no means thoroughly bad: nevertheless, the Turville furore, which is still blazing in 1996, raises in perfect microcosm the question of whether the responsibilities of the wealthy to the improvement of our society go beyond simply paying tax at the higher rate.

It may be naive to do so in these circumstances, but I would still like to hope that the debate on isolation, alienation and indifference, called for in the *Guardian*, might take place. The debate should not have to wait until the wave of moral hysteria that follows a terrible crime. Nor should it allow as a premise the fatalistic belief that nothing can be done since it is this as much as anything which leads to indifference. The debate should range widely across family, school and Church as well as the criminal justice system. This book is intended to contribute to that debate, at least in relation to education and the role of learning in society. If the global agenda described in the opening section of this chapter is the first justification for radically rethinking education, the need to challenge the isolation, alienation and indifference revealed so starkly by the Bulger case is the second.

The Crisis in Education

Education policy has been the site of bitter controversy for a decade or more now. A sense of crisis pervades the education service. On the face of it this is very odd because more young people are achieving more than ever before. Indeed, if the available indicators are to be believed, there has never been a period in British history when standards have risen so fast. There was a steady improvement in achievement in the examination at age sixteen – the General Certificate of Secondary Education – for six consecutive years, which stabilised, probably temporarily, in 1995. Over 53 per cent of those entered for GCSE achieved grades A, B or C, equivalent to the old O Level passes achieved by fewer than 30 per cent of exam entrants as recently as 1987. What is more, the percentage of the age group entered for exams has also risen. There has been a steady improvement in performance at A Level too over recent years. More dramatic still is the huge rise in the numbers staying on in education after the age of sixteen. In 1979–80 only 35 per cent of sixteen- and seventeen-year-olds were in full-time education. Over the next eleven years there was a steady rise to 51 per cent. Yet by 1995 the figure had leapt to over 70 per cent. In part this was due to the recession, and of course there is no guarantee that those staying on are necessarily making effective use of their time; nevertheless in the space of a few short years we have at last become a society, like most others in the developed world, where the general expectation is that young people will remain in full-time education until the age of eighteen. Moreover, there has also been a dramatic rise in the numbers remaining in education beyond the age of eighteen. The Age Participation Index (i.e. the percentage of a given age group entering higher education) has already exceeded 30 per cent, a target that not long ago another former Secretary of State for Education, Kenneth Baker, thought would not be reached before the millennium. This startling evidence of success raises two questions. Firstly, why has no one been shouting from the rooftops about this remarkable turn around? And secondly is it appropriate to talk of crisis at all?

The answer to the first question is bound up in the complex politics of education which Chapter 2 is intended to disentangle. Suffice to say at this point that for much of the 1990s there has been a conspiracy of silence. The government has been so determined to justify its constant stream of reform that it has chosen not to celebrate the successes which stare it in the face. Instead – as John Patten did when the GCSE results were published in 1992 – it has often preferred to side with the right-wing critics of the education service who perceive every rise in levels of achievement as evidence of a decline in standards. The government has often been joined in the conspiracy by its critics. Within the confines of the party-political dogfight there is no benefit to the Opposition in giving public recognition to progress under a Tory government. Meanwhile the teacher unions, whose members have been largely responsible for the success, often fail to point it out lest it undermine their interminable campaign for more resources. When they do, their view is often dismissed as the voice of self-interest.

The answer to the second question is that there is indeed an educational crisis. There is the global challenge (described in the first section of this chapter), compared to which the progress in education looks frankly inadequate. There is the moral state of affairs (described in the second section), which demands urgent attention from those in the education service. Either alone would justify the use of the word 'crisis', but there are in addition some other uncomfortable factors that cannot be ignored.

One is that, in spite of the progress of recent years, international statistics reveal that, compared to some of our major competitors including France, Germany and Japan, our education service is still relatively ineffective, especially for those young people outside the top 20 per cent of the ability range. Tables 1 and 2, prepared by Andy Green and Hilary Steedman for the Report of the National Commission on Education (1993), make the point vividly.

Table 1: Sixteen-year-olds in certain countries reaching equivalent of GCSE grades A–C in mathematics, the national language and one science, 1990–1

Country	Percentages
Germany	62
France	66
Japan	50
England	27

Source: Green, A. and Steedman, H., 1993

Table 2: Young people in certain countries obtaining a comparable upper-secondary school qualification at eighteen-plus, 1990

Country	Percentages
Germany	68
France	48
Japan	80
England	29

Though there has been progress since these statistics were gathered, the gap remains. For example, the *Times Educational Supplement* reported on 19 January 1996: 'English 10 year olds are much worse at arithmetic than their European peers despite having been at school 18 months longer.' Their report describes work undertaken by the National Institute of Economic and Social Research (*Laying the Foundations of Numeracy* by Helvia Bierhoff, NIESR, 1996), showing that English pupils spend less than two-thirds of the time that their counterparts spend on number work and are often two years behind by the age of ten. Swiss and German children spend much more time consolidating their arithmetic.

David Burghes, Professor of Education at Exeter, reported on an international study of achievement in mathematics (the Kassel Project) in the *Sunday Times* on 18 February 1996. The shocking results are included in Table 3.

As if to affirm the conclusions of these international studies, Sir Ron Dearing's report on post-sixteen qualifications, published in March 1996, sets out the ambitious National Targets for Education and Training and then, with devastating simplicity, points out that: 'These targets, for the year 2000, have already been surpassed in Germany and Japan.' Moreover, it is apparent that the jobs of the future will demand more skill and a greater ability to innovate, think, apply and analyse knowledge and work in teams than ever before. If so, then even to stand still – as it were – standards need to rise. Thus, although analysis of the key statistics reveals a gratifying upward slope on the graph, it is still clear that standards are not yet nearly high enough.

Table 3: Percentage of correct answers from representative samples of pupils aged thirteen-plus years to three questions

	Question 1: $60 \times 450 = ?$	Question 2: Solve $x + 1 = 3 - x$	Question 3: $2.4 \times 1\frac{1}{4} = ?$
England	33	28	5
Scotland	40	23	3
Germany	71	38	20
Finland	61	20	10
Poland	81	48	42
Holland	65	35	29
Singapore	89	75	63

Finally, it is important to recognise that amid all the evidence of progress there is also evidence of a deterioration in some specific aspects of education and among some particular groups of children and young people. There is, for example, some – albeit contested – evidence of a decline in reading standards at primary level in recent years. The studies of the government standards watchdog (the Office for Standards in Education) and the National Foundation for Educational Research point in this direction. Their conclusions are confirmed circumstantially by the evidence that the teacher unions have gathered showing that during the implementation of the National Curriculum between 1989 and 1992 teachers gave less time and priority to the basics such as reading. Perhaps most worrying of all is the testimony of a growing number of secondary heads who, though they do not trumpet it loudly for fear of offending their primary colleagues, tell you behind closed doors that they are admitting ever more eleven-year-old children to their schools with reading ages of nine or less. Studies published by the Secondary Heads Association in 1995 and OFSTED in 1996 confirmed this whispered testimony.

If this evidence at one end of the educational spectrum creates anxiety about standards, the facts about recent school-leavers do nothing to alleviate it. The Basic Skills Agency recently reported that as many as 15 per cent of twenty-one-year-olds have limited literacy skills and

20 per cent limited competence in mathematics. Meanwhile, four out of every ten students starting their further education at age sixteen or more required additional help with basic skills.

On the face of it, therefore, the facts we have about standards are puzzling. The surge of progress in public examinations and staying-on rates is sandwiched between concern about basic skills at both primary and further-education levels. There are several possible explanations for this paradox.

One, beloved by right-wingers on the traditionalist wing of Conservatism, is that the examination system has gone soft. According to this view the statistics at GCSE and A Level show nothing about actual student performance and everything about sloppy marking and inconsistent examining. The problem for these critics is that standards have moved steadily on upwards even after the government, responding to their attacks, has implemented a new code of practice (in 1993) and new severe limits on the coursework element at GCSE (in 1994).

The government, with its often blinding admiration for the market, has, however, left the examination boards competing for business. As heads of departments in schools wisely shop around they naturally seek out the boards with the highest proportion of high grades in their subject. Thus there is a commercial incentive for boards to award high grades. It is therefore possible that the rise in recorded levels of achievement includes both real improvement and an element of grade inflation. However, the critics, by focusing on the basic skills which are undeniably important, miss the fact that GCSE is designed to give credit to a much wider range of types of achievement than its predecessor, the O Level. In English at GCSE, for example, an oral presentation to the class is included in the examination. It is not 'soft' to recognise this kind of performance; on the contrary it makes the examination more demanding. Nevertheless the evidence of rising standards should not blind us to a disturbing lack of competence in some basic skills among very large numbers of young people. Regardless of the extent of improvement this remains an educational problem of the highest priority waiting to be addressed. It perhaps ought to be pointed out in passing that age sixteen is hardly the appropriate moment to assess the basics of literacy and numeracy. They should surely be in place by age eleven at the latest, and tinkering with the examination for sixteen-year-olds is not going to solve this problem.

It does not require an attack on the examination system to explain the paradox in any case. Even if 53 per cent achieved five higher-grade GCSEs in 1994, that leaves 47 per cent who did not. Among them we are likely to find the very young people who had low reading ages on admission to secondary schools and who, if they go on to further education, would require assistance with their basic skills. Often these young people, a disproportionately high percentage of whom are boys (as Chapter 3 will reveal), have drifted through the secondary years hiding their incompetence through misbehaviour or truancy. Schools have responded in three ways. Some have moved heaven and earth to provide rigorous programmes to help them catch up. Many, with headaches enough to attend to, have simply allowed them to continue to drift in and out of class. A minority have responded by patronising such young people. These poor youngsters, the line runs, are so hard done by that we will make exceptions for them when the coursework deadlines arrive, we will step over the boundaries of professional advice and give them direct help with exam work. Where we can we will mark up, not down. Thus beguiled by well-meaning but naive and transparently unprofessional teachers, these youngsters arrive in work, further education or the social security system with a deadly combination of poor skills, low self-esteem and a confused notion of what successful learning really means. In short they have been betrayed.

Thus, improbable though it may seem, it appears that we have rising standards and falling standards at the same time. While they are rising for the many, they are low for perhaps 40 per cent and perhaps falling for a significant minority of this group. In this failing group white working-class males are predominant. It should also be pointed out that, while standards have risen for advantaged, average and disadvantaged young people (if such crude categories can be used for a moment), they have risen faster for the already advantaged, while the rate of improvement among the disadvantaged is markedly slower. Talk of the development of an underclass or something approaching J. K. Galbraith's two-thirds/one-third society would seem to be close to the mark. This too would on its own be enough to justify the use of the word 'crisis'.

There was once a German mayor who had the honour of receiving a visit to his small town from the Holy Roman Emperor himself. He was embarrassed, however, that he was unable to lay on the traditional twenty-one-gun salute. He apologised to the emperor immediately. 'Sire,' he said, 'there are three reasons why we were unable to provide a twenty-one-gun salute. The first is that we have no gunpowder—' The emperor interrupted him. 'My dear Lord Mayor, I think you might spare me the other two reasons since the first is clearly sufficient.'

Like that mayor, I sense that I am open to the accusation of overkill in my argument for the use of the word 'crisis'. There is, however, still one more point I want to make in its support. The visible reported crisis of recent years has sadly (but perhaps inevitably) had much less to do with standards, moral panic and the global challenge, and much more to do with the bitter conflict between government and teachers, first over pay and then over the nature of education reform. Chapter 2 concentrates on this aspect of the crisis but some conclusions from it need to be drawn at this point. The result of a decade of conflict is that parents and much of the rest of society are, to put it as gently as possible, bemused.

No wonder that according to data we collected in 1994 at Keele University on parents' attitudes to testing – a major flashpoint in the contest – one-third were found to favour the government's tests, one-third opposed them and one-third didn't know. There could hardly be clearer evidence of the confusion created by the propaganda war of charge and counter-charge over the last few years. Confusion, however, is not the only result. In the unsavoury scramble to sling mud, both sides, government and teachers, have lost credibility. Many parents are uncertain about the testing debate, the curriculum debate and the funding debate. What most people, and particularly parents, do know is that education policy is a matter of dispute, that educational standards are not what they might be and that there is concern – more a dull ache than a sharp pain – about the state of young people today. The words 'crime', 'drugs', 'sex' and 'violence' soon emerge in conversations about 'the youth of today'. Often in people's minds the education crisis (government versus teachers) and the crisis about young people today (the Bulger case and after) are quite separate subjects. In fact they are inextricably linked and the reform of the education service is central to the solution of both.

Helen

It is all too easy in examining these profound and disturbing questions to become gloomy and even fatalistic. It sometimes seems that, whatever is attempted, the outcome is failure. Though it is part of my argument that we should hide neither the extraordinary challenge of the twenty-first century which will face the next generation, nor the inadequacy of our present education service in preparing them to meet it, this book is intended to be optimistic.

My optimism is reinforced whenever I go into schools, which I do all the time. There are many outstandingly good headteachers and teachers who, in spite of all the difficulties they have faced in recent years, are doing a magnificent job. There are increasing numbers of evidently improving schools, and OFSTED, the government inspection agency, reports a fall in the proportion of inadequate lessons between 1994 and

1995. At over 20 per cent it is still far too high, but at least the trend is positive. In schools and elsewhere, I come across young people, too, who are superbly prepared for the future that awaits them. Take the countless talented young people that one meets, for example, at school awards evenings: take Helen, whom I met at one such evening.

She steps up on to the stage in front of a school hall packed with proud parents and expectant teenagers. It is midsummer, and parents and young people alike have been fanning themselves with the programme throughout the awards evening. A succession of young people – boys and girls – have preceded Helen on to the stage. They have made that nerve-racking journey from their seat, up the steps on to the stage to shake the hand of the local mayor invited to give out the prizes. Achievement of every conceivable kind has been recognised. Academic, musical, sporting, social and even horticultural contributions have each had their moment of glory. Progress, improvement and effort as well as absolute achievement have all been honoured.

Helen's prize, however, is for her all-round contribution to the school as a community. She is tall for her fifteen years and walks with poise and quiet confidence across the stage. She is neatly turned out in a white blouse and immaculately pressed navy skirt. Her long fair hair is tied back. She shakes the mayor's hand with a firm confident grip (if the truth were told he is probably a great deal more nervous than she is) and accepts the Everyman copy of *The Return of the Native* that she has chosen for her prize.

The headteacher makes a brief but glowing speech about Helen's contribution to the school. Her academic performance is sound, she tries hard, her attendance is impeccable, she has captained the girls' soccer team and organised a group of fifteen-year-olds who give up time after school to assist those eleven-year-olds who have difficulty with reading. She has been a stagehand in the school play and – it is known to the school – was a pillar of strength for her grandfather, who lives near by, during the long, painful and terminal illness of his wife, her grandmother. There is a tremendous round of applause. Helen blushes, but not too much, and then steps up to make a brief and thoughtful speech, thanking the parents for attending, the staff for their efforts and the guest for handing out the prizes. There is another round of applause. Helen smiles with pride at her achievement and relief that the ceremony is over.

The young people currently in our schools *are* capable of accepting their awesome destiny and solving the problems it will bring. My belief that this is so is based on meeting people like Helen in every school I set foot in. If all young people arrived on the threshold of adulthood with an array of talents, different to hers but as wide-ranging, with her determination to contribute to the communities of which they are a part and with her poise and confidence, then the next century might see the realisation of the kind of humane and democratic world order which for previous generations has been no more than a utopian dream.

It is possible, but at this moment it has to be admitted that that prospect seems as distant as it ever did.

PART TWO

As It Was

2 · Education and the Cultural Revolution

> History is nothing more than a tableau of crimes and
> misfortune.
>
> Voltaire

On the Eve

People in education tend to date the era we are currently living through
– the era of accountability – from the autumn of 1976. That was when
James Callaghan, the then Labour Prime Minister, made a speech about
education, which for a prime minister at that time was an unusual thing
to do. Ruskin College, Oxford was the ideal setting for the speech: a
city with a centuries-old tradition for excellence in education; a college
committed to education for workers and the trade union movement. He
knew he was creating a stir.

> There have been one or two ripples of interest in the educational world
> in anticipation of this visit. I hope the publicity will do Ruskin some
> good and I don't think it will do the world of education any harm. I
> must thank all those who have inundated me with advice: some helpful
> and others telling me less politely to keep off the grass, to watch my
> language, and that they will be examining my speech with the care
> usually given by Hong Kong watchers to the China scene. It is almost
> as though some people would wish that the subject matter and purpose
> of education should not have public attention focused on it; nor that
> profane hands should be allowed to touch it.
>
> I cannot believe that this is a considered reaction. The Labour move-
> ment has always cherished education: free education, comprehensive
> education, adult education. Education for life. There is nothing wrong
> with non-educationalists, even a prime minister, talking about it again.

Having reviewed the problems as he saw them, he summarised:

> I do not join those who paint a lurid picture of educational decline
> because I do not believe it is generally true, although there are examples

which give cause for concern. I am raising a further question. It is this. In today's world higher standards are demanded than were required yesterday and there are simply fewer jobs for those without skill. Therefore we demand more from our schools than did our grandparents.

There has been a massive injection of resources into education, mainly to meet increased numbers and partly to raise standards. But in present circumstances there can be little expectation of further increased resources being made available, at any rate for the time being. I fear that those whose only answer to these problems is to call for more money will be disappointed. But that surely cannot be the end of the matter. There is a challenge to us all in these days and a challenge in education is to examine its priorities and to secure as high efficiency as possible by the skilful use of existing resources.

Let me repeat some of the fields that need study because they cause concern. There are the methods and aims of informal instruction; the strong case for the so-called 'core curriculum' of basic knowledge; next, what is the proper way of monitoring the use of resources in order to maintain a proper national standard of performance; then there is the role of the Inspectorate in relation to national standards; and there is the need to improve relations between industry and education.

Reading Callaghan's words twenty years later, they seem mild, cautious and even tentative, but, at least among people in education, they generated massive controversy at the time. There are some educators who even now have not got over it. They resented the implied criticism in Callaghan's speech and they questioned his motives. They believed that they had been accused unfairly by a prime minister attempting to deflect blame for the country's dire economic straits. With hindsight, it is difficult to characterise this response from the education establishment as anything other than a roughly equal measure of defensiveness and arrogance.

What, in fact, had the avuncular Prime Minister said? He had suggested that standards might not be all they should be. He had hinted that the curriculum of schools was insufficiently relevant to the needs of industry and society and he had argued that the teaching profession ought to be more accountable. Gently though he phrased his critique, he had unerringly identified the three themes that would dominate the debate about education in the last quarter of the twentieth century.

The most interesting historical question about the Callaghan speech is why it was so long before the crisis became anything more than a war of words. The limping Labour government of the late 1970s achieved little. For the first seven years of the Thatcher administration, the secretaries of state for education, Mark Carlisle (1979–81) and Sir Keith Joseph (1981–86) operated at snail's pace. Within the education system itself there were far-sighted people who recognised that unless they acknowledged the breeze blowing in the direction of accountability it would become a whirlwind. For example, Tim Brighouse, then Chief Education Officer in Oxfordshire, gave great emphasis to the idea of school self-evaluation.

Overall, however, there was little in the way of dramatic change. The crisis of action as opposed to words actually began with the long-running and fateful teachers' pay dispute of the mid-1980s. This had three under-lying causes. Firstly, the Conservative governments of the 1980s were hostile to unions in general and to public sector workers in particular. The Conservatives were also suspicious of those who claimed professional status, seeing them, in George Bernard Shaw's terms, as a 'conspiracy against the laity'. Teachers were guilty on all counts. In the early 1980s a number of national policy-making bodies on which teacher unions and government were jointly represented, such as the Schools Council, were abolished. As a result, by 1984, relations between the government and the teaching profession were characterised by mistrust on both sides.

Secondly, the government was determined for both ideological and economic reasons to reduce local government expenditure. It attempted to do so by various means. The most effective technical means of reducing it was, ironically, the poll tax, which was politically lunatic. Teachers' pay was an inevitable target of this cost-cutting drive since it was, and remains, the largest single item in local government expenditure. If that could be held down, the government thought, then the broader political task of reining in local government expenditure would be significantly easier to achieve.

Thirdly, because of a fall in the birth rate in the 1960s and 1970s, the number of pupils in school fell steadily from the late 1970s onwards. This led to an apparently endless round of school reorganisations and closures, which substantially reduced promotion prospects and sapped teacher morale. Simultaneously, it provided a justification of the govern-ment's determination to restrict expenditure on education, although in the short term it increased unit costs. As many companies have dis-covered, 'downsizing' is temporarily expensive.

Faced with these pressures and three years of disappointing pay offers, teachers embarked on a campaign of industrial action involving working to rule, withdrawal of goodwill and a series of strikes that lasted, on and off, from 1984 into 1987. The six different teacher unions, squabbling endlessly among themselves, led their members into a bewildering array of temporary alliances, splits and divisions.

The leadership of the action rested primarily with the NUT and NASUWT, then the two largest and most militant unions. Their incorrigible determination to disagree, which is a continuing feature of the education scene even now, led ultimately to the teaching profession's public humiliation. In May 1986, Kenneth Baker was appointed Secretary of State for Education. The ever-smiling Cheshire Cat of the Tory 1980s, he exploited their disarray. In 1987, teachers' pay negotiations were suspended, a pay settlement and contract imposed and a government-appointed advisory committee established to make recommendations on teachers' pay in the future. It, in turn, was replaced by a review body a few years later and negotiation of teachers' pay was consigned to history, where, probably, it belonged.

That same year, 1987, the Conservatives won their third consecutive overwhelming election victory. Prior to the election, the right-wing pressure groups like the Centre for Policy Studies, to which Thatcherism owed so much of its intellectual energy, had developed a coherent programme for education based on market principles. Meanwhile, in December 1986, Kenneth Baker had announced – characteristically during a television interview – that the government intended to introduce a statutory national curriculum. (Apparently, Margaret Thatcher told him shortly afterwards, 'Kenneth, never underestimate the effectiveness of simply announcing something.' He never did.) The Tories' 1987 election manifesto thus included the most radical package of educational reform ever put to the electorate. It promised a national curriculum, national tests at seven, eleven, fourteen and sixteen, the delegation of the bulk of school finance from local education authorities (LEAs) to schools themselves, the opportunity for schools to opt out of local authorities altogether, and the break-up of the largest LEA in the country, the Inner London Education Authority. Thus the newly elected government was immediately ready to turn the piercing Thatcherite eye on education. It had both the power and the programme to embark on what became a cultural revolution in education.

The basic premise behind the government's programme, which ultimately became the 1988 Education Reform Act, was that market forces would solve problems in the public sector just as they solved them in the private sector. Anything that might interfere with a free market – above all teacher unions and local education authorities – was therefore part of the problem, not the solution.

The government's reform programme was so radical and so universally rejected by people in education that there has been a generally accepted assumption that it caused the crisis of the late 1980s. Opponents of the reforms believed at the time that it was necessary only to point out the logical flaws of a market approach to a universal public service and it would all go away. As a Labour candidate in Henley-on-Thames in the 1987 election campaign, I can remember adopting precisely this stance during an education meeting for all three candidates. Michael Heseltine, the sitting MP, did not turn up to that (or any other) public meeting. He was represented instead by a local Conservative councillor, who was less than equipped for the debate that ensued.

The Liberal and I won what amounted to standing ovations from a predominantly teacher audience by repeatedly attacking the Tory programme. Michael Heseltine's hapless representative was left to parrot a party line he did not begin to understand. Though we won easy applause at the public meeting, the Liberal and I had missed two fundamental points on which a more competent opponent might have nailed us to the ground. Firstly, we offered no credible alternative to what was perceived by the public at large, if not in that public meeting, to be an inadequate existing state of affairs. Secondly, we had completely failed to identify a series of underlying social changes which would sooner or later have forced a radical shift in education policy, whether we liked it or not. It was these changes that caused the crisis, not the market reforms which the Thatcher government drove through. In short, we lacked both a vision of the future and an understanding of the past. No prizes, incidentally, for guessing who won on election day in Henley constituency.

The next section of this chapter outlines the shape of the education system under the post-war settlement and then goes on to identify those underlying social changes which were destined to blow it apart.

Before the Flood: the Butler Settlement

Even while the outcome of the Second World War hung in the balance, a handful of civil servants were mapping out a radical programme for post-war education. They were cooped up in the unreal surroundings of the Branksome Dene Hotel in Bournemouth, where they were avoiding the Blitz. Nevertheless, they were sensitive to the huge popular ferment in favour of education reform. This movement brought together such diverse strands of opinion as the Labour movement, the Anglican Church led by Archbishop William Temple, most of the press, urged on by *The Times* and its *Educational Supplement* (*TES*) and, of course, the teaching profession and its fellow educators in the universities and elsewhere. Overwhelmingly, what drove these advocates on was the idealistic desire to build a New Jerusalem after the defeat of fascism. They believed that the time had come to move beyond the class-ridden stagnation which had characterised the pre-war years. Their campaign had tremendous popular support and, judging by the small ads in the *TES* of the time, there was an inexhaustible thirst for public meetings on the theme.

Ronald Gould, the young, ambitious and talented President (and later General Secretary) of the National Union of Teachers captured the flavour of the time in his autobiography:

> The propaganda work in which I was engaged was exacting . . . Train journeys were often interrupted, there were no dining cars and trains were sometimes unheated. One wintry Sunday, I left home at 7.00 am, drove to Bath to pick up a train to London, where I intended to have lunch and then go by train to Nottingham and by bus to Worksop to address a public meeting. The train to London was delayed. I rushed by taxi to St Pancras, missing the meal. The train to Nottingham was unheated and of course had no restaurant. The bus arrived late at Worksop, the ground was covered with snow and the meeting had already begun. So, stiff with cold and hungry from a fast of more than 12 hours, I addressed the meeting. Bombing, too, interrupted train schedules and on many nights prevented sleep.

In R. A. Butler, who became President of the Board of Education in 1941, this broad progressive movement found a young politician with the ambition and political acumen to drive education reform through a deeply Conservative Parliament in spite of both the demands of total war and the initial reluctance of the Prime Minister, Winston Churchill.

There is no need here to go into the details of how Butler brought about his great reform. It established universal free education up to the age of fifteen. Provision was made for raising the school-leaving age to sixteen, 'when practicable'. Education between the ages of five and fifteen would be organised in successive stages. From age five to seven, children would attend infant school, and from eight until eleven junior school. At that age they would transfer to one of three types of secondary school, each offering a different type of curriculum. These were concisely described in the Norwood Report, published the year before Butler's 1944 Education Act.

> First, [for the grammar schools] there would be a curriculum of which the most characteristic feature is that it treats the various fields of knowledge as suitable for coherent and systematic study for their own sake apart from immediate considerations of occupation, though at a later stage grasp of the matter and experience of the methods belonging to those fields may determine the area of choice of employment and may contribute to success in the employment chosen.
> The second type of curriculum [for the technical schools] would

be closely, though not wholly, directed to the special data and skills associated with a particular kind of occupation; its outlook and its methods would always be bounded by a near horizon clearly envisaged. It would thus be closely related to industry, trades and commerce in all their diversity.

In the third type of curriculum [for the secondary modern schools] a balanced training of mind and body and correlated approach to humanities, Natural Science and the arts would provide an equipment varied enough to enable pupils to take up the work of life: its purpose would not be to prepare for a particular job or profession and its treatment would make a direct appeal to interests which it would awaken by practical touch with affairs.

In practice, the technical schools barely got off the ground and for most children at eleven the choice was between the grammar school (for the most academically able 20 per cent or so) and secondary modern school (for the rest). Butler and his colleagues expected that selection for the grammar school would be based on a combination of IQ tests – the eleven-plus – and discussion between parents and teachers. In reality, the test became sovereign.

In terms of making policy, Butler assumed a continuation of the partnership which had developed between central government, local government and the teaching profession in the 1920s and the 1930s. Broadly speaking, he expected policy-making to be consensual. There would be few issues which could not be resolved by an informal meeting or two with the General Secretary of the NUT. The Act had strengthened central government's ability to give direction but left it dependent on its partners to implement any real change. The aim was – to use what became a cliché in educational circles – a national system, locally administered.

The engine room of the post-war education system was the LEA. It planned the provision of school places, built schools (and closed them sometimes), recruited teachers and other staff and provided public accountability through the education committee of the local authority. Each LEA's plans for the post-war era had to be submitted to central government for approval, but generally this proved straightforward because local and central government, at least for the first fifteen to twenty years after the war, shared broadly the same goals, regardless of party control.

The teaching profession, in which until the 1980s the National Union of Teachers was the predominant force, was able to negotiate its pay and conditions through national committees established for the purpose. The school curriculum (what was taught) and pedagogy (how it was taught) were the responsibility of headteachers and their staff. It was not until the 1980s – ironically under an administration elected to 'roll back the frontiers of the state' – that central government in England and Wales sought to prescribe what children should be taught.

Thus a fundamental feature of the post-war settlement was the extent to which it distributed power and influence among the three main partners. Butler drew attention to this in his speech on the second reading of the Education Bill on 19 January 1944.

> Perhaps this Bill owes its welcome to an appreciation of the synthesis which it tries to create between order and liberty, between the voluntary agency and the state, between the private life of a school and the public life of its district, between manual and intellectual skills and between those better and those less well endowed.

Once his Act was in place, Butler assumed that it would take a generation or more to implement and that he had provided sufficient flexibility within his legislation to allow his successors to refine it as and when it was necessary. He turned out to be right on both counts. His model lasted intact, broadly speaking, until the 1980s. It resulted in a period of steady and unprecedented expansion of provision which lasted into the early 1970s. The number of pupils in state schools increased from about five million to over nine million in the twenty years after the war. In the same period, the percentage of the nation's income spent on education increased from 3 per cent to 4.5 per cent. The number of teachers more than doubled in the thirty years after the war, and from the 1960s on there was rapid expansion of the provision of higher education, which has continued more or less until the present day.

Butler was right, too, about the flexibility he had built into the structure of the education service. There were two major changes in schooling in the 1960s, both contained within the 1944 legislative framework. The first of these was the introduction of comprehensive schooling at the secondary stage. A few local authorities had moved towards comprehensive schooling in the 1950s. Often these were shire counties which found it was more economical in some small towns to provide one comprehensive school rather than both a grammar and a secondary modern school. However, by the 1960s a much more powerful force was driving forward the comprehensive idea. It was becoming increasingly clear that the test on which selection at eleven was based – the so-called eleven-plus – was an unreliable guide to children's performance after that age. Indeed, the whole notion underpinning it – Cyril Burt's view that intelligence was general, inherited and fixed – was becoming discredited.

Furthermore, the majority of parents found that their children were being denied access to the grammar schools. They were increasingly dissatisfied with what everyone perceived to be second best: the secondary modern school. Butler's view that grammar and secondary modern schools would have parity of esteem could not have been further from the mark. A British society riddled with class tension ensured that difference was transformed into hierarchy. The division provoked particular bitterness when the eleven-plus split children within the same family. There are many adults now in their forties and fifties who will testify that 'failing' the eleven-plus damaged not only their education but also their relationships with brothers and sisters who 'passed'. (In 1995, I interviewed a candidate for a PhD course. He already had a degree, a Masters qualification and thirty years' experience of work. He said he hoped his approach could be 'practical'. I replied that a deep understanding of the theory in his field would be essential in any PhD. He said this worried him: 'I'm a practical person, I failed the eleven-plus.') Worse still, research evidence showed that the grammar schools were predominantly and increasingly filled with white middle-class children and the secondary modern schools with their working-class contemporaries.

A Labour government in the egalitarian 1960s could not countenance such a situation. In 1965 Harold Wilson's first administration required all local authorities to draw up plans to become comprehensive. Implementation took longer than might have been expected. Some Conservative local authorities dragged their feet and in any case the wheels of bureaucracy turned slowly. Although Labour lost power in 1970, the Conservative government that followed continued the process. History, therefore, records the delicious irony that the Secretary of State responsible for the creation of more comprehensive schools than any other was one Margaret Thatcher. By 1979, well over 90 per cent of the nation's secondary school population was being educated in comprehensive schools.

The second major change of the 1960s was the triumph of the child-centred approach to education in primary schools. The idea that education was a matter not so much of teaching information and skills to children as of allowing children to learn through their own experience had a long and honourable tradition. In the British primary schools of the late 1960s and early 1970s – suddenly freed from the pressures of preparing children for the eleven-plus – it reached its apogee.

This was the time when primary classrooms shifted from the serried ranks of uniformed children learning their tables into the informal, cheerful, buzzing places they tended to be in the 1980s. Of course it was not that simple: the formal approach maintained support throughout in some places, and the informal, child-centred approach was adopted with varying degrees of enthusiasm. Research on which approach was more effective was never conclusive. The truth turned out to be that the quality of the teaching matters much more than the philosophical approach.

Nevertheless, the highly formal primary school education that I experienced as a pupil in the early 1960s is rare in the state sector these days. Our classroom was organised with desks in pairs facing the front. Every Friday we were tested in spelling, mathematics and mental arithmetic. Where one sat the following week depended on one's score in the tests. The person who came top sat at the back in the left-hand corner of the room as the teacher looked at it. The person who came last sat at the front on the teacher's right with the remaining forty-two pupils ranged in rank order somewhere in between. The school was streamed, with four classes in each year group. A1 was the top stream, A2 the second and then B and C. In our reports there were comments and grades in every subject and the parent was informed of the child's overall position in the class. On my 1965 report – which for some reason I still have in my desk – I was ranked fourteenth out of forty-four. This was a standard primary school experience at the time.

By the time my own children attended primary school, everything had changed. They were in mixed-ability groups. It was rare for the whole class to be taught together, and each child was supposed to be following an individual programme, established every few days, designed to meet her or his particular needs. The curriculum was not divided into subjects as mine had been but, in theory at least, was held together by some overarching theme or project: perhaps 'the weather' or 'the way things move'. The idea of ranking children, or dividing them in any way according to ability, was considered anathema because it 'labelled' children. The point at this stage is not to judge either system, but simply to observe that within the space of one generation a revolution had taken place.

While these two shifts – one affecting secondary schools, the other primary schools – occurred, there were also developments in the 1960s and 1970s at national level. Perhaps the most important, in the light of later events, was the growing emphasis on what was called 'curriculum development'. In the 1960s, a national body with representatives of central government, local government and teachers was established to promote development in curriculum, assessment and examinations. The Schools Council, as it was called, tended to be dominated by the teacher representatives and spawned over the two decades of its existence a series of curriculum development projects. The most famous, perhaps, was the Schools Council History Project, which reflected avant-garde thinking in that subject. Instead of kings, queens, battles and treaties, the emphasis shifted to teaching the skills of a historian: evaluating and interpreting documents, creating a story on the basis of conflicting evidence and empathising with people in different situations in the past. However, the Schools Council philosophy brooked no central direction. It was up to individual teachers and schools to decide whether or not to take them up. It did not challenge the view that the curriculum was a matter for the teaching profession to control. The result was that its impact was patchy and uneven. After its demise it would be accused of expending a great deal of energy for relatively modest results. Its most lasting legacy was perhaps the significant number of teachers who learnt to link change in the curriculum with improvements in their professional practice.

The same period also saw the parallel development of the Certificate of Secondary Education, or CSE. This was an examination designed for the majority of the school population for whom O Level was considered too academic. CSE was an examination largely designed and developed by teachers and might be considered the assessment equivalent of the Schools Council curriculum projects. It opened up to many pupils for the first time the opportunity to achieve recognised qualifications, and through it, also, many teachers learnt new assessment skills.

The Schools Council, however, was responsible for one increasingly apparent failure. Though secondary schools had become almost entirely comprehensive by the early 1980s, the examination system, with its separate O Levels and CSEs, was still designed for the old grammar and secondary modern system. The lack of direction in the Schools Council, combined with the faintheartedness of Shirley Williams, Secretary of State under Jim Callaghan (1976–79), resulted in a failure to reform this obviously inadequate state of affairs.

It is another of those remarkable ironies of educational history that the Secretary of State who abolished the Schools Council and provided much of the intellectual underpinning for the post-1988 cultural revolution also introduced a common examination at sixteen appropriate for the comprehensive system which he abhorred. This is precisely what Sir Keith Joseph achieved when he introduced the General Certificate of Secondary Education (GCSE) in the year – 1986 – he gave way to his smooth-talking but determined successor, Kenneth Baker. At the time of his demise, Sir Keith Joseph had few friends in education, largely because of the bitterness caused by the pay dispute. A few years after he had gone almost everyone remembered him with affection. 'Bring back Sir Keith,' people would say, 'all is forgiven.' This was because, whatever his faults, he cared deeply about education and had an integrity and sheer intellectual honesty which were wholly admirable. One of many (possibly apocryphal) stories about him concerns the popular children's soap opera set in a school, *Grange Hill*. Sir Keith received a number of letters critical of it from right-wing advisers to whom he was sympathetic. He felt unable to reply since he had never heard of it. He decided, therefore, that he – the Secretary of State – a senior civil servant and Her Majesty's Chief Inspector of Schools would sit down to watch an episode before drafting a reply. The civil servant was worried that Sir Keith would be drawn into a completely unwinnable political row about what was undoubtedly a popular TV programme. They watched for half an hour, riveted. When it finished, Sir Keith rose and, walking out of the room, commented curtly: 'I had no idea children could act so well.' This same honesty explains why he implemented the GCSE in spite of his misgivings about comprehensive education.

By another twist of fate, the National Union of Teachers, which had advocated a GCSE-style examination for seventeen years, decided, as part of its action in the mid-1980s pay dispute, to urge a delay to its introduction and called on its members to boycott training for the new examination. This was the start of the era in which nothing was quite what it seemed and when paradox ruled. The cultural revolution was about to begin.

Six Causes of a Cultural Revolution

On the surface, Butler's post-war settlement appeared, even in the 1980s, to be relatively stable and flexible enough to adapt to the changing social demands placed upon it. From this perspective, what happened in the late 1980s and early 1990s – which I term the cultural revolution – was that Margaret Thatcher and her ministers decided to destroy Butler's distribution of power because of their hostility to local government and their devotion to market forces. As an explanation of a revolution this is too shallow. In fact there were at least six underlying causes of the crisis of the 1980s. The cultural revolution cannot be understood unless these are taken into account.

The first of these was a growing social diversity. Butler and his colleagues had assumed social homogeneity, if not in terms of social class, then at least in culture, religion and broad outlook. In 1944, with the war turning in favour of the Allies, there was a tremendous social solidarity, and a shared assumption that the brutal divisions according to class which had characterised the 1920s and the 1930s would be banished for ever. By the mid-1970s, despite thirty years of unparalleled prosperity, these assumptions no longer applied. The 1960s challenged the old homogeneity and legitimised a much wider variety of lifestyles. The influx of people from the Caribbean and the Indian sub-continent in the 1950s meant that by the 1970s the cultural, religious and ethnic constitution, particularly of Britain's large conurbations, had changed irreversibly. Above all, there was an increasingly influential international mass media changing people's perceptions and aspirations. Younger generations were demanding as entitlements for all what had been the privileges of a few in previous generations.

Secondly, there was growing dissatisfaction with the output of the education service. Bluntly, it failed too many young people too much of the time. This was true in relation both to international comparisons and to the demands of the newly assertive young people of the 1970s. It was true in spite of the expansion of the school and higher education systems of the previous decades. Butler's system had assumed that offering an academic education to 20 per cent of the population would meet society's needs. By the mid-1970s, this was no longer acceptable, as no less an authority than James Callaghan, the Prime Minister, pointed out in his famous speech.

It seems incredible, looking back, that we as a nation tolerated a school system under which, as recently as 1985, only just over a quarter of sixteen-year-olds achieved five O Level passes or the equivalent. Keith Joseph, Thatcher's longest serving Secretary of State, used to complain about the poor performance of the 'bottom 40 per cent' of young people. He was right. Talent was being wasted on a monumental scale, as the improvements since then in achievement at sixteen and staying-on rates beyond sixteen demonstrate incontrovertibly. One local example shows this vividly. In the 1980s, Stoke on Trent had the worst staying-on rate in England and Wales. In the 1990s, Keele University, as part of its contribution to raising aspirations among local people, has offered some places through its local access scheme. As a consequence, some young people from inner-city Stoke schools have been admitted not on the basis of a standard offer of, say, three grade Bs at A Level, but on teacher recommendation and minimum A Level entry requirements. The performance of these students has been monitored, and turns out to be indistinguishable from that of students admitted through the standard entry route. Yet in the 1980s young people of similar potential would have taken a semi-skilled job in the Potteries at sixteen and would never have considered higher education.

The third cause of crisis was growing dissatisfaction with the performance of the British economy in comparison with that of competitor countries. The oil crisis of 1973 revealed the extent of Britain's relative economic failure and, predictably, politicians turned to education for part of the explanation and, less worthily, for scapegoats. This was the context for Callaghan's Ruskin speech with which this chapter began. Ever since that time, the fate of the education system has been linked inextricably in the minds of politicians to economic performance. Thus, in Tony Blair's words at Manchester in 1994: 'Education is not just the basis of a healthy society, it is the foundation of a wealthy economy. Looking at Britain's problems today, their roots lie above all in our failure to educate and train the majority of our people.' Or, as he put it more crisply at the 1995 Labour Party Conference: 'Education is the best economic policy we have.'

The government's view as expressed in the 1994 White Paper on competitiveness is similar. John Major's foreword argues that: 'my aim is to create a climate in which our companies can beat the best. That is what this White Paper is all about . . . we must give our young people the highest standards of education and training. Their skills will be the key to our future.' Sir Ron Dearing's 1996 Report makes a similar point: 'The only strategy for a nation seeking to maintain and enhance a high standard of living lies in concentration on advanced products and services, a high level of innovation, challenging and constantly improving standards of achievement and competitiveness, based on a highly educated, well-trained and adaptable workforce.' Most people recognise that the relationship between economic prosperity and education is by no means a simple one, but few deny that it exists. Everyone recognises that, for the kind of high-skill, information-based economy that Britain aspires to in the twenty-first century, a successful education system is a pre-condition, but on its own it will not be enough.

As Will Hutton reported in an important *Guardian* article on 8 January 1996: 'while there is no disputing the value of education and training, recent research is sobering about how much they can achieve themselves. The necessary expenditure to close income inequality, raise skill levels and lower unemployment is vast: the pay-offs are slow and . . . the results are likely to be variable at best.' He then reviews the economic evidence of the importance of skill levels and training:

Richard Freeman and Larry Katz say in one American study (*Working Under Different Rules*, Russell Sage, 1994) that between seven and 25 per cent of rising inequality is due to inadequate skills; while Steve Nickell and Brian Bell (*Oxford Review of Economic Policy*, Vol II No 1) found that in Britain the decline in real demand for unskilled workers contributed up to 20 per cent of the long run increase in unemployment between the 1960s and the 1980s . . .

Will Hutton's conclusion is that: 'The larger point is that the industrial world is suffering from a multitude of shocks to which education and training can only offer a partial response ... education and training cannot stand alone, but to say and do more means moving beyond the policies of apple pie and motherhood – and challenging the interests of the powerful.' This surely is right and, to me, sobering. It implies that a good education service is essential; but also that even if we were able to create a perfect education system, much else would remain to be done before we had a good society.

The economic crisis of the mid-1970s had a more direct impact on the education system which provided the fourth underlying challenge to Butler's settlement. Public spending had to be controlled. As Tony Crosland put it famously: 'the party is over'. Much of the history of education in the last two decades can be explained as central government seeking the powers to restrict local government spending, particularly on its largest single element: education. As we have seen, this was part of the motivation behind the government's determination to restrict teachers' pay rises in the mid-1980s. It also prompted a bewildering series of laws and regulations designed to limit what local authorities could spend. Rate-capping was followed by the poll tax before, on the back of another envelope, the council tax was invented to save the Conservatives from election defeat in 1992. The end result is that now only a tiny fraction of what local authorities spend is actually raised locally. There has been a corresponding loss of the local discretion on which Butler's settlement rested. In terms of central government's original narrow aim of restricting expenditure, it has – after fifteen years – finally succeeded. He who pays the piper really does call the tune.

The issue of finance led directly to a fifth factor in the demise of the post-war arrangements. Once there was pressure on public expenditure, it was inevitable (and right) that questions would be asked about how effectively public money was spent. Accountability therefore became a central issue across the public services. In education, this economic pressure for accountability coincided with a *cause célèbre* which raised the same issue from a different perspective. As a result, professional autonomy was dealt what, with hindsight, can be seen to have been a fatal blow.

William Tyndale, for most of us the name of the author of the first translation of the Bible into English, is also the name of a junior school in Islington. In January of 1974, a new headteacher, Terry Ellis, was appointed to the school. Under his direction, the school embarked on an experiment which tested the limits of teacher autonomy and led to a state of affairs best described as anarchy. In their attempts to be 'progressive', the majority of the teachers abdicated responsibility for the learning process and failed even to keep records of the pupils' progress. They took an extreme view of professional autonomy. On one occasion the

headteacher told a governor that he 'did not give a damn about parents
... or anyone else ... teachers were pros at the game and ... nobody
else had any right to judge them'. 'In any case,' he added, 'parents were
either working-class fascists or middle-class trendies out for their own
children.' Robin Auld QC, who conducted the inquiry into the Tyndale
affair, concluded that, among other things, it showed that the LEA had:

> No policy as to:
> 1. standards of attainment at which primary schools should aim;
> 2. the aims and objectives of the primary education being provided
>   in its schools . . .;
> 3. the methods of teaching to be adopted in its schools.

In the absence of answers to these questions (which, to be fair, few
LEAs would have been able to answer in 1976), it is difficult to make
clear judgements about quality. Thus, in the context of a burgeoning
interest at national level in the accountability of public services, it became
evident that, under the Butler settlement, holding the education service
to account was virtually impossible. Since the Tyndale affair there has
been a series of attempts not only to answer the three questions asked
by Robin Auld, but also to decide whose responsibility it should be to
ask them. Oddly, however, in spite of the confluence of pressure for
accountability in the late 1970s, there were few policy developments on
the issue in the following decade. Instead the education service drifted
towards crisis. Again with hindsight, what is so striking about the decade
between 1976 and 1986 is the complete absence either in government or
in the teaching profession of a sense of direction.

This raises the final pressure for change in the 1980s. Least debated
but by no means least important is the fact that, under the Butler settlement, the decision-making process was painfully slow: far too slow for
a world in which social, cultural, economic and technological changes
were gathering pace and would continue to do so.

Butler himself had brought about consensual decisions fairly rapidly
(it was three years from the moment of his appointment to the passing
of the 1944 Education Act), but of course the ideas in the Act had been
fermenting for a generation. Meanwhile, the Act's implementation was
expected to take a generation, as indeed it did. The school-leaving age
was not raised to sixteen until 1972, which would have surprised everyone
involved in the 1944 debates except that arch-realist Ernest Bevin, who
had argued in 1943 for implementing a school-leaving age of sixteen
straight away in case post-war governments lost their nerve. Even more
staggeringly, the Hadow Report of 1926 had recommended that all-age

elementary schools should be reorganised into primary and secondary departments. Yet, in spite of universal approval for the recommendation, it was not until forty-five years later that the last all-age school was reorganised. More recently, the GCSE, floated as an idea in the National Union of Teachers headquarters in the 1960s, was not implemented until 1986. The fact is that the partnership model of decision-making, after which many educators still foolishly hanker, was demonstrably inadequate by the 1980s.

For all these reasons, therefore, it is a mistake to see Thatcherism as the cause of the educational crisis of the late 1980s. A crisis was coming anyway. Thatcherism's contribution was to shape decisively the solutions that have been attempted. From the range of possibilities available for dealing with the problems outlined in the preceding paragraphs, the Thatcher government chose solutions based on a radical combination of market forces and centralisation. Historians writing twenty years from now will be able to tell us if they worked.

The Cultural Revolution

The 1988 Education Reform Act was the most important piece of education legislation in the second half of the twentieth century. It set out to create a market within the school system. This required three steps. Under local management of schools (LMS), LEAs were required to delegate over 85 per cent of funding – including that for staff salaries – to the individual schools. They were required to allocate funds among the schools on the basis of a published formula, the largest element of which, by far, had to be pupil numbers. Under the Act's open enrolment sections, schools were required to recruit up to their physical capacity. The result of these three stipulations was that a school's budget depended on how many pupils it attracted. As Kenneth Baker said in an interview in 1996, these measures created 'a voucher system in all but name'. *De facto* a market existed. Schools found themselves in competition for pupils. As a consequence, schools have made far greater efforts to project themselves to parents. Management courses for headteachers on public relations have mushroomed and school brochures have become glossy (as well as, on the whole, more informative). In places this has been taken to extremes. I heard of a school which was offering a free shower fitting to all parents who chose it. This bizarre offer resulted from the fact that one of the governors owned a shower-fitting company. As the parent of three daughters and the owner of only one shower, I have often speculated what I might have done with the two spare fittings. Either way, it illustrates the point that market forces began to operate in earnest following the passage of the 1988 Act.

The framers of the Act did not stop there. It was not sufficient, in their view, to put schools in competition with one another. It was also necessary to ensure that parents had a variety of schools from which to choose. There is no point in creating a market, they reasoned, if the choice is between a number of uniform LEA-run comprehensive schools. To free up the supply side, to use the market jargon, the Act also allowed for the establishment of privately funded city technology colleges (CTCs) and made it possible for schools – if the parents so decided – to opt out of their LEA and receive funding directly from central government. They would become grant-maintained schools, or self-governing state schools as they were later described. Thus the LEA monopoly would be broken and diversity encouraged. The same sections of the Act, by enabling schools to threaten to opt out, forced LEAs to become much more responsive to their needs. The boot, as it were, was suddenly on the other foot.

Some of the lobby groups behind the government would have liked them to stop there: create a market and get out of the way. Others, however, were as much concerned with what was taught as with how the system was structured. The 1988 Act, drawing on the 10 years of desultory debate which followed the Ruskin speech, provided for the implementation of a national curriculum consisting of ten subjects and RE (with Welsh as an additional compulsory subject in Wales). The National Curriculum was intended to cover the whole five-to-sixteen age range. There would be national tests at the ages of seven, eleven, fourteen and sixteen as promised in the Tory manifesto. In this way the Act not only provided for a market, but also for a standardised means of checking which schools appeared to be performing best within it. Actually, rather than a free market, it was, as Stephen Ball, sharp and critical as ever, pointed out, more a franchise-restaurant model. The government's message to schools was: 'You run the restaurant, we set the menu.' Indeed, Stephen Ball even talked of a Kentucky Fried Curriculum.

The ease with which this radical programme was constructed and enshrined in law is remarkable. Partly it was because the ideology behind it had been clearly thought through in the right-wing pressure groups over nearly two decades. Parts of it, indeed, had been tried out at local level, most notably in Croydon, where the Chief Education Officer was that talented and genial ogre, Donald Naismith.

Naismith was the arch-advocate of parental choice who, having set the agenda for the 1988 Act while in Croydon, then moved to Wandsworth and attempted to set a new market agenda for the 1990s. By then the government was less responsive to external promptings, not least because the concentration of new powers in ministers' hands gave them delusions of grandeur and, for a brief but fatal spell in 1992 and 1993, a belief in their own infallibility.

The smooth passage of the legislation was also due to the demoralisation of the teaching profession. The NUT – still perhaps unaware of its decline in influence – booked the Albert Hall for a mass rally against Baker's Bill, but was unable to draw a decent audience. The half-empty rotunda became a symbol of the defeat the profession had suffered in the mid-1980s. A combination of the Thatcherite supremacy, growing public concern about standards and the teaching profession's own internal divisions had profoundly weakened the confident profession which Ronald Gould had led into the post-war era.

The 1988 Education Reform Act was not, as it turned out, the end of a legislative process, but the beginning. Acts affecting education and the teaching profession came thick and fast: one in 1991, two in 1992, the longest Education Act of the twentieth century in 1993 and another in 1994. In the seventh year, God (for the Secretary of State now had near omnipotence) rested. The government announced that this side of a general election there would be no further legislation.

In part this was because the government had by then acquired all the powers it could possibly want, and in part because the process of implementing the reforms which it had introduced had become an educational and political nightmare. It had learnt the hard way what King Charles I had been told – shortly before losing his head: 'there is more to the doing than bidding it be done'. Either way, in early 1996 it proved unable to resist the temptation to break the promise and tamper once more with the legislative framework, albeit in a marginal way, and a White Paper in the summer of 1996 promised still more legislation in 1997.

During the period of cultural revolution, there were no fewer than four secretaries of state for education. Kenneth Baker (until July 1989), John MacGregor (July 1989 to September 1990), Kenneth Clarke (September 1990 to April 1992) and John Patten (April 1992 to July 1994). During the same period, there were four permanent secretaries at the Department for Education: David Hancock (until 1989), John Caines (1989–92), Geoffrey Holland (1993–94) and Tim Lankester (1994–95). Following the merger of the Department for Education and the Employment Department, Tim Lankester departed and Michael Bichard became the fifth Permanent Secretary in eight years.

There was a similar rapid turnover in the senior positions at the crucial agencies responsible for implementation. The National Curriculum Council (NCC) had two chief executives and three chairs in its five

years of existence. The same was true of the Schools Examination and
Assessment Council (SEAC). By a remarkable coincidence, five of the
six teacher unions also found themselves with changes at general secretary
level. Given this extraordinary turnover in senior posts in the education
service, it became extremely difficult for the crucial informal relationships, on which smooth implementation of change depends, to develop.
Furthermore, at any given moment memories were short, the lessons
learnt from the recent (never mind the more distant) past few and the
urge for people to demonstrate their authority endless.

This rapid turnover cannot be put down solely to unhappy coincidence. The process of cultural revolution actually depends to some extent
on turnover. The longer a minister or an official is in post, the greater
the likelihood is that she or he will begin to accommodate the establishment. For example, one of the reasons why John MacGregor's tenure
was so fleeting was that the right-wing ideologists accused him of 'going
native'. Also, the growing assertiveness of ministers, who were taking
advice from outside pressure groups rather than from the civil service,
led to growing tensions between them and officials. What made the
confusion even worse was that each of the agencies like the NCC was
shadowed by civil servants at the Department for Education. Inevitably,
relations between the two sets of officials were frosty at best.

Duncan Graham, the first chair and chief executive of the NCC,
described this extraordinary state of affairs in a passage in the book (*A
Lesson for Us All*, Routledge, 1993) he wrote after his resignation.

> Then [in 1989] the roof fell in. A posse of civil servants descended on
> York to tell NCC that it could not continue work on nor publish the five
> booklets [on cross-curricular themes such as economic and industrial
> understanding]. They were a dangerous distraction, funds were not
> available, and work would have to be delayed until 1993 when the
> National Curriculum was due to be fully implemented.
>
> Clearly alarmed by what he had been told by the civil servants,
> Kenneth Baker wrote a detailed two-page letter to the Council in May
> 1989 in which he told it to abandon [this work]... In the future
> nothing should go to formal meetings of the council for approval until
> it had been seen and approved by the Secretary of State. Here was
> the question of independence in a nutshell...
>
> At that point I decided that I had to see Baker and telephoned him
> at home. I was well received. He asked how the council was getting
> on, showed some surprise that we had not seen each other more often,
> and asked what the problem was. I told him bluntly that he had signed
> a letter which would have had electric consequences on the future of
> the council and would lead to him parting company with his industrial
> friends who wanted a rounded curriculum. I also stated that I wanted

to be perfectly sure he fully appreciated what was happening. He showed great concern and said that we should meet urgently without civil servants. His first available date was 16 June in Betws-y-Coed, North Wales, where he was staying overnight before going on to do a half marathon for charity the following morning. As it happened I was in Wales that weekend for a meeting of the Curriculum Council for Wales, so we both had perfect cover.

A helicopter was waiting for Baker in a field behind the hotel. I went with some trepidation as I wondered whom he would have with him. Dressed in his running gear, he came out of the hotel alone to meet me and shook me warmly by the hand. We went into the hotel and found a room where we talked over coffee. We started with the letter and its implications. He looked at it and could not believe he had signed it. It was one of those magic moments in life. We then discussed whether he really wanted the publicity that would follow the sudden cancellation of the working groups. He asked why I thought the civil servants had advised him so strongly and accepted that he had been persuaded by the argument that work of this sort could prove to be a distraction.

Still talking, we walked out to the helicopter. He said he was very angry and shaken by what had happened and that we should meet more regularly, whereupon he climbed into the helicopter to be whisked off to the start of his half marathon.

Some civil servants dispute Duncan Graham's account of how difficult it had become to meet the minister, but Kenneth Baker himself confirms it. Whatever the exact nature of events, the policy process had become bizarre to say the least. There is a line in a Peter Cook and Dudley Moore sketch which often sprang to mind during that extraordinary period in educational history: 'Is that the way to run a f***ing nightclub?' Clearly similar thoughts passed through the minds of those who were, like Duncan Graham, caught up in the collective madness.

Instability at leadership level was only part of the problem. It was compounded by a failure to enlist teachers, the group responsible for the implementation of reform. Indeed, the teaching profession began the reform period demoralised, became alienated and eventually, as we shall see, in the face of extreme provocation became angry.

Politically, the cultural revolution fell into three distinct phases. The first lasted from the passage of the 1988 Act through to the appointment of Kenneth Clarke as Secretary of State for Education in the autumn of 1990. During this period, though both Kenneth Baker and John Mac-Gregor were clearly committed to the market reforms, they were broadly pragmatic about implementation. The ministers were accessible to teacher leaders or, for example, representatives of the inner London boroughs who were to take over responsibility for education in the capital from the ILEA. Baker would receive deputations in his office on the fourteenth floor of the then Department of Education and Science, next door to Waterloo Station. Behind him, through the vast window, was a magnificent panorama of central London. He would listen, ooze his confident replies and occasionally make pragmatic concessions in order to ensure smoother implementation. MacGregor was even more receptive to deputations. He seemed genuinely to understand the problems that were occurring, whereas for Kenneth Baker the whole exercise appeared to be a political charade. Under Baker and MacGregor, therefore, in spite of the sense of confusion, implementation of the 1988 Act proceeded steadily. I therefore refer to this period as the era of free-market pragmatism.

The autumn of 1990 changed everything. In September, Kenneth Clarke, a politician in a hurry and with a reputation for bashing professionals, became Secretary of State. Two months later the unthinkable occurred. Mrs Thatcher drove away from Downing Street with tears rolling down her cheeks and John Major became Prime Minister. Though in his first year he presented an image as the pragmatic face of Thatcherism (most notably in his haste to escape the poll tax), in education his effect was the precise opposite. Free-market pragmatism was dead. The government now took the view that the 1988 Act was inadequate because it did not go far enough in implementing the market agenda. Hence, in Clarke's eighteen months of tenure, the Further and Higher Education Act (1992), which introduced a more competitive market among colleges and universities, was put on the statute book. Simultaneously, the 1992 Education (Schools) Act gave the Secretary of State power to require the publication of performance tables of schools' academic progress or other aspects of their work and, most remarkably, proposed the creation of a market for the inspection of schools. Under its original proposals, schools would have been required to put their inspection out to tender just as a company appoints its own auditors. In the end, only as a result of a Labour amendment, the process became a market heavily regulated by the new Office for Standards in Education (OFSTED). OFSTED was given the responsibility of appointing a team of inspectors for every school. The market idea was also extended in this period to the initial training and continuing professional development of teachers. Meanwhile, the idea of grant-maintained status was elevated to the extent that the government presented it as the eventual goal for secondary schools and perhaps all schools, although at the time only a few hundred had actually opted out. This era is best thought of as the era of free-market purism. It was followed by the April 1992 election, the appointment of John Patten as the Secretary of State for Education, and another shift of gear.

Free-Market Stalinism

People have forgotten now, but for his first six weeks in office John Patten said virtually nothing. An article in the *Spectator* in which he regretted the passing of people's belief in heaven and hell created a minor stir, but otherwise there was silence. One reason for this was that the Conservative election manifesto had created a major administrative problem which required urgent attention.

The grant-maintained option had been introduced in the 1988 Act mainly in order to allow schools in what the government described as 'loony left' LEAs to escape and become funded by central government. For the 1992 election, however, the Conservative Party elevated 'opting out' from being an option for a minority of schools into the chief plank of its education policy, at least for secondary schools. The new minister, therefore, envisaged a situation in which, over his period of office, most (perhaps all) secondary schools, as well as many primary schools, would become grant-maintained. This raised two issues. Firstly, if there were now to be literally thousands of grant-maintained schools, it would no longer be sensible to fund them on the basis of the levels of expenditure prevalent in the LEA of which they had previously been a part. Secondly, while the Department for Education had been able to provide the administrative supervision of a GM sector of a few hundred schools, overseeing thousands would require a bureaucracy of a different order. In any case, there was the obvious political danger to the Secretary of State of having direct responsibility for all those schools. If one of them failed, or if what the Audit Commission called 'the green shoots of impropriety' became sturdy plants, he would be directly in the political firing line.

The government's solution to these problems was published in the 1992 White Paper, *Choice and Diversity*, which emerged three months into John Patten's period of office. It proposed the establishment of yet another quango. The Funding Agency for Schools (FAS) would be given the task of distributing funds to grant-maintained schools and providing national supervision of the sector. As if to make clear that the department was no longer politically responsible, it was decided that the FAS would be headquartered 200 miles away in York.

The pursuit of this policy created a minefield of detailed administrative problems, with some schools becoming overseen by the Funding Agency in York and others remaining with the LEA. Which would decide the admissions arrangements in any given area, York or the individual LEA? Which would decide school closures? Which would decide about the opening of new schools? What about places for special educational needs? The answer was different in each of these cases, but in all of them the Secretary of State took to himself the ultimate power in case the FAS and individual LEAs did not agree. The result was a monstrously complicated piece of legislation on education, which grew in length as it passed through Parliament during 1992 and 1993. It was amended over 1,000 times, mostly by the government itself making policy up as it went along. It was said that, soon after it became law, the first printed copies were distributed with thirty pages missing, but it was so dense that nobody noticed. Whereas the 1944 Act can be read and understood by a moderately intelligent adult in an evening, the 1993 Act is beyond comprehension to anyone but a lawyer, and even a lawyer would have difficulty staying awake.

It was supremely ironic that, at the moment the Act became law, the stream of schools voting to opt out became a trickle. By the summer of 1994, even the trickle had virtually dried up. Instead of the 1,500 GM schools promised by April 1994, the number reached only 1,000 in August that year and the prospects for many more seemed remote. Even by mid-1996 there were only just over 1100. Paradoxically, given the original purpose of the idea, the majority of them were to be found not in former 'loony left' LEAs, but in traditionally Tory shires like Kent and Essex.

The 1993 Act was more successful in improving the rights of children with special needs and in unifying the different responsibilities of the NCC and SEAC under one agency, the School Curriculum and Assessment Authority (SCAA). This was timely because, by 1993, assessment and testing had become the decisive issue in education policy. Indeed, it was the dispute over testing that brought an end to the cultural revolution and its third phase. Given John Patten's contradictory drive to extend the market while simultaneously increasing the powers of the Secretary of State, I have described this phase, which lasted from April 1992 to the appointment of Sir Ron Dearing in 1993, as the era of free-market Stalinism.

This brutal description might have been considered an exaggeration had it not been for the extraordinary policy process which developed during that year. The mixture of tinpot arrogance and rank incompetence cost both the government and the education system dear. It was, without doubt, the most catastrophic year in twentieth-century educational history.

Partly this was the result of John Patten's personality. Few holders of the office since the war have relished the prospect of being Secretary of State for Education so much. John Patten saw it as a historic opportunity to improve education and tackle the moral lassitude which manifestly disturbed him. He is a flamboyant character, liable to talk off the cuff, unpredictable and lacking in judgement. He is also greatly concerned about his image, convinced of his own views (regardless of the evidence) and easily threatened by contrary advice. For these reasons, his civil servants found him hard to deal with. His problems were compounded by the fact that his Minister of State was the bullish Baroness Blatch, a forceful and able character known to be a close confidante of the Prime Minister. His authority was, therefore, permanently on the line. Worse still, he was ill advised about relations with the teaching profession. The prevailing view among officials was that the teacher unions were weak and unrepresentative of their members. Thus, for the government to gain support for its policies, talking to union leaders was not important; instead ministers should appeal over the heads of union leaders to the broad mass of teachers at grass-roots level – the group John Patten called, rather unhappily, our 'mostly excellent teachers'. Furthermore, the new minister was advised that the key to success was winning the support of the general public, and especially parents, who would be likely to support the government's programme of opening up the secret garden of education.

There was, in fact, little objective evidence to support this advice. The relative ease with which the government had been able to introduce reform owed much more to the demoralisation of the profession in the Baker era and the divisions among the unions that led to it. Any Conservative politician worth his or her salt ought to be able to divide the six unions fairly easily. As often as not, they split without external prompting. The one certain means of uniting them was to ignore them equally. This became John Patten's approach. Worse still, the civil servants had failed to identify or take seriously the burgeoning resentment of the National Curriculum and testing and the workload they caused. In discussions with the NCC and SEAC, the six unions had not found it difficult to co-operate since 1990, because all teachers, regardless of which union they belonged to, shared a collective anger about the lack of consultation and the slipshod process of implementation. The officials at the quangos knew, because union leaders told them, but the Secretary of State, it seems, was never properly informed, or if he was he ignored the warnings.

Thus, with poor advice reinforcing his personal inclination, John Patten began to make policy by shouting at people. At the same time, he studiously avoided all meetings with leaders of the profession. In twelve months, he turned down seventeen requests from the NUT to bring a deputation to him. He refused to attend the conference of the National Association of Head Teachers. In the autumn of 1992, Baroness Blatch emerged from the laager to talk to the Girls' School Association, but managed only to inflame this most upright of groups which represents mainly independent girls' schools. Apparently she told the cab driver who took her to the station exactly what she thought of the GSA and its President: it did not make happy listening. We know this because the cab driver's next passenger was the President herself and he spilled the beans.

In January 1993, John Patten made a decision which symbolised this brief and disastrous era. He turned down an invitation to speak at the education calendar's most prestigious event, the North of England Education Conference. For as long as anyone could remember, the Secretary of State had spoken to this huge gathering of educational leaders. John Patten, sticking to his 'strategy' in letter and in spirit, chose instead to go on the Jimmy Young show: 'forget the professionals: it is Essex man and woman that count' appeared to be the motto.

He compounded this affront to the profession by making public statements that oscillated between the insensitive and the insulting. He commented unfavourably on the weight of the General Secretary of the NUT and, most famously, described one chief education officer as 'deeply lippy' and another as 'a nutter'. The latter remark landed him in court, where he was forced to apologise to Tim Brighouse, the Chief Education Officer in question, and had undisclosed damages awarded against him. The episode revealed both his unpredictability and his contempt for LEAs. There is no doubt that these wild remarks contributed to undermining the last remaining shreds of his credibility, which had been fragile from the beginning.

More fundamentally, all this was evidence of the increasingly eccentric policy-making process he had inherited from his predecessors and then driven to its logical conclusion. In its purest form it operated in the way illustrated in Figure 1.

A particular policy example might help explain the cycle. The Centre for Policy Studies had consistently advocated that educating teachers in universities caused problems. Instead, the CPS argued, consistent with its market approach, schools should train the teachers they need when they need them. Over a long period, stories appeared from time to time in papers friendly to the government (such as the *Mail on Sunday* and the *Daily Express*) about either the poor quality or the political extremism to be found in university departments of education. In March 1993, John Patten announced that the training of teachers wholly in schools would be piloted from September 1993. In June – *three months before the pilots*

Figure 1: The policy process under free-market Stalinism

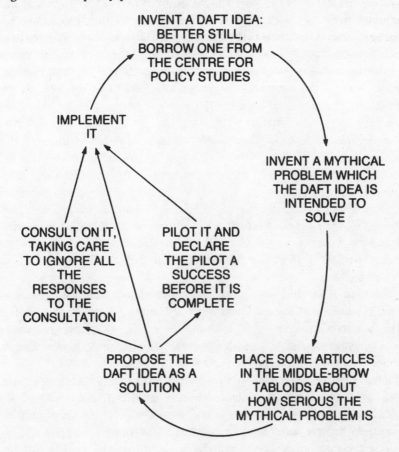

began – a government circular stated that because the new scheme was so popular it was likely to be extended. In December 1993, after a handful of pilot schemes had been running for only three months, legislation was introduced making it possible to extend this scheme nationally. The teaching profession had little or no input at any stage of this process. Such research evidence as there was on the subject was ignored. OFSTED's view was flatly contradicted. The pilots were announced without any consultation. There was no plan to involve the teaching profession in overseeing them or evaluating them. While there was some consultation about the plans for legislation, its overwhelmingly critical message was completely ignored. Fortunately, Patten's successors moved with caution on this issue, but as an illustration of the policy process it is instructive.

This approach to making policy might conceivably be successful in short bursts and with bold, skilled politicians driving it. If – to use Andrew Arden's term – the unthinkable becomes the habit, and if the politician in charge is less than skilled, it is doomed to failure. This was the case under free-market Stalinism. John Patten achieved what no politician or teacher leader had achieved for thirty years. He united the teaching profession, at least temporarily. That, in turn, resulted in the downfall of free-market Stalinism and, ultimately, of John Patten himself.

The issue which led to that fleeting unity and the downfall of the hapless minister was assessment and testing.

Annus Mirabilis

Teachers of English are a sensitive lot, and in the early 1990s the government kicked them once too often. When the National Curriculum began in the late 1980s, it was possible to predict that English would be an area of conflict.

Kenneth Baker had set foot in this controversial territory as early as 1987. He had established a Committee of Inquiry under Sir John Kingman (inevitably a scientist) to examine the teaching of English because he believed that sensible English teaching 'had virtually ceased in British schools, where [it] had fallen victim to the ludicrous political fashion which argued that language was an instrument of class'. Kingman managed to produce a report which teachers of English found unexceptionable. Baker, however, liked it less and suggested that Kingman and his team 'had become infected with fashionable nonsense'.

The prospects of achieving agreement about the National Curriculum in English after 1988 appeared to be at best small. English teachers feared the worst when Professor Brian Cox, a right-wing scourge of state education in the 1970s, was appointed to chair the group which would shape the National Curriculum in their subject. Amazingly, however, Cox found a way through the maze and produced a report which met the apparently contradictory requirements of Margaret Thatcher on the one hand and the English-teaching fraternity on the other. Diplomatic skill of the highest order was behind this achievement. When his draft proposals were published, Cox attached to them a list of recommended texts for primary pupils. The press focused entirely on the absence from these lists of Noddy and Biggles. Cox became, as he described it later, 'the villain who put his knife into Noddy and his boot into Biggles'. Simply by dropping the list altogether when the final proposals emerged, Cox ensured a good press reception. Noddy, as it were, was back. Meanwhile, the major issues his report inevitably raised were left relatively unexplored.

Had the government left Cox's proposals alone, all might have been well. But the right-wing pressure groups were not satisfied. Moreover, Kenneth Clarke had appointed some of their number to key positions on the National Curriculum. They wanted a required list of classics, greater emphasis on teaching reading through phonics and a clearer definition of standard English. Therefore, in 1992, only two years after Cox's triumph, a review of English in the National Curriculum was ordered. Teachers of English were understandably offended in principle. They also groaned at the thought of revising, again, all the schemes of work they had so recently revised.

To add insult to injury, John Major, in his first big speech on education, attacked another of their sacred cows, coursework assessment in English GCSE. Many pupils were working on syllabuses for GCSE which were entirely coursework assessed and had no final examination: many schools had based a large proportion of their assessment on coursework even in the old days before O Level was replaced by GCSE. In order to ingratiate himself with the right-wing Centre for Policy Studies (founders: M. Thatcher, K. Joseph), John Major told their conference in July 1991 that there was far too much coursework, it lacked rigour and the proportion of it allowed should be cut to 20 per cent. Teachers of many subjects were offended: teachers of English were outraged.

It was against this background that the government began to pilot English tests for fourteen-year-olds. The first small pilot in 1991 was a disaster. Ken Clarke dismissed the tests of that summer as 'complicated nonsense'. In the summer of 1992, with John Patten now at the helm, the science and maths pilot tests for fourteen-year-olds went smoothly. The much smaller pilot English tests ran, once again, into trouble. In spite of this, John Patten announced that in the following summer – 1993 – there would be compulsory tests for fourteen-year-olds in English as well as maths and science. He announced in September 1992 that the tests would include questions on one of three Shakespeare plays, that there would be some selected extracts of readings too – but that details of the tests would not be announced until the spring.

Teachers of English had now been pushed too far. Meanwhile, behind the scenes, the government had given the test-development contract to a new company and during the autumn was still piloting tests (on fifteen-year-olds) only months before the first full compulsory run.

Teachers of English began to whisper, and then shout, the word 'boycott'. They also began to write to their unions in greater and greater numbers throughout the autumn of 1992. On 12 December 1992, the NUT Executive decided to conduct a consultative ballot of its members who taught English to find out whether they would be prepared to take the risk of boycotting tests. Other members were asked whether they would be prepared to take action in defence of any teachers who boycotted the English tests. In January 1993, the results came back and astonished even the most militant NUT leaders. Over 90 per cent of those who voted favoured a boycott and, overwhelmingly, teachers were prepared to support members who might be disciplined for implementing one.

Two factors help to explain this groundswell of anger. Many other teachers, including infant teachers and those who taught maths and science, already had experience of the government's tests. These had been implemented professionally, but that did not mean teachers liked them. They began to see an opportunity to throw off this burden. In any case, hardly any teachers welcomed the prospect of the publication of test results which was about to begin for public examinations at sixteen and eighteen, and which the government planned to introduce for the statutory tests for eleven- and fourteen-year-olds too.

A confident government with a competent minister overseeing the impending crisis might conceivably have been able to drive through this agenda. The reality could not have been more different. The shattering blow to the government of 'Black Wednesday' in September 1992 had destroyed the public's confidence in it as a whole and indeed its own confidence in itself. John Patten, meanwhile, aided and abetted by the ill-informed Lord Griffiths, who chaired the government's assessment agency (SEAC), was a public-relations disaster. When, in late 1992, Lord Griffiths described the English tests as the best-prepared assessments in the history of education, the air of unreality reached a new level.

However, even in early 1993, Patten could have quite easily saved the government's testing programme, its curriculum and, conceivably, his career, had he shown an iota of flexibility. All he had to do was announce that the English tests were not yet ready as a result of mistakes in 1991 and 1992, and that therefore the 1993 tests would be a voluntary pilot, while maths, science and the tests for seven-year-olds would go ahead as planned. Either he was too proud or he was too out of touch. Early in 1993, the six teacher unions published a joint statement condemning the English tests and urging John Patten to think again. A few months later, in a unique display of unity, the six unions, along with all the organisations which represented independent schools, published proposals for the revision of the National Curriculum. The display of unity was immensely powerful, but it was fleeting, temporary and fragile, as we shall see.

The NUT's sensational ballot of teachers of English, not surprisingly, provoked its arch rival, the NASUWT, to attempt to trump it. The NASUWT argued that the NUT's proposed boycott – on educational grounds – of the English tests would fall foul of the law since it could not be construed as a legitimate trade dispute. It argued, however, that a boycott on grounds of workload would be legitimate, but in this case it would be irrational to boycott just the English tests: instead there should be a boycott of all the workload resulting from the testing programme.

An overwhelming majority of its members supported this line, and before Easter the NASUWT implemented a boycott of all assessment-related work. The baton had been passed from the groups representing English teachers, to the NUT, and now to the NASUWT. Members of other unions now began to lobby their leaders to follow the NASUWT. Meanwhile, John Patten's public-relations skills did not improve. In February 1993, he described representatives of parents as 'Neanderthal'.

The attention now shifted to the third major classroom teachers' union, the ATL. John Patten was due to address their annual conference, which opens a few days before those of the NUT and NASUWT. The seriousness of his predicament had become apparent to him. The decision he announced there in Cardiff turned out to be his best: a classic example of a good decision taken for the wrong reasons.

By announcing that the whole National Curriculum would be reviewed by Sir Ron Dearing in order to make it more manageable, he opened up the whole curriculum agenda and put in charge of the task a skilled, open-minded pragmatist who, in addition, was a man of integrity. This was an extraordinary breath of fresh air and led eventually to the restoration of the National Curriculum's credibility.

But Patten's objective in announcing this was to save his testing programme, including the absurd English tests. In this he signally failed. Immediately after his departure from ATL's conference, the normally excessively moderate association voted overwhelmingly to join the boycott. A few days later the NUT followed suit. It is standard practice in negotiations to sacrifice the short-term for a long-term gain. John Patten, by contrast, sacrificed the long-term for the short-term, an unusual tactical gambit, and lost the short-term nevertheless.

The boycott itself, far from being the climax of these stirring developments, was literally a non-event. May and June came and went and the tests stayed unopened in their packages. It was a complete success. As Charles I said of a different crisis, 'not a dog barked'. Parents, school governors and local education authorities all had reasons to despise government in general – there was, after all, a recession on – and John

Patten in particular. The government was entirely isolated in a sea of testlessness. Not a single individual was ever disciplined for defying the law. A government which had spent much of the last few years taking new powers to itself was manifestly powerless.

In spite of this miraculous success, which demonstrated the power of a united profession working with its allies, the temporary alliance did not survive. The *annus mirabilis* was no longer than that.

Building Bridges and Improving Schools

Amazingly, and in spite of his obvious failure, John Patten was not sacked by the Prime Minister in the 1993 reshuffle. This can only have been because the government – with so much at stake – felt it could not admit to failure, however apparent it was.

However, after his illness during the summer of 1993, John Patten was evidently less influential. His propensity to blunder remained, as his remarks about Tim Brighouse revealed, but for much of the rest of 1993 and well into 1994 Ron Dearing was the real power in the land. His combination of shrewd insight, tactical awareness and openness proved irresistible. He became everyone's favourite uncle. More importantly, in his two reports – one in August 1993, the other in January 1994 – he unravelled the curriculum and assessment knots in which the government had tied itself up. The details of his proposals were important to teachers at the time, but the underlying principles are all that matter here.

The curriculum was simplified, the bureaucracy associated with it cut back, and the words in which it was described clarified. The perspective of the serious, practically minded teacher who had to put it into practice was applied to it at last. Suddenly it all began to make sense. More importantly, Dearing reasserted the importance of professional discretion. He had listened carefully to representatives of teacher unions saying to him that the reason the National Curriculum had driven teachers out of the zone of indifference was that it had undermined their professionalism. He took this seriously. He understood that this was a question not just of the nature of a profession, but also of quality: a teacher who was focused on ticking boxes on forms and trying to make sense of the old National Curriculum's excessive detail was a teacher distracted from the learning needs of pupils, a teacher whose flexibility and room for manoeuvre – so important for inspiring pupils – was undermined. He understood the danger that the prescriptive National Curriculum, which Kenneth Baker had consciously conceived to make sure that 'lazy and inadequate teachers' did not 'skip the important parts', was destroying the profession's confidence and creating a culture of dependency.

He restored teachers' professionalism. In his report he argued: 'the excessive prescription of the National Curriculum [should be] removed, particularly outside the core subjects. This is a recognition that the professionalism of teachers must be trusted. Trust carries with it, however, the duty of accountability: the greater the trust, the clearer the accountability must be.' Here were the terms on which a new, more effective relationship between teachers, government and society could be built. Dearing had done all he could. It did not lead to immediate or complete recovery. As long after his report as February 1996, for example, I found myself discussing the issue of teaching styles with a group of secondary headteachers from a large shire county. 'We are not sure which way we should go on teaching styles. OFSTED seems confused. When are they going to tell us what to do?' they said. 'You have two options,' I replied. 'You can wait for OFSTED to come to a clear view about how to teach and then tell you, in which case you will wait forever . . . or you can debate it among yourselves and with your colleagues, look at the research evidence, evaluate practice, and see what works.' There is, in fact, no alternative to professional assertiveness. It cannot be given to teachers: they have to take it and the responsibility which goes with it.

Dearing understood this: we still await a similar understanding emerging among the leaders of the teaching profession, who tend to place arguments about resources ahead of any reconstruction of the profession. In doing so, they fail to recognise that the latter is a necessary precondition of the former. Dearing, in any case, cleverly turned the argument about professionalism back to teachers by linking it to public accountability. This put the ball firmly back in the profession's court, but on this too its response has been muted: it does not like performance indicators, it opposes inspection, yet it fails to suggest credible alternative models. It is not enough to accept accountability in theory; there must be practical proposals for how educators will be held to account. Only then can public confidence in teachers be rebuilt and the necessary popular support established for greater levels of investment in education.

Dearing's triumph was to regain the initiative for a government which had allowed itself to be run ragged. His proposals to restrict national tests to the core subjects of maths, English and science were straightforward common sense. This, combined with the curriculum reforms, evidently reduced the workload implications of the National Curriculum, which in turn was the key to ending the boycott, at least as far as two of the three major classroom unions were concerned.

Meanwhile, by this time – January 1994 – a quiet shift had happened inside the Department for Education too. Sir Geoffrey Holland, who had been appointed Permanent Secretary in January 1993, had experienced an unenviable year in office. Lumbered with a disaster-prone minister and an unfolding crisis made by others before his appointment, he nevertheless was responsible for two far-reaching decisions. First, he persuaded ministers that they should appoint Ron Dearing to head up the curriculum review even though, apparently, Baroness Blatch, Patten's deputy, had already offered the post – over dinner – to David Pascall, the right-wing chairman of the National Curriculum Council at that time.

Secondly, Sir Geoffrey commissioned Coopers and Lybrand to review the functioning of the Department for Education. They made thoughtful recommendations which greatly improved the performance of the department. It was urged to become much more open, more in touch. Without mentioning the test boycott, the report made it clear that during the disasters of 1993 the department had demonstrated an extraordinary absence of 'antennae'. It had not sensed the mood among educators or parents. It had not provided ministers with the advice they needed, partly because few officials in the Patten era were willing to give ministers the bad news. This, incidentally, is a classic characteristic of dictatorship and very often causes its destruction. Following the review, the department also reorganised itself structurally and established a school-effectiveness division with a brief to deal with the schools that were found, through inspection, to be failing, and to ensure that the department was in touch with the growing body of excellent research about what made schools effective and how they could achieve effectiveness.

In spite of these successes, Sir Geoffrey Holland left the DFE after little more than a year in post. This precipitate departure was said to have resulted from his frustration with ministers, and in particular with John Major's decision to leave John Patten in office after the 1993 test débâcle. He was succeeded by Sir Tim Lankester, who rightly gave high priority to the department's school-improvement work, a process which was greatly encouraged by ministers after John Patten had been sacked.

Dearing's second report, published in January 1994, provided a golden opportunity for the whole education service to put the tortuous and destructive conflicts of the early 1990s behind them. It was a chance to shift the emphasis of policy to the central issues: how could Britain improve its educational performance to achieve European or Pacific Rim levels? What should be done about the very poor schooling provided in many inner-city areas, evidence of which had been highlighted by the report of the National Commission on Education in the autumn of 1993 and an influential OFSTED report entitled *Access and Achievement in Urban Education*? And what should be done to ensure both steady investment in education and a fair distribution of that investment? How, in short, could the challenges set out in Chapter 1 be met?

This was an immense, rich, pressing agenda in the spring of 1994, but the opportunity of giving a concerted response to it was missed. The simmering tensions among the teacher unions boiled over. The NASUWT and the ATL decided Dearing had done enough.

The NUT decided that Dearing's efforts had been inadequate, that his proposals were a sham and that John Patten could not, in any case, be trusted to implement the settlement. It decided to boycott the tests alone in 1994. It is possible to understand this decision. Relying on John Patten, given his track record up to that date, did appear to be a risk. Furthermore, many teachers remained deeply suspicious of the government and its testing programme. To the NUT there appeared to be an opportunity to gain members at the expense of their rivals: the remorseless logic of the market – and the battle for members it demanded – had been temporarily put in the shade during 1993, but it remained powerful, as it always does. As if this were not enough, the union's General Secretary faced re-election in 1994, and selling the Dearing compromise to a union membership which included a powerful left wing may have looked too daunting.

Nevertheless, the consequences of the NUT's decision were, in my view, deeply damaging. For a start, it opened the way for the NASUWT to persuade government to spend up to £30 million on an inefficient system for externally marking the tests. This money might otherwise have been committed to improving teachers' skills. More fundamentally, the opportunity of building a concerted service-wide drive for school improvement was missed. The teacher unions returned to the public bickering that had characterised their nadir in the mid-1980s.

The 1994 boycott did effectively disrupt the tests, but none of the teacher unions acting alone could do more than disrupt. Whereas, the year before, the joint union proposals for the curriculum set the agenda which the Dearing Review largely followed, in 1994 there was no similar professional agenda for assessment or for school improvement. In effect, the 1994 boycott surrendered these issues to the government.

In the second half of 1994, a number of developments brought home to the NUT the realisation that it had walked into a cul-de-sac. John Patten was replaced by the highly competent and emollient Gillian Shephard. It might be argued that the 1994 boycott caused Patten's demise, but surely he was doomed anyway, particularly once Tim Brighouse had won the 'Nuttergate' case in the civil courts. The undisclosed damages awarded to Brighouse were, ironically, used to improve education in Birmingham, the city that John Patten had so often publicly criticised.

More important, from the NUT's point of view, was the emergence
under Tony Blair and David Blunkett of 'new Labour', with its emphasis
on raising standards, dealing with failing schools and providing the public
with performance data about the education service. When the league
tables were published in the autumn of 1994, David Blunkett criticised
them, not for their existence, but for providing insufficient information.
Before the new Labour revolution, there might have been a case for
resisting the government's tests until the election of a Labour government
which would then have swept them away. This was no longer an option,
since a Blair government would clearly maintain the testing programme.
The shrewd Mrs Shephard helped the NUT leadership to play a canny
hand in sliding out of the boycott sack. The promise of a full review of
the national assessment programme – which turned out to be a very
low-key affair – enabled the NUT to claim a victory.

It also, a year later, paved the way for school improvement to reach
the top of the policy agenda at last. The quiet work which had begun
at the department in John Patten's last months now emerged into the
light. Occasionally in 1995, leaders of the NUT complained that it was
the government and its inspection agency, OFSTED, that were driving
school improvement. This was wrong on three counts. Firstly, it was
the union's boycott that ensured it missed the school-improvement bus.
Secondly, and more profoundly, a combination of a powerful body of
research and a growing interest within schools in using that research to
assist improvement was already in place. Indeed, many researchers and
schools were waiting impatiently for a national lead. Thirdly, the era of
free-market Stalinism had been replaced by a new pragmatism. The
government had rejected pure ideology and set out, at last, to seek
evidence of what worked. The Blair revolution meant that the Opposition,
with less ideological baggage to drop, was seeking the same thing.

What worked, they both discovered, was school improvement. This
chapter has examined the tortuous conflicts of government and educators
since the war: it might be thought of as the producer's story. Before
examining the issues of school improvement in depth in Chapter 5, we
need, in Chapters 3 and 4, to gain a consumer's perspective. A concluding
point about the government reforms does, however, need to be made.
In spite of their blunders, they had brought about progress in four
important respects: funding had been successfully delegated to schools,
national standards had been established, public accountability demanded
and the producer stranglehold on policy loosened. Wrong though ministers often were in the decade of reform, about these four principles they
were fundamentally right.

PART THREE

As It Is

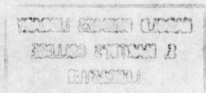

3 · Young People and their Attitudes to School

Boredom is . . . a vital problem for the moralist, since half the sins of mankind are caused by the fear of it.

Bertrand Russell

Ups and Downs

'I hate school and the work. I only go because my mum wants me to. I won't ever need any of the stuff we are learning now. I don't work as hard as I could as I'm not bothered . . . the teachers . . . are really boring.' This is not a chapter for the faint-hearted. The database of Keele University's Centre for Successful Schools records the attitudes of over 30,000 young people to all aspects of secondary schooling. Though not all of them by any means are as disaffected as this young man from a Midlands school appears to be, the printouts do not make pretty reading. The disturbing evidence from this data provides the basis for much of my argument in later chapters, but there are positive findings too, with which I want to start.

Nearly 90 per cent of young people say they are happy at school. Most pupils would probably agree with the pupil who said simply: 'I like school but it has its ups and downs.' Almost all young people believe that it is sensible for them to stay on in education after the age of sixteen. Eighty per cent say they work as hard as they can and about the same number believe that the school they attend is a good one. Over 90 per cent believe that their school work is important (even, in some cases, while they are not doing it) and about three-quarters believe they get on well with all or most of their teachers. At one point the survey asks the pupils whether the school and they are like 'good friends', 'friends', 'distant relatives', 'strangers' or 'enemies'. About 60 per cent place the school in the first two categories, with another quarter choosing 'distant relatives'. Only 9 per cent choose 'strangers' and as few as 8 per cent 'enemies'. The fact is that schools are generally places where pupils feel welcomed.

The Disappeared

In spite of this, the research demonstrates beyond doubt that for many young people in this country secondary school fails to inspire. For some this is a gross understatement since they have opted out of school entirely. On the rare occasions that I visit my home in inner London during the school day, I cannot help noticing a small group of boys in their early and mid-teens sitting on a wall opposite. Sometimes they wander the length of the street and vanish, but rarely for long. Once in a while I have seen them all climb into the back of an unmarked, rusting van which is driven away by a young man, aged perhaps eighteen. I have known one of them since he was a small boy. He has several older brothers who gave him a hard time when he was young. They used to play this game with him: he lay on the pavement and they cycled towards his head. The winner was the one who could brake latest without actually hitting his head. He grew up smaller, slighter, weaker but also more friendly than the older boys. He often offered to wash our car to earn the entrance money for the football. He has the misfortune of being an Arsenal fan.

When I ask him why he isn't in school, as I have done from time to time, he picks one of a range of excuses. There is the predictable 'I'm not well today,' the desperate, 'I'm changing school next week,' or the resigned, 'I ain't going in today.' He is one of many young people who have decided, long before the leaving age of sixteen, that school is not for them. His parents have colluded in his decision to opt out of school. Presumably his school has too. So have I, to my shame, since I have never rung either the school or the education authority about his absence.

This young Arsenal fan is not alone, except perhaps in his undying enthusiasm for Britain's most boring football team. There are thousands like him up and down the country who have opted out. In 1994, at the Council of Local Education Authorities Conference, Tim Brighouse, the dynamic Chief Education Officer of Birmingham, had the courage to draw attention to this issue which many in education would prefer to forget.

> I am moved to run the risk of offence . . . I would like to look at a
> social trend which disturbs most of us: that is the growing number of
> youngsters in adolescence whom we choose to classify as emotionally
> or behaviourally disturbed . . . I am alarmed by the growth in the

number of youngsters excluded from secondary school: moreover, it is a number which I am sure will grow with the expansion in education of pupil referral units. I note that in most cities – indeed, most medium-sized towns where there is more than one secondary school – the pattern of exclusion, having been almost exclusively confined to Year 11 (age sixteen) youngsters ten years ago, has shifted first to Year 11 and Year 10; then to Year 11, Year 10 and Year 9, and finally until now there is a strong representation of Years 11, 10, 9 and 8 among those permanently excluded from the school in which they were originally enrolled in Year 7. Moreover, the overall numbers have escalated through that 10-year period.

Brighouse pointed out that this was just the tip of the iceberg.

For we all know of the parents who are persuaded to withdraw their child from a school where he is a non-conformist and where 'Mrs Smith' – it is always the mother – says 'it would be better for Jim' – it is almost always the male of the species in the teenage years – 'if he were to be in another school better suited to his particular interests and character.' To these considerable numbers of adolescents add the others who absent themselves on the basis of 'you don't bother me and I won't bother you.' I believe that for every one officially excluded from secondary school there is another who has voluntarily withdrawn in search of another school and perhaps three others permanently absent as a result of 'collusion'. If that is right, one way or another there are up to 10 per cent of youngsters between Year 8 and Year 11 who are finding their secondary education outside secondary schooling altogether.

Tim Brighouse is not prone to exaggerate. If his estimate of 10 per cent is near the truth then the country faces not only a serious educational problem but a whole series of interlocking social problems too. I can perhaps illustrate this best by describing a chance conversation I found myself involved in at the Oval in August 1994. While England were striding towards their rare victory over South Africa, I tried out the Tim Brighouse '10 per cent' argument on the people sitting with me. They turned out to be a group uniquely qualified to confirm it. One was a social worker in a north London borough whose main responsibility was young offenders. Some of the young people he had contact with had not been to school for ages. The borough had no accurate records and the schools generally denied all knowledge of them. Worse still when he succeeded in persuading the courts to keep them out of prison he found it very difficult to find any school prepared to take them on. Once their contact with him, which resulted from the non-custodial sentence, came to an end, they drifted back into the ranks of the disappeared.

In his experience, once one of these young people 'at risk' had been out of school for even a few weeks, it was very difficult for them to return successfully. The longer they were out, the harder it became. Thus the procedures that were in place – involving temporary custody, exclusion from school and so on – actually made a return to routine school life harder not easier.

In his excellent piece entitled 'The Thief of Brixton' in the *Guardian* (31 August 1994*)*, Nick Davies described a not untypical case.

> By the time [Daniel] went to secondary school, he was well used to the sight of children smoking spliffs and by the time he was in the third year, he had joined them. The teachers didn't allow it, but he says it was easy to do, and a big minority of the 14 year olds were smoking routinely. He'd build several spliffs on the way to school and then he and his friends would disappear down the dark cracks between buildings or just hang out on the far side of the playground where they could see the teachers coming. He liked it and pretty soon he was smoking every breaktime and lunchtime.
>
> Around this time, certain things began to frustrate Daniel. One of them was that his parents refused to buy him new Nike trainers like everyone else had. How could he show his face in class with these cheap old clothes they expected him to wear? And then there was a new teacher who told him on the first day he taught him that he had his eye on him as a trouble-maker. Daniel was indignant. The man didn't even know him! He was just going by some report he'd read. This teacher was always on his back, trying to follow him and his friends round the place as if he didn't have anything better to do. Daniel got more and more angry. He thought school was rubbish. Then he got kicked out.
>
> He was 15 when it happened, just about to take his exams. A history teacher noticed he had a cigarette packet in his pocket. She took it from him but she didn't seem too worried until she looked inside and saw his little spliffs. She walked him down to see the headmaster. The headmaster said there was nothing to discuss and told the secretary to write a letter. And that was it. He was out of school.

In a better world, this moment would be the beginning of a new stage for Daniel, in which new opportunities to prove himself would arise. Instead, Daniel was left confused.

> The way Daniel saw it, he knew he was sometimes out of order and he spent too much time hanging round the girls, but he thought he was doing OK really and he was planning to work hard on his exams. He felt like they had just been waiting for an excuse to get rid of him. He had never even been suspended before. But they had sent him away.

Now, he was really angry. The next time his dad tried to beat him, he told him to get off him – he was too big to be beaten. When his mum arranged for him to go to a special school, he just stayed at home and slept. And when his dad finally exploded and hit him over the head with a monkey wrench, he knew for sure they didn't care about him and he went to live with one of his sisters in Herne Hill. But she only shouted at him and complained that he showed disrespect to her boyfriend and then one day when he was trying to annoy her by sharpening his flick knife in the front room, she called the police on him.

He talked his way out of that but, a little while later, she called the police again and told them she felt threatened by him, so they pulled him out of the house and dumped him on the street.

Next to the social worker at the Oval was a security guard from a large south London shopping centre. He pointed out that from morning till evening there were young teenagers roaming the centre. Obvious though it was that they should be in school, hardly anyone ever challenged them. What is more, he said, when challenged, even by the police, they did not seem to care. 'When I was young', said the security guard, 'if a policeman told you to jump, you jumped. Not any more.'

On the other side of me was an inner London educational psychologist. The secondary school pupils referred to him were fed up with school. They misbehaved or opted out to try to hide their poor literacy skills and the increasing gap between what they felt able to do and what was expected of them. What is more, he believed that the few that came his way were a drop in the ocean.

For evidence, however, it is not necessary to rely on a conversation among cricket lovers. Those who never darken the doors of schools are the tip of an iceberg. According to the Keele data, though individual schools vary greatly, the national pattern is now startlingly clear. As many as 15 per cent of fourteen- and fifteen-year-olds admit to truanting 'sometimes' or 'often'. Among sixteen-year-olds the equivalent figure is even higher. Even among those in the first year of secondary school, when most teachers find pupils a delight to teach, as many as 8 per cent admit to skipping school from time to time. These are national averages: in urban schools the figures are often much higher. There is a statistical trick here too. The Keele questionnaires are handed out and completed in school time. It must be assumed that some of the most persistent truants will not be there on the day the questionnaires are filled in. The figures for truancy therefore err on the side of caution.

The Disaffected

Truancy is only one of the indicators of disaffection in the Keele data. In addition to those who vote with their feet, there are those who remain in school and express their dissatisfaction through their behaviour. Almost 30 per cent of pupils admit they behave badly 'sometimes' or 'often'. A third of all pupils state that others in their class disrupt lessons every day and in Year 11, the year young people take their GCSEs, 92 per cent of pupils state that others in their classes disrupt lessons at least 'sometimes'.

The Keele questionnaire encourages pupils to add any comments they want to at the end. The theme of disruption by others in the class is one that they write about over and over again. Some comments are mildly critical:

I enjoy most of the lessons, even though it is very noisy in our class.

In the main it is talking that is the problem.

If you want to learn then you can, but you have to try hard because of the noise and students messing around.

In other comments, the sheer frustration leaps from the page:

I think this school would be much better if the teachers showed more discipline towards students and if the students tried harder to get on with work instead of playing around.

I feel that I am a hardworking student . . . However sometimes lessons can be disrupted. Most of the students have no respect for the teachers.

Badly behaved pupils are allowed to hold back and impair the performance of [others].

General disruption is clearly a matter of concern, and by no means only in inner-city schools. Nationally almost half of all pupils say that others often make fun of pupils who work hard. More worrying still is the fact that 15 per cent of pupils in their early teens state that fellow pupils make their lives miserable. Slightly more than this are bullied sometimes. Three per cent say they are bullied every day. The overall picture is, to say the least, alarming. In the comments pupils volunteer, bullying and intimidation are often mentioned. Again this is an issue for every secondary school, however advantaged its intake. The following are taken from a selective secondary school with a highly privileged intake:

I think the playground situation is not very good, the big kids knock you over a lot.

Overall pupils at this school are pleasant to know but there appears to be a disturbing amount of racism, mostly against Asian members of the school.

Even harsher comments were made by pupils at a rural comprehensive.

Bullying is the worst thing about the school. Before you start you are promised that if anyone does in any way bully you, steps will be taken. This is not true. A group of us were bullied right up to the third year and we were just told to stay away from them, they were not stopped even when one of us was hit . . . The headmaster just tries to ignore the issue.

In this school there is a wonderful community in the eyes of many of the staff, especially the headmaster, who tries to ignore the fact that bullying takes place. Two of my friends and I have been on the receiving end . . . The best the teachers could do was make us promise to stop slagging each other off. It went on for three years and resulted in all of us being hit . . .

In an urban setting, for a significant number of pupils, school was an ordeal:

it is difficult to find happiness because there are a lot of bullying people in this school.

sometimes it is making me angry like all day I fight with some student. Some student is swearing . . . all that is making me angry . . . I said to my dad to change me the school because of all the problems I have . . .

Some pupils in this school are over-tolerated when they should be expelled as they disrupt the class and stop others from working.

These two girls betray their vulnerability vividly:

what I don't like is because I'm fat people call me names and take the mickey and I get scared and because I'm big they want to beat me up because they think I'm a good challenge.

I feel so scared when the fourth years push you out of the way when you bump into them by accident and when they start having a go and everybody crowds round . . . I hate it when the second years take the mickey out of me. They say how I stink and that my legs are so skinny, and they cuss my mum . . .

The pupils in their comments tend to lay the blame for these difficulties firmly at the door of their peers. As one pupil put it: 'here the teachers are kind but the pupils are bad'. Nevertheless it is also clear that disruption and intimidation sometimes poison what might otherwise be positive relations with teachers. In schools where there is substantial evidence of disruption there are many comments from pupils urging their teachers to be more strict. These are typical comments at one inner-city school:

> The school could be better if the teachers were stricter.

> I think there should be stricter punishments than just fines and detention. I think we should reintroduce corporal punishment.

The theme is by no means confined to inner urban areas. The following pupil in a rural school is typical of many.

> Most of the teachers are strict enough but some can't keep control of some of the class.

Once a significant level of disruption is established in a school it raises, in heightened form, another theme which is constantly in the minds of secondary pupils, fairness. One student commented:

> I think that some of the teachers victimise some of the students unfairly because they have been in trouble before.

Another in a different school suggested that the school 'could become better by not concentrating so much on the hard-working and clever well-behaved people and give everyone a fair chance'. Pupils clearly hate it when they feel that they are innocent bystanders caught in the crossfire: 'I think when somebody misbehaves they should be the only one that gets punished, not the whole class.'

There is substantial research evidence to show that changing the peer-group pressure in a secondary school is one of the keys to success. From these pupils' comments it is easy to see how a negative peer culture undermines the quality of relationships between pupils and teachers and makes lessons less interesting and more a scene of conflict. Reversing this downward spiral is extremely difficult. Nevertheless it is clear that even in the most troubled schools there are teachers who through a combination of force of personality and pedagogical skill manage to engage young people. One pupil who was fiercely critical of her school said that 'Mrs X is a brilliant teacher who is strict but pleasant and polite [and] takes time to listen.' The same teacher was described by another pupil as 'the BEST teacher ever'. It will be argued later that an essential element of any national strategy to improve the quality of education is to create the conditions that enable many more teachers to succeed. At this point, it is necessary to reach the depressing conclusion that a minority, perhaps 10–15 per cent nationally but much more numerous in some particular schools, are disrupting education for the majority of pupils and impairing the quality of teacher–pupil relationships through-out many schools.

The Disappointed

In addition to the disappeared and the disaffected, there are the dis-appointed. The levels of disruption may help to explain, at least partially, the evidence in the Keele data of a much more general lack of motivation affecting perhaps 40 per cent of all pupils in secondary schools. Almost 60 per cent of pupils agree that they 'count the minutes' to the end of their lessons. Over 20 per cent believe that work is boring. Over 40 per cent believe lessons are too long and almost a third take the view that they would rather not go to school. 'Nowadays school life seems to be like one big chore, which you hate doing. It's so boring and there's never any spice in the school,' says one pupil in a comment which represents the views of many. Another suggests that 'some of the subjects are very boring and we cover totally uninteresting areas'. Of course, attitudes such as these are not necessarily new, but that is of no comfort. Whereas in the past society tolerated and sometimes even encouraged an education system in which most pupils failed, this is no longer acceptable.

Clearly, too, pupils' motivation is greatly affected by the quality of particular teachers. Comments such as the following are common:

> This school has a fair number of very good teachers. However there are at least three teachers who are exceptionally poor . . .

> Sometimes school can be boring, like I really like Mondays but when it comes to Thursdays I feel like pretending to be sick.

Research shows the quality of teaching to be the single most important factor in successful education. Young people did not need research to tell them what their daily experience makes obvious. Reading their com-ments, and between the lines of their comments, it is possible to pick out what pupils think are the characteristics of good teachers: strict, fair, enthusiastic, able to listen, able to take a joke and always able to mark work promptly with care and attention. This is a theme taken up in Chapter 8.

At this point it is necessary to identify negative characteristics of teachers that contribute to boredom and frustration. One is a failure to make things clear. 'I often find,' says one pupil, 'that teachers don't explain things properly and expect you to know the answer to the question.' Another that attracts more criticism than any other is when teachers fail to mark work promptly. 'Some teachers are hopeless at marking books,' comments one boy. Another says with fascinating accuracy: 'Only six out of 10 teachers regularly mark my work.'

Pupils can easily be demoralised when teachers fail to respond to what they see as genuine requests for further information. The following are typical of this line of criticism:

Some of the teachers in my school give you the impression that you're stupid when you ask them to explain more than once. Especially the biology teacher . . .

The teachers never explain anything, they're always on people's backs like that's wrong, that's pathetic, you're thick.

Teachers favour the more intelligent students in our class and don't help us less intelligent students enough . . .

Worse still is the bruising pupils feel if teachers humiliate them in front of their peers. 'I think that teacher should not make fun of you in front of everyone,' pleads one student. Another says that 'there are two teachers who are always calling students names such as "tart" or "fat boy". I don't like this because it is disturbing . . .' Abuse of this nature is completely out of order, but the picture is not always that simple. In the same school teachers will be criticised by some for being too strict and others for not being strict enough or by some for giving too much attention to the most able and others for concentrating on the least able. Whatever else one learns from analysing pupils' attitudes it is evident that being a teacher is not easy. Those who succeed are without doubt people of exceptional talent.

There is consistency, however, in the demands of pupils that they be treated with respect. Sarcasm and put-downs are profoundly damaging. Pupils also hate being patronised or ignored. The following is a cross-section of views on this:

I also feel it is important that the teachers listen to what we have to say as usually we have something useful or important to say.

Basically we are patronised and treated as though we are little kids.

Some teachers are rude towards pupils in a personal way and pupils cannot do anything about it because they do not have any authority.

The teachers think they know everything and some of the male teachers are sexist towards the female students.

The teachers don't even try to understand you.

This raises another theme. Many pupils in school feel anonymous. They want recognition both as a group and as individuals. One pupil suggested constructively that: 'there could be more scope for pupil/teacher contact in interviews . . .'

It is not enough for a school simply to urge pupils on or to reaffirm its values continuously, unless the day-to-day reality conforms to the image. At one school there were a number of comments similar to this pupil's:

> The head is obsessed with school image . . . There is too much emphasis on 'care, community and commitment'. We come here to learn not to . . . conform to the headmaster's ideas.

Another commented acidly: 'They keep telling us that we should commit our whole lives to supporting the school in the community. In reality we only go to school because we have to . . . We are constantly reminded we have a contract with the school but really we have never agreed to one.' Not all pupils are budding Rousseaus like this one, but nearly all of them have an unerring eye for hypocrisy.

Of course, the disturbing lack of motivation and the disappointment with school is not entirely explained by factors within school, but it is evident from pupils' comments that such factors are extremely important. This is one reason why research demonstrates again and again that academic performance can vary dramatically even between schools with very similar intakes.

Nevertheless factors external to the school are important too, and to ignore them would not only do an injustice to teachers and schools, it would also prevent the analysis necessary if we are to bring about significant improvements in our education service. The lives of young people outside of school fall beyond the scope of this book, but all the evidence suggests that being young in the 1990s involves facing up to a range of pressures which previous generations did not face. Of course, there is unparalleled opportunity too, but in a way that simply adds to the burden. At this point it is necessary only to draw one or two conclusions on the basis of the Keele data in order to continue to develop the argument. About one-third of young people spend more than twenty-eight hours a week watching television. That is to say they spend more time watching television than they do in class. Almost all watch television for over fourteen hours a week. It is therefore impossible to conclude other than that television is an important influence on the lives of young people. Since there is no question of turning the clock back to the days before television, it becomes essential to think creatively about how television as a medium – and the new technologies – could be better exploited educationally than at present.

However, it is also important to think about what young people might do instead of watching television. Analysis of the Keele data strongly suggests that pupils in more effective schools do more homework and watch less television. It also suggests that many pupils are desperate for additional activities organised by the school but outside of the formal school day. Over and over again pupils write comments like this boy's:

I think there should be more trips abroad, adventure weekends, art galleries, museums . . .

Another argues that 'We should be allowed to use the sports facilities lunch time and after school,' while a third says: 'We should be able to use the library everyday.'

The enthusiasm of many pupils, especially in inner-city schools, for involvement in extra-curricular activities is one of the most positive aspects of the picture pupils paint of their school experience. It may be that here is another key to significant school improvement. Overall, however, it is hard to escape the conclusion that the disappointed are disturbingly numerous and represent around two-fifths of all young people in secondary school. The picture has its bright spots but its general tenor is bleak.

The Keele data has all been accumulated over the last three years. It is therefore not possible to deduce from it whether the state of affairs is improving or deteriorating with time. My own experience of schools – which is broadly confirmed by the Office for Standards in Education – is that secondary schools have improved in recent years. Certainly, as we have seen, the trend in examination results is upwards. Tim Brighouse in his speech to the Council of Local Education Authorities in 1994 made a similar point:

First, the evidence . . . suggests that secondary schools in urban areas are more not less disciplined places than they have been for some time . . .

Secondly, I believe that secondary teachers and their heads are more capable and doing a better job than has ever been the case before.

If he is right it renders the picture more disturbing, not less, since it makes the task ahead seem Herculean. There are a number of possible explanations. Schools may have been even less happy, less motivating places ten years ago. They may have improved but found themselves increasingly overwhelmed by forces such as drug abuse, family break-down, poverty and unemployment, which are largely beyond their control. Or both might be true. About this we can only speculate. What is beyond a shadow of doubt is that the reality in schools in the middle of the 1990s falls far short of meeting the global challenges outlined in Chapter 1. There I described the destiny of the students currently in school as awesome. It is impossible to avoid the conclusion that at present school fails to prepare many of them adequately for it.

Can All This Be True?

My immediate reaction to the Keele data and even to re-reading the previous sections of this chapter is to decide that it simply cannot be true. I would very much like to discover that everything recorded here about pupils' attitudes is simply wrong. No doubt others will react the same way. Some will therefore rightly turn to question the quality of the Keele data and the research methods that have been used. I hope some researchers will take up this challenge, since all research of this kind is open to question.

To assist the process let me point out here and now where the defects in the research might lie. First of all the data: though it is collected from schools in all kinds of areas – rural, suburban, urban and inner city – and though it includes the views of a large number of young people, it is not based on a carefully constructed random sample. In all cases either the schools or the local education authority chose to be involved. There may be biases in the results for this reason. On the face of it I would expect a sample made up of volunteer schools to paint a picture likely to err on the rosy side of anything, but one cannot be sure. Secondly, it is important to emphasise that the results relate to pupil perception. We have not shown that 17 per cent of fourteen- and fifteen-year-olds play truant 'sometimes' or 'often', but that they say they do. This is not necessarily the same thing at all and this applies to the data as a whole.

Thirdly, the questionnaires are filled in by 25 per cent of pupils chosen randomly from the school roll under conditions laid down by Keele University. It is, however, left to the school to organise the process. If it chooses not to follow the Keele procedure the results from that school may not be valid. For example, if pupils were asked to fill in the questionnaires on a wet Friday afternoon after the others had gone home, one might expect a higher level of disaffection among pupils to be recorded than would otherwise have been the case. It is clear in any case, from looking at the pupils' comments, that while some of them welcome the opportunity to give their views, by no means all do. One pupil for example wrote on the end of his form, 'This is such a rubbish questionnaire,' while another recorded that filling it in was 'such a waste of ******* valuable time and effort'. Pupils in that frame of mind are unlikely to be giving considered answers to the multiple-choice questions.

Fourthly, there is not necessarily any consistency across schools or even individuals in the definition of some key words. For example, if two young people agree that they are usually happy at school, that does not mean that they are equally happy, since one might have a very different view of happiness from the other. Similarly, if school A finds that 95 per cent of its pupils say they are happy and school B that 85 per cent do so, it does not follow that the pupils in school A are objectively happier than those in school B, since we do not know what the levels of expectation of happiness are among the pupils. In short, Keele's research findings, like all such findings, need to be treated with caution. Hopefully, they will provoke other researchers to explore the field and confirm, refine or refute the Keele results.

In the meantime the Keele findings stand. Moreover, I have now discussed them with hundreds of secondary headteachers across the country and, though the results are to say the least challenging from their point of view, headteachers have almost always acknowledged, rather than rejected, them. In addition, as more and more schools participate in the surveys, the findings are reinforced. Finally, the results are broadly similar to a smaller study of pupil attitudes to school undertaken by the NFER for the National Commission on Education. It showed that among fourteen-year-old pupils:

- over half say that most of the time they don't want to go to school;
- one in four thinks teachers are too easily satisfied;
- one in four admits to having played truant; and
- one in five denies being happy at school.

Though there are differences in detail here, the overall impression is similar. It would be comforting to reject the Keele data as simply untrue, but it looks as though we will have to live with it and begin, as a matter of urgency, to do something about it.

Adolescence

The discussion so far has tended to lump all secondary-school pupils together, regardless of their age or gender. In fact these variables are important. This section examines how pupils' attitudes to school change as they get older, while the next section looks at the differences in attitude between boys and girls.

Sometimes I describe to teachers how, according to Keele's data, pupils' attitudes change with age. They show little sign of surprise. When pupils start secondary school at the age of eleven they are predominantly positive. They are generally highly motivated, get on well with their teachers and feel supported by their parents. Over the next two years their attitudes slide. There are increasing signs of lack of motivation, disaffection and cynicism. We have followed up the surveys in some schools and encouraged teachers and pupils to try to explain this slide. It seems that just at the point when the school work becomes more difficult in Year 8, pupils find they receive less support from parents and teachers and that winning praise becomes harder. The relatively easy ride they had in the first year of secondary school has deceived both them and, to some extent, their teachers.

By school Year 9 when pupils are aged thirteen to fourteen, the downward slide in motivation has slumped further. Parents are still less likely to offer support, and relationships with teachers have become more difficult. By Year 10 – the year young people begin their GCSE courses – the bottom of the trough has been reached. Only in Year 11 with GCSE examinations fast approaching does the curve begin to rise again. Here, while parental support has continued to fall, there is evidence of more positive attitudes and improved motivation, though there is no return to the cheery outlook with which young people began secondary school. It seems that, as the examinations at sixteen-plus loom, large numbers of young people begin to buckle down and the adrenalin, at least a little, begins to flow. Simultaneously, however, a significant minority becomes even more disaffected and joins the ranks of the disappeared.

This then is the general shape of pupil attitudes from age eleven through to age sixteen. It is tempting to dismiss the downward slide as the inevitable consequence of adolescence. After all every parent knows only too well that the adolescent years are often heavy going. There are the dramatic changes of mood and the anxiety about self-image which sometimes crosses the border into narcissism. There are fears and fantasies about relationships and the need to strike out for independence. The same young person who demands recognition as an adult one minute, wants the comfort expected by a child the next.

It is easy to forget how hard life in adolescence can be. Perhaps because of this schools are sometimes inadvertently insensitive places. Reading the pupil contributions at the end of the questionnaires is one way of rediscovering how adolescence feels. Uniform, which parents are generally enthusiastic about, is often a bone of contention: 'All teachers think about is how the uniforms LOOK, not how they FEEL which is much more important.'

A few other comments from pupils in that same small-town comprehensive give uncanny insights into being adolescent:

> School is boring. Girls should be allowed to wear make-up and more jewellery and I also think that we should have a girls' football team. I would like school more if the buildings were made more interesting, i.e. [pictures of] Take That. No more homework. (I don't do it anyway.) Drop RE (no need to do it). Helpline (boyfriend trouble). Allowed to have more say in what goes on, drop all exams. We should be allowed to go on more trips. School is too sexist (boys always). Get rid of detentions (cause no one turns up for them).

> I think what people wear on their feet or what type of hair style they have does not really matter. Yet teachers still make a fuss . . . I think that pupils should be allowed more than one pair of pierced earrings, just do not wear them for games. I think we are old enough now to know whether we need a shower after games.

> I think we should be able to go out at lunchtime. I think we should be able to have our hair however we want and have our ears pierced again. Teachers should care more for their pupils and not embarrass them. We should have shower cubicles.

The pupils describe many concerns in these expressive comments and neither the National Curriculum nor academic success seems to register at all. Some of the causes of conflicts between adolescents and schools, especially those over appearance, are perennial. I can remember my own arguments as a pupil with my headteacher. My hair was too long and I remember him describing the slippers I turned up in one day as 'too informal'. Such a gentle rebuke, it seems, looking back. Less than a decade after my long hair had been the subject of controversy, a pupil in the school where I had begun my teaching career was sent home for having his hair too short.

There are some fronts where the battle between generations will always rage, or at least fizzle, and maybe it is no bad thing if the subject is as unimportant as hair length. In the same way it might be argued that the general slide in pupil attitudes, noted by the Keele research, is inevitable and no more than a statement of the obvious. To reach this fatalistic conclusion would be a grave mistake for a number of reasons. One of the most remarkable findings in our research is the extent to which pupil attitudes vary from one school to another. The fact is that, as Figures 2 and 3 show, a decline in motivation during adolescence is not inevitable.

Secondly, adolescence is not best perceived as a problem. I was recently

Figure 2: Pupil commitment to learning (percentage of maximum score): School A

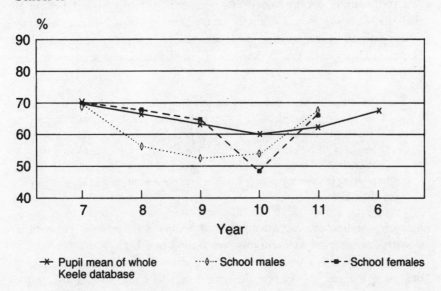

Figure 3: Pupil commitment to learning (percentage of maximum score): School B

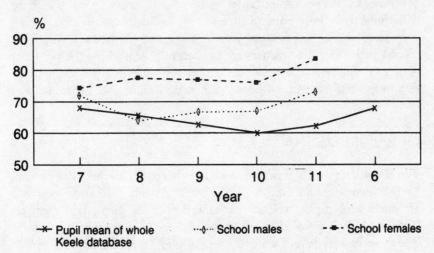

challenged on precisely this point by a headteacher in Birmingham. 'Why do you keep talking about the problem of adolescence?' he argued. 'There is a tremendous energy and creative potential among young people at that age. Our job in schools is to take advantage of it.' The same view was expressed in rather different language nearly seventy years ago. The Hadow Inquiry into the Education of the Adolescent opened with the view that:

> There is a tide which begins to rise in the veins of youth at the age of 11 or 12. It is called by the name of adolescence. If that tide can be taken at the flood, and a new voyage begun in the strength and along the flow of its current, we think that it will 'move on to fortune' ... Transplanted to new ground, and set in a new environment ... we believe that [young people] will thrive to a new height and attain a sturdier fibre.

It is easy to become carried away with Hadow's rhetoric; it is possible to consider his view as incurably romantic; but I believe it to be true.

Each of the characteristics of adolescence – the violent mood-swings, the concern about self-image, the need to criticise and to establish independence – has within it immense educational potential. The key surely is to provide the educational opportunities and the quality of teaching that can unlock this potential. Easy to say but, as many teachers will testify, difficult to do. Nevertheless, teachers will also testify that it can be done and, what is more, that there are few more satisfying professional achievements than doing so. Enabling more schools and teachers to succeed in this respect is one of the central themes of the last three chapters of this book. Two points need to be made at this juncture. One is that there is nothing more important to success than an intellectually challenging and varied curriculum taught by enthusiastic and talented teachers. The second is that if more teachers are to succeed in unlocking the potential of more young people in adolescence, then the issues of attitudes, motivation, pupil self-esteem and peer-group culture must take centre stage.

Girls and Boys

The Keele data provides the evidence for what many teachers and parents have known for a long time: girls are better students than boys. Girls are more likely to be well motivated and positive, they tend to get on better with their teachers and they spend more time on their homework. They are less likely to be disruptive, to play truant or to be bored at school. They also have higher expectations of themselves and are more enthusiastic about staying on in education after the age of sixteen.

There is no way of telling whether girls were that much more positive about school a decade ago. What we do know, however, is that in terms of achievement at age sixteen girls are now leaving boys trailing in their wake. The change over a decade is dramatic. In the mid-1980s, though girls were more successful than boys in English, modern languages and history in the old O Levels, they were some distance behind in mathematics and science. In terms of overall performance the difference between boys and girls was not all that great. At that time, after the age of sixteen, boys strode ahead – being more successful at A Level, more likely to go to university and more likely to achieve a first-class degree once they were there.

In the years since then there has been what amounts to a revolution. In the subjects traditionally associated with girls, the girls' lead over the boys has increased. In English in particular it is now massive. By contrast, in the subjects traditionally associated with boys the girls have steadily narrowed the gap and in science in 1993 they overhauled the boys for the first time.

It was this that prompted interest in these shifts from outside a small circle of researchers. Charles Hymas, the then *Sunday Times* Education Correspondent, and his colleague Julie Cohen wrote a ground-breaking full-page feature on 19 June 1994 which began a major public debate.

> Boys now outnumber girls by two to one in Britain's schools for children with learning difficulties ... In special units for pupils with behavioural or discipline problems, there are as many as six boys for every girl.

> In nearly all the important measures of school achievement, boys are trailing girls. Even in science, once a safe haven of male dominance, girls have finally outperformed boys at GCSE after years of campaigning by the equal opportunities lobby to encourage more girls in the subject.

> By contrast, boys have fallen further behind in the 'female' arts subjects and particularly in English and reading, the skill that is fundamental to success in even the most menial of modern jobs.

> The gap is so wide that girls are now almost twice as likely to get an A grade at GCSE in English as boys. They are more likely to get top grade GCSEs in all but three subjects, they are outperforming boys at A-level, now outnumber men at university and are less likely to end up unemployed after graduating.

> It is a pitiful performance by boys that now requires a radical rethinking of attitudes to equal opportunities. The question is: have

girls had it too good for too long while society has complacently
accepted that boys will be boys?

No doubt the fact that girls are better students helps to explain their
much greater academic success. It is generally assumed, with good reason,
that encouragement from parents and praise from teachers contribute to
improving student motivation. Yet our data suggests that girls have more
positive attitudes and greater success *in spite* of the fact that they receive
less parental support and less praise from teachers. Confusing the issue
still further is the fact that girls appear to have lower self-esteem than
boys. One of the Keele survey questions asks the pupils to assess their
own ability. Fewer girls than boys believe themselves to be 'able' or 'very
able'. More girls than boys think that they are 'below average'. Yet, as
the examination results show, girls are in reality performing much better.

Thus, though the attitudinal data helps to explain the irresistible rise
of the female sex, it falls well short of providing a full explanation. In
any case, revealing that girls are better students simply begs the question
why that should be so.

Some psychologists have pointed to innate characteristics of girls as
opposed to boys – suggesting, for example, that they are steadier, are
more self-contained, have more stamina and have greater mental powers
in relation to socio-linguistic areas of thought. By contrast they suggest
boys are more likely to need external encouragement, have less staying
power and have strength in the mathematical rather than linguistic areas
of intelligence. Others argue that boys are more likely to be risk-takers
and that therefore they will provide more high-fliers but also more failures, whereas girls will thrive where the examination gives most recognition to steadiness. These suggestions of innate differences are not
universally accepted and in any case, though they might contribute to
the discussion, they do nothing to explain the huge change in the relative
performance of girls and boys in the last few years.

Another factor in the burgeoning debate is the nature of the GCSE
examination itself. It appears to be generally assumed that one of the
reasons for the more rapid progress of girls in recent years is that the
GCSE has had a much more substantial coursework element than O
Level. The view seems to be that the steadier girls are more likely to
succeed with a continuous assessment model while boys benefit from the
'Big Bang' examination. To use a football analogy on this theory, girls
would be more likely to be League Champions while boys would do
better in the FA Cup. This has a ring of plausibility, but turns out to
be at variance with the evidence which, as Janette Elwood has shown,
reveals that girls do better in the timed examination element of GCSE

as well as the coursework. Thus, though additional coursework may be a contributory factor, it seems that girls would do better even without it. No doubt further analysis of results will provide us with important new insights.

In the meantime all we can do is continue to speculate. One factor that ought certainly to be noted is that during the 1980s there was an emphasis on equal opportunities for girls. This was given high priority in primary as well as secondary schools. My own daughters, for example, attended inner-London primary schools in the early 1980s where there was a tremendous effort to encourage girls to think positively about academic achievement.

For them the experience of moving to Zimbabwe in the early 1980s while they were still of primary age proved a rude awakening. When national tree-planting day came round in December, each class tramped out into the rainy-season heat. The boys dug a hole and planted a tree in it while the girls waited patiently. Then, just when my daughter assumed it was now her turn, the class was marched back inside. It was never intended that the girls should do more than watch. My daughter then aged nine was outraged by this flagrant infringement of what she saw as her rights.

Those same cohorts of girls attended secondary schools which emphasised equal opportunities for girls too. Schools saw it as part of their mission to challenge low expectations among both teachers and girls themselves of what girls could achieve, especially in the traditionally male bastions of mathematics and science. There was great emphasis on providing girls with role models, past and present. There was, for example, a growing demand for posters of Marie Curie and other women scientists. In the mid-1980s the ILEA became the first education authority to have more women headteachers than men. Others have followed, though there is still a long way to go.

The National Union of Teachers and other teacher organisations made equal opportunities a major focus during that decade. They campaigned with stunning success for maternity benefits for women teachers, for improved promotion opportunities for women, for retraining for women returning to the profession and, in one notable campaign, for 'equal opportunities for girls and boys' (in that order).

The cohorts of girls who experienced school during that decade are now taking GCSE and the results of the rigorous equal-opportunities policies are being revealed. The leaders of that social movement ought to be dancing in the streets; it has been a remarkable success.

Now, at the moment of triumph, is the time to review the nature and direction of this aspect of equal-opportunities policy. The task is to recognise and challenge underachievement in all its forms. In 1994 the most significant underachievers are working-class boys. We are witnessing a new and, to me at least, frightening social phenomenon. New thought needs to be given to how their underachievement might best be challenged. Before discussing solutions, however, a central and obvious (but easily overlooked) point needs to be made. We are not dealing here with a zero-sum game. A strategy aimed at raising achievement levels among disaffected boys need not be at the expense of girls. Indeed the evidence of the last decade would suggest the opposite. It is not that girls have improved as boys have declined but that, while both have improved, the rate of improvement among girls has been faster. If there were an equal-opportunities programme focused on raising levels of motivation among boys, girls would benefit too. We have seen after all earlier in the chapter how deeply frustrating many pupils, especially girls, find the disruption of their lessons by other pupils.

In case this line of argument is dismissed as the feeble rantings of a male professor in defence of his own sex, it should be stressed that there are indications that the Equal Opportunities Commission itself has recognised the importance of a rethink. Anne Madden of the EOC told the *Sunday Times*:

> We have spent a lot of time raising girls' achievement and aspirations. We have got to the stage where we are thinking they are doing extremely well but boys are doing quite badly. The girls' improvement in 'male' subjects has not been replicated by boys in 'female' subjects.

Part of any new strategy would need to be based on an examination of the relative failure of boys in literacy and English. For good or ill we live in a society in which one can say, even with pride, 'I'm hopeless at maths,' but where to admit to illiteracy is deeply damaging to self-esteem. People go to extraordinary lengths to avoid revealing their illiteracy. This is one major reason why some boys disappear from school altogether. Research into boys' problems with literacy would have to reach back not only into primary school but to the earliest years of childhood. Kim Reynolds of the Children's Literature Research Centre told Charles Hymas that there was a long tradition, perhaps a century old, of boys preferring factual books and perceiving novels or poems as 'sissy'. She went on: 'If you want boys to read you have to give them stories that get them involved, not just with a series of facts, but with narrative as well. If you want equal opportunities . . . you have to change things for the boys.'

Already in the early years of primary school, teachers notice differences in attitude to literacy between boys and girls. Girls are more likely to sit quietly and talk and listen. Boys, even at that age, are more absorbed by computer games. Is literacy something that young boys perceive to be broadly a woman's domain? After all, their mothers are more likely to read with them at home and their teacher in primary school is almost invariably a woman too. These are complex issues, many of which are taken up in later chapters. In particular it should be emphasised that strategies which improve motivation among young people of both sexes are likely to be central to solving the problems raised here.

The differences in attitude and performance between girls and boys also add a new twist to another debate which is just beginning about how we group children within schools. The relative merits of mixed-ability grouping, streaming and other options are a matter of fierce controversy. At this point single sex-education merits comment. Following the *Sunday Times* article of June 1994 a number of schools found themselves under the spotlight. Two schools in Chelmsford which, though mixed in intake, segregated girls from boys for lessons were repeatedly mentioned. Their contribution to the debate turned out to be rather disappointing. One school had chosen to segregate on the ground that the other was doing so. The other segregated not on the basis of an educational philosophy but because twenty years earlier the Chairman of Essex Education Committee had suggested that by doing so it would be able to compete more successfully with neighbouring single-sex grammar schools. A couple of other schools, one in Gloucestershire and one in Durham, were about to embark on the experiment which may in time have interesting results, but they have little to contribute at this stage.

Another oft-quoted headteacher was Alan Leech of Bohunt School in Hampshire, where boys and girls do equally well. He rejected out of hand the Chelmsford approach. In his view the route to success lay in concentrating on the individual talents of each pupil and avoiding stereotyping. He was proud of the rigour of his school's equal-opportunities policy and believed that co-education had important social benefits which should not be overlooked.

This, of course, raises the more general issue of single-sex schools. There was a steep decline in their numbers during the comprehensive reorganisations of the 1970s and early 1980s. Among the remainder, the evidence suggests that, on the whole, girls' schools are highly successful and very popular with parents. The same cannot be said of boys' schools. As a result it is common to find that in areas where there are both single-sex and mixed schools, as in much of inner London, the girls' schools are oversubscribed and the boys' schools under-utilised. Therefore the mixed schools inevitably have significantly more boys than girls, to the detriment of both. As long as the number of boys and girls born remains roughly equal – as it has done since the beginning of time – it is not possible to construct an education system in which there are girls' schools and mixed schools with equal numbers of boys and girls, but no boys' schools. This leaves only two available options.

One would be to require all schools to become co-educational, which would be deeply unpopular, would be extremely difficult to implement and would drive much of the Muslim community out of the state sector altogether. It would involve heavyhanded and destructive social engineering of a kind that would not be in the spirit of the times.

The alternative is to give attention to making boys' schools more successful. Again, some of the proposals later in the book ought to play a part in this process. It is, however, an area which, like the whole issue of boys' underachievement, needs new research and analysis. This chapter has been written at a time when a major debate is only just beginning. It is a description of the thin end of a potentially large wedge.

4 · Parents and their Attitudes to School

We must ensure that the wishes of parents . . . are not thwarted
by unreasonable behaviour on the part of education authorities
. . . Some are even campaigning against the wishes of
parents . . .

John Major

More needs to be done with those parents who simply will
not discharge their responsibilities adequately.
David Hart, General Secretary, National Association
of Headteachers

Trotsky's Problem

One of the seminal moments during the cultural revolution described in
Chapter 2 was a speech by John Major at the Café Royal on 3 July 1991.
The conference was organised by the Centre for Policy Studies, so the
fledgling Prime Minister was among friends. He had been Prime Minister
for only eight months, most of which had been dominated by the Gulf
War. Prior to becoming Prime Minister, his career had largely been at
the Treasury, with a brief interlude at the Foreign Office. In terms of
the great domestic issues of the day – health, crime and education –
John Major's CV was what might be described as thin. Labour's Shadow
Education Spokesperson at the time, Jack Straw, taunted him – perhaps
unkindly – with the statement that if all John Major's views on education
expressed in Parliament were cut out of Hansard and glued together
they would just cover the back of one postage stamp. The speech at the
Café Royal was to put that taunt to flight with a vengeance.

The importance of the occasion from the Prime Minister's viewpoint
was heightened by two further factors. One was the approach of a general
election, before which he would need to stake out some ground on the
critical domestic issues such as education. The other was that the CPS
had been the ultimate Thatcherite think-tank. It was to Thatcherism

what the Jesuits had been to the Counter-Reformation. Though the Thatcherites had generally supported Major in the leadership ballot following the coup in which Thatcher had fallen, the young Prime Minister was still very much on probation.

All this explains why, at the Café Royal, the Prime Minister gave the Centre for Policy Studies large doses of what they wanted to hear. The free-market think-tank must have been delighted by the contribution. For the Centre for Policy Studies, parents choosing in a free market was *the* way to raise standards. The leading figure in the CPS in the early 1990s was one Sheila Lawlor, officially its Deputy Director. It seemed for a while, at that time, that whenever the radio or television wanted a pure right-winger to say pure right-wing things, they turned to her. In a beautiful upper-crust accent which, in her throat, appeared to unite with a slightly breathless sense of panic, she intoned the virtues of the market and attacked all things bureaucratic. Since a number of those associated with the CPS were appointed to education quangos in the free-market purism era, it is a wonder that she never was. Kenneth Clarke, the Secretary of State for Education in 1990–92, came close, however, by appointing her husband to the assessment authority. It may be mischievous, but one can't help wishing that the disastrous English tests of 1993 were first hatched in their pillow talk.

Sheila Lawlor, however, was no fan of the National Curriculum. She wanted the curriculum, like everything else, to be left to the market. Then, if parents did not like a school, they would vote with their feet – or, more accurately, with their children's feet – and another bad school would bite the dust.

Small wonder that in these circumstances the Prime Minister drew heavily on already published CPS pamphlets and put his emphasis firmly on parental choice.

> We must ensure that the wishes of parents and governors are not thwarted by unreasonable behaviour on the part of education authorities . . . Some are even campaigning against the wishes of parents . . . which leads me back to accountability. Accountability first and foremost to parents . . . We have sought to make room for parents within the cosy relationship between local education authorities, their schools and their advisers and inspectors. All this is part of our long-standing intent to empower parents within the education system so they can make better-informed choices about what is best for their children. But – as no one knows better than parents – the quality of education depends on the quality and commitment of our teachers . . .

The conference audience warmed to it. The Prime Minister no doubt hoped he had scored electorally too. The problem was that neither John

Major, nor his various secretaries of state for education, have ever had any clear picture of what parents actually want. Indeed, by 1993, the gap between government and parents was such that about two-thirds of them actually supported the teachers' boycott of the tests. John Patten, as we have seen, proved how far he had failed to understand parents by publicly describing their leaders as 'Neanderthal', a spectacular own-goal by any standards. Increasingly, it seemed that the reforms being carried out in the name of parents did not have their support. Opponents of the government's reforms, above all the National Union of Teachers, were quick to latch on to this division. They revelled, for example, in the findings of the Keele survey of parents which showed that, in the summer of 1994, only one-third of parents supported the government's tests. The trouble was that, in their enthusiasm to co-opt parents to their cause, they were in danger of falling into the same trap that the government had fallen into: they were no better informed about what parents wanted. Both government and teachers, in short, were tied in knots when it came to parents.

The government had what might be called Trotsky's problem. Trotsky, it will be remembered, had decided in the 1920s that the party – the Bolsheviks, that is – was always right. To put it in his words, 'an individual cannot be right against the party'. This is fine as long as the party does what you want it to do. It is a less comfortable position to hold when the party is run by your arch-enemy – in Trotsky's case, Stalin – and does what he wants. Question: what does a politician who believes the party is always right do when he disagrees with the party? Answer: retreat to Mexico.

The government's version of the Trotsky dilemma can be expressed in similar terms. Question: what does a government do when, having argued for several years that parents will always be right, parents evidently disagree with its reforms? Answer: in John Patten's case, call parents 'Neanderthal'; in Gillian Shephard's case, shift the focus of the education debate and take less advice from Sheila Lawlor.

For the teacher unions, the predicament was different but no less difficult. Parents make marvellous allies when there is a campaign to run, whether it is for resources or against testing. Their support enables the teachers to demonstrate that their advocacy is a matter of children's entitlements rather than self-interest. On the other hand, if they have performance data about schools and a degree of choice or if they dominate governing bodies and exercise their extensive powers, they can potentially limit teachers' own room for manoeuvre or, worse still, make life difficult for them. Thus, through the 1980s, parents were treated by teachers as a stage army to be wheeled on when they were needed as allies, and wheeled off again as soon as the campaign was over. Extensions of parental power from the Taylor Report in the late 1970s, which proposed elected parent governors, through to the 1988 Act, were almost without exception opposed by teacher unions.

Yet it was the 1988 Education Reform Act, also bitterly opposed by the teaching profession, which created a new configuration of these tortuous relationships between government, parents and teachers. The government, through extending the rights of parents, no doubt expected to co-opt them as allies, just as in the early 1980s they had co-opted tenants by offering them the right to buy. Parents, as a group, turned out to be an ungrateful lot. As it does to the rest of the electorate, government inevitably seems distant and their views of it are more likely to be influenced by the state of the economy than by whether they are represented on a school governing body. By contrast, they feel very attached to, and interested in, the school their children attend and the teachers who teach them. The government, by giving schools extensive autonomy to run their own affairs, thus unintentionally provided a genuine and practical basis for a teacher–parent collaboration. Ironically, therefore, a government hoping to co-opt parents as allies provided a platform on which teachers and parents could unite against it. The 1993 test boycott was one outcome. The 1995 campaign for better school funding and reduced class sizes was another. And, in some schools, school improvement is a third. At the level of the school, therefore, community of interest is genuinely possible. However, to leap from that conclusion to the view that at national level either government or teachers can rely on parental support is to misunderstand reality.

Halibuts and Whingers

In fact, parents, like any other large and diverse social group, are uncertain and varied in their views about education and about the schools their children attend. Indeed, on many issues it is difficult to claim that there is what might be called a 'parental view' at all. For example, as we saw in Chapter 2, in 1994, in the Keele survey, about a third of parents thought national testing helped children to learn, a third thought it did not, and a third did not know. In short, they were confused, which considering the extent of the controversy over the question in the preceding two years was hardly surprising.

This raises a further point: as opinion polls on other subjects show, people's attitudes can change quite rapidly on questions such as these. By 1995, for example, those who believed national tests had beneficial effects made up over 42 per cent of those surveyed, while the negatives and 'don't knows' had correspondingly fallen away. While it is helpful to know this, it provides no basis for policy or for steady implementation. A government which tries to build its policy purely on the shifting sands of public – or in this case parental – opinion will surely fail.

Furthermore, even where an overwhelming majority of parents believe something, this does not necessarily mean they are right. Parents, like everyone else, are victims of fashion, trends and media portrayals of education. For example, in one school where both pupils and parents were surveyed, the parents thought it was marvellous – one of the best we had ever surveyed – but the pupils gave it disturbingly low ratings.

If parents are not always well informed about what characterises a good school, it is hardly surprising. They have, after all, few opportunities to find out about schools other than the one their child attends. Nevertheless, it is clear that parents' views are, and ought to be, a crucial element in the decision-making process at both school and national level. Whether or not their views are finally adhered to, it is vital that they have been taken into account. The problem is that, while many people claim to know what parents think, there is a paucity of hard data about what they actually do think. At school level, heads' and teachers' views of parents and what parents think are inevitably coloured by the handful that they meet regularly. Among this one small but powerful group are the constructive activists. These are the parents who tend to get themselves elected to the governing body or run the PTA.

From time to time their enthusiasm gets the better of them. I tried to parody this type of parent in a column, written ostensibly by an irascible headteacher, Satterthwaite, in *Education* magazine in 1993.

Don't get me wrong, I'm 100 per cent committed to the idea of PTAs. But, like staff meetings, they have a tendency to spend the greatest amount of time on the least important matters. They also draw into action that unique category of parents who are both wonderfully committed and dreadfully irritating.

The backbone of our PTA is a remarkable woman by the name of Polly Clone. She devotes all her conscious hours, and a good many unconscious ones too, to fund-raising for the school. At last night's meeting where I wanted to generate parental outrage about the government's attack on primary teacher training, Polly wanted to discuss the halibut which had been a prize in the recent grand raffle. The problem was that the parent whose name was on the winning ticket was unable to produce his stub.

I was all for giving him the halibut and getting on to teacher training. But Polly felt, with considerable vehemence, that this was setting a poor precedent. Anyone who couldn't keep a raffle ticket stub didn't deserve a prize, still less a prize halibut. The meeting was split down the middle. The debate was greatly prolonged when someone asked where the halibut was at the moment, and was it alive or dead. It emerged that it was dead and in Polly Clone's freezer. Those present drew the obvious conclusion, and for a while the vote seemed to go in my favour. Then Polly played her trump card.

If there was any implication of a green shoot of impropriety here, she argued, then she saw no alternative but to resign her posts, as secretary, treasurer, membership secretary, chief fund-raiser, and open-day organiser, all of which she felt she had held with distinction for more years than she cared to remember.

We fell for this – as we do every time – hook, line and sinker. Never one to get out when she's winning, Polly burst into tears and continued the emotional blackmail. In the end, it required a gushing speech from me about her remarkable contribution before calm was restored.

Deeply embarrassed and keen to avoid inheriting any of Polly's array of responsibilities, most of the committee shot off at the end of the meeting. I had no alternative but to invite Polly for a drink in the Mock Turtle, where she told me about the Singalongathon she has planned for the autumn . . .

I don't know what fund-raising does for halibuts, but it certainly isn't good for the soul.

Believe it or not, this is based on a true story, though to protect the innocent, I changed the salmon into a halibut. Nevertheless, the constructive activists make an immense contribution to the life of a school, as any head will testify, and their views, almost always supportive, may be influential. The opposite group, most of the time equally small, are the whingers. These are the people for whom, whatever the school does, nothing will be right. The parents' evening will be on the wrong day, or at the wrong time, or both. The school bus driver will be surly and probably late as well, and the pupils from the school will be poorly turned out and antipathetic to the (unfortunate) child of the whingeing parent. A head of a much improved school told me recently that one of the indicators of improvement as far as she was concerned was that the number of whingers had fallen substantially. These parents sap morale and are doubly damaging because they hide or disguise the real complaint. Still, such people are an occupational hazard, well known across the public services.

There are then the mass of ordinary, law-abiding parents who are recognised by the head and on friendly terms with her or him. On the whole, this group will choose to give the school the benefit of the doubt and keep their views about it, whether positive or not, to themselves.

It was to address this problem that the Keele survey of parents' attitudes was developed. It was designed to help individual schools gain a clearer picture of how parents perceived them. They became popular partly because schools found themselves increasingly at the mercy of the local market as parental choice became influential, and partly because the Total Quality Management fashion encouraged schools to find out what their customers thought. The chief motivation, however, for heads I discussed it with was that they hoped it would help them to improve their schools.

The national aggregation of this data, which, by 1996, includes the views of over 8,000 parents, provides perhaps the clearest picture yet of parents' views of secondary schools. Not surprisingly, the picture is a mixed one. However, what is shown most vividly is that parents are very positive about the schools their children attend and the teachers who teach them. Judith Judd commented on the preliminary findings in the *Independent* on 22 July 1994:

> Parents are happy with standards in their children's schools and most feel welcome, according to one of the biggest research studies into parental opinion.
>
> The findings of the national survey . . . challenge the belief that there is widespread dissatisfaction with schools, which government ministers have used to justify education changes. It appears to contradict polls showing that parents think standards are falling . . . Nearly 87 per cent of parents . . . would recommend the school their children attend . . . 83 per cent thought their child's school was either good or of a very high standard, and only 16 per cent worried about their school's examination results . . . More than 97 per cent of parents felt welcome in school.

Judith Judd puts her finger on a central issue. When parents are asked about education, schools and standards in general, they are victims, like everyone else, of the media portrayal of falling standards and poor state schools. When asked about the school they know, their views are much more positive. The fact is that, even with all the public information on examination results, parents find it hard to judge quality. It is too early to say whether the cycle of inspections which requires each school to be inspected every four years will change this. It certainly ought to have an impact. The inspection process must include a meeting for parents with the inspection team: it also requires the school to send a summary of the report to every parent. The system has been in operation for three years, but the early evidence suggests that it has not yet had a major impact on parents' opinions of the school their child attends, except where serious underperformance is reported. Partly this is a matter of the style of the reports: the word OFSTED-ese has been coined already to describe the bland platitudes that pass for judgements in some inspection reports. More importantly it is, I think, the case that we tend to underestimate parental commitment to the school they have chosen for their child. They have chosen it. They desperately want their child to succeed. And therefore they desperately want to believe that it is a good school. In most cases, they convince themselves that it is and, of course, often it really is. Sometimes, however, the school could be better and, in spite of all the information to which parents now have access, it is not clear that they are in a position to recognise when that might be.

Sometimes, too, the school is poor and the evidence suggests that even then parents are more than likely to rally round it. Generations of chief education officers have discovered that the one guaranteed means of generating parental support for a school is to propose its closure. The least-loved and most mediocre schools suddenly become popular. Of course there is a simple statistical reason for this in many cases: parents who do not like the school have already withdrawn their children; those who remain are thus a self-selected sample of devotees.

For this reason, I fully expected a massive parental campaign to save Hackney Downs School when its closure by a central government appointed team was proposed in 1995. In fact, the parental response was muted. Only thirty or forty attended the consultation meeting, and they expressed a range of views. Others joined the demonstration, though only eight signed the petition handed in to Gillian Shephard. This relative lack of support is rare, and probably indicates that, in the case of Hackney Downs, parents had read the writing on the wall.

Nevertheless, the evidence of the Keele survey, and of numerous examples of school closures, is that parents are strongly supportive of the school their child attends. This fact tends to be given a positive interpretation, particularly by teachers. They argue that the gap between parents' support for their own child's school and their concern about standards of schools in general is a measure of the malevolent influence of the press on the debate about education.

Another interpretation of this evidence is possible, however. It could be that parents are complacent about the school their child attends: that parents, like society as a whole, have low expectations, both of children and of schooling, and that the standard achieved as a matter of course in, say, maths by German, Swiss or Korean children at age eleven is simply not considered possible, never mind likely, in this country. Certainly international studies suggest that one reason for higher levels of performance in, for example, Pacific Rim countries is precisely that parents there have far higher expectations of the education service than parents here.

If parents' views of the status quo border on complacency, it is more disturbing still to discover that they are reluctant to see change in schools. If the matter were left to parents, it seems probable that, far from the rapid change schools have seen in recent years, there would be very little change at all. While 55 per cent of parents in the Keele survey agree with the view that some things should change, when offered a list of what should change, there is not a majority for any of the possibilities. Only 20 per cent, for example, want change in reports on pupil progress; as few as 11.5 per cent want changes in examination results; and only 20 per cent think the curriculum should be altered. Even the buildings – which in many places are a national disgrace – are acceptable to over three-quarters of parents.

The two areas with the largest proportion of parents urging change are school discipline (36 per cent) and pupil dress (28 per cent). Even in these categories caveats need to be made. While the overwhelming majority of those who want change in these respects want stricter discipline and uniforms, a significant minority included in each of those figures believe that discipline is too strict and that a move away from uniforms would be beneficial.

Involvement in Schools or Involvement in Learning

Consistent with this lack of demand for change among parents is the clear message that, on the whole, they do not want to be more involved in running schools. Less than 20 per cent want more involvement in schools, over 30 per cent do not know what governors do, and 60 per cent do not know who the governors of their school are.

Further evidence of this lack of interest in school governance is provided by the poor turnouts at the annual meetings governors are required to provide for parents. These were introduced under the 1986 Education Act as a new element of accountability. Just as company boards are required to report annually to shareholders, so school governors must now report to the wider parent body.

In practice, few parents take the opportunity to find out what the school governors have been doing. It is common for attendance to be in single figures and, indeed, for the governors to outnumber parents. Cynics among the teaching profession – those who have resisted every attempt to open up the secret garden – delight in telling stories about the failure of those meetings to generate interest. One head told me that his chair of governors had failed to attend the annual meeting. On the way home, the head had called in on the chair to find out why he had not come. Apologising profusely, the chair had said, 'Were you very embarrassed?' 'No,' the head had replied, 'no one else turned up either.' Both had then cheerfully gone to the pub to celebrate this abject failure to communicate with the people in whose name the two of them carried out their responsibilities.

At the school where I was chair of governors in the early 1990s, we had a disastrous meeting for the opposite reason. We decided to flex every muscle to persuade parents to attend. The teachers mounted a magnificent display of children's paintings all round the hall on the first floor of the Victorian three-decker building. We bought wine, soft drinks, cheese, biscuits and crisps. We laid on a crèche.

And the parents came – forty or more of them. A small proportion of the total parent body, it's true, but nevertheless this was four times the national average attendance at such events, and that average includes secondary schools. The first sign of trouble was that, as a result of a work commitment, I was late. Nevertheless, the excellent headteacher and the enthusiastic vice-chair started the meeting with great competence. Soon after I arrived, the second cloud emerged on the horizon. One of the parent governors was sitting very close to the wine and appeared to be filling her plastic cup with alarming regularity. My fears were confirmed when she gave her parent governor's report in a slurred version of Cockney. Matters became worse when she was involved in a vicious altercation with another parent who apparently bore a long-standing grudge against her, following a dispute on their housing estate.

The mellifluous headteacher managed to smooth ruffled feathers, and the meeting proceeded more or less calmly until – two cups of wine later – the parent governor staggered across the hall, sat down next to the other parent governor, a very upright West Indian man, and put her arms around him. The meeting never recovered from the ensuing chaos. The parent governor slid to the floor in a stupor; her comrade-in-arms tried desperately to hide his embarrassment, and her rival from the housing estate stormed off demanding a resignation. All that remained to do was to look at the children's magnificent artwork all round the room and to reflect on the gap between the theory and practice of parental involvement.

With regard to the involvement of parents in the governance of schools, according to Michael Fullan, one of the world's leading authorities on educational change; 'there is little evidence to suggest that parent involvement in governance [of schools] affects student learning . . . although there may be other benefits and indirect effects'. (*The New Meaning of*

Educational Change, Cassell, 1991.) Again the Keele survey would appear to confirm Fullan's conclusions. The vast majority of parents are simply not interested in involvement of this kind. Thus the government's emphasis on parental involvement in governing bodies is unlikely to bring about significant improvements in education standards, though it can be, and in my view is, justified on other grounds, not least as a means of encouraging teachers to account for their performance.

Parents' reluctance to play an active part in school governance is, on reflection, hardly surprising. Parents are people with children. They have the rest of their lives to get on with. Their work, or lack of it, their personal relationships and even painting the front bedroom are matters of concern. Part of the virtue of school is that it actually ensures that for five hours or more on 190 days a year parents know that – generally speaking – their children are gainfully employed in a safe environment. Even if they did want to be more involved in schools, many parents could not easily find the time.

The fact that they do not wish to be more involved in schools should not be confused with the view that parents do not care about the education of their children. Most do, deeply, if the Keele evidence is to be believed. Over 90 per cent also believe that their children are well cared for. Over 95 per cent hope fervently that their child will stay on in school after age sixteen. They find that teachers are approachable and generally treat them as partners in the education process.

Though they do not want more involvement on the whole, between a quarter and a half of all parents do want more information. Over 70 per cent want more information on the measurement of pupil progress: this is the one area where the government's information revolution has ensured that extensive information is available, with more to come. Another potent demand is for more information on extra-curricular activities. About half of all parents would like to know more about clubs and other out-of-school opportunities. This would appear to be a forceful plea for more provision in this area of schooling. Extra-curricular pro-vision appeals to two powerfully held parental views: a genuine, altruistic concern for their child to have a broader, deeper educational experience; combined with a more cynical hope that someone else will take the little blighter off their hands.

Over 50 per cent would like to know more about the curriculum, while nearly 55 per cent believe they do not know enough about the National Curriculum. This confirms previous research which shows that parents are keen to know what their children are supposed to be learning. Slightly fewer – about a third – would also like to know more about how their children are being taught. And they are keen to help their children learn. Over 90 per cent of parents think homework is important. Almost 50 per cent check homework 'often' and another 40 per cent check it 'sometimes'. About 50 per cent feel able to help their children in most or all of their subjects and another 40 per cent can help them in a few.

Michael Fullan identifies four different forms of parental involvement:

1. Parent involvement at school (e.g. volunteers, assistants);
2. Parent involvement in learning activities at home (e.g. in assisting children at home, home tutors);
3. Home/community–school relationships (e.g. communication);
4. Governance (e.g. advisory councils).

The first two forms of involvement have a more direct impact on instruction than do the other forms . . .

Fullan goes on to argue that involvement of parents in instruction can have significant educational benefits in terms of improving learning. He points out that, while many parents are enthusiastic about this kind of involvement, a significant minority are not. The Keele survey confirms this view. Many parents do want to know more about and to contribute better to their child's education. Given the benefits of parental support of this kind, the rest need to be encouraged. Where a large number of parents at a given school show a lack of enthusiasm for this kind of involvement, then it is incumbent on schools to attempt to change that attitude.

Many schools genuinely aspire to increase parental involvement and to communicate more effectively: few would claim they have solved the problem as they see it. Ultimately, it depends on the extent to which the general aspiration is turned into practical strategies. At one primary school I know they chose, following very poor results in the seven-year-olds' English tests, to give priority to English for the next academic year. In addition to rethinking teaching approaches and investing in teachers' skills, they urged parents to read with their children at home. They produced a clear, simple, five-point guide for parents on the contribution they could make, and they translated it into community languages too.

At another primary school, the class teachers write a letter to the parents of children in their class, setting out what learning is planned for the children that term and how the parents can contribute. It suggests to parents, for example, that they practise specified 'times tables' on the journey to and from school or at home, and that they make sure the weekly spellings are learnt. Simple, low-cost initiatives such as these can make all the difference.

At many secondary schools, children and young people have 'day books' or 'homework diaries'. These record homework assignments, but often also provide space for parents and teachers to write comments. They create, therefore, the possibility of three-way communication between teacher, parent and learner. Too often, however, the good idea is not turned into reality, for it depends on teachers and parents giving it priority and implementing it rigorously. With one of my own daughters, for example, we filled it in assiduously for the first three weeks of a bright new school year, only to find that, long before half-term, no one at the school – including our daughter – was making use of the book any more. On the other hand, where they are rigorously implemented, they are appreciated by teachers, parents and students.

Ideas such as these do not, on their own, change the world but, as with so much in education, it's the detail and the practice as much as the bold ideas that make the difference between success and failure. This is certainly true of communication between schools and parents. In the end, it is often a matter of where a school places such communication in its scale of priorities. For many, it is considered a good thing, but is not in practice a priority. Yet the evidence suggests there is tremendous untapped potential for raising standards if, collectively, we can make advances in this area.

As Fullan argues: 'the evidence shows, once teachers and parents interact on some regular basis around specific activities, mutual reservations and fears become transformed, with positive results for the personal and academic development of students and for parent and teacher attitudes'. If this is right, then one might deduce from the Keele survey that schools in this country have a sound foundation for the development of interactions around specific activities, as Fullan calls them. The survey reveals, I think, that parents and teachers in general have a good but perhaps too distant relationship. Many parents do want more information about crucial aspects of school life, and not all get it because, of course, schools vary dramatically in this as in other respects. In short, what parents want is not so much involvement in schools as involvement in their child's learning.

Information about what the school has planned for children, such as that mentioned above, is important, but often it is not enough. Parents often have specific anxieties or questions which relate to the progress of their own child. Whether they are able to find a satisfactory response depends on two separate factors: whether the school is sufficiently welcoming and makes opportunities available for individual parent consultations; and whether, when the parent arrives at the consultation, the teachers are well enough informed and confident enough to deal with the parent's concern.

Many schools have made great efforts to become more welcoming, and the Keele survey suggests that they have been broadly successful. This is a significant achievement, given the trepidation with which many parents face the prospect of going to see a teacher or a head. Too many parents can recall only too well the sense of anxiety, fear or even humiliation they associated with such consultations when they were themselves at school.

But being generally welcoming is often not enough. Some schools have gone further, and have instituted what have become known as home–school contracts. These set the mutual expectations that parents and the school should have of each other and, in addition to dealing with straightforward matters, such as parents ensuring that their child arrives on time, in uniform, with the right equipment, may also provide parents with an entitlement to consultations at formal parents' evenings and perhaps at other times too. Such contracts are constructive, but they do not solve all the problems of communication either.

Parents must also overcome anxiety that if they complain or challenge the school their child will be victimised. The overwhelming majority of teachers are far too professional to allow this to happen, but the fear, nonetheless, is real. Reducing that fear and parents' other anxieties depends ultimately on the quality of all the minute contacts a parent has with the school. What is the tone of letters home? What kinds of questions does the head ask parents when they meet by chance in a school corridor or playground? Do teachers at parents' evenings appear harassed and overworked and keen to see the next set of parents as soon as possible? In short, it is a matter of culture. There are examples of schools taking this bull by the horns. The City Technology College in Derby, for example, has an open week when parents can spend as much time as they like in the school and see any part of it in operation that they choose. It is a splendid gesture of openness which every school could reasonably easily follow.

None of these strategies addresses the second question: whether, when the parent consults the teacher over a specific anxiety, the teacher is informed, confident and able, therefore, to address it. It is worth briefly comparing teaching to another profession, medicine. All parents know the experience of taking a child to the doctor. Understandably, parents often fear the worst. For example, the child gets a headache and the parent – particularly when the issue has been in the news – fears meningitis. How does the doctor deal with this? Some, it is true, are arrogant and make the poor parent feel impossibly small. There is an extensive literature on this in medical circles. Most doctors, however, make a series of checks against known criteria and reach a firm diagnosis. They are able to state with confidence that it is or, in most cases, is not meningitis. And they are able to instruct the parent on what he or she should do to cure the child's ailment. There are, of course, from time to time, errors, but these are rare.

Consider, against this background, the nature of parents' conversations with teachers. One concerned and thoughtful parent described to me recently a discussion she had with a concerned and thoughtful teacher. It was a standard parents' evening in a primary school. The parent had seen the daughter's school books and gazed lovingly at her pictures on the classroom wall. The child's education was going well; her reading was improving, her maths was good; she was happy and a good citizen of the class. But the parent had an anxiety and wanted reassurance. She explained to the teacher that she thought her daughter's concentration span when at home seemed very short: she chopped and changed, one minute enthusing about this, the next deeply involved in that, but never in anything for very long. 'Should I be worried about this?' she concluded.

A number of possible replies from the teacher to this inquiry spring to mind. She could have said that the girl's concentration in lessons was excellent and there was nothing to worry about; she could have said that the girl showed similar characteristics at school, but it was normal for an intelligent eight-year-old, and part of the plan at school was to help her improve her ability to concentrate, and then she could have described what strategies this would have involved. Or she might have said that she, too, was worried, that the school was working on it and that the parent could contribute by using complementary approaches at home. The teacher, in fact, did none of these things. Instead, her brow furrowed into a worried frown and she replied with a question: 'Do you think her concentration's a problem?'

This simply reinforced the parent's anxiety. It revealed the lack of professional confidence that so many teachers feel. This was a good teacher. A good teacher should surely know in some depth about the concentration spans of eight-year-olds, not only from experience, but also from research. Yet, though many teachers do acquire enough experience to hazard a good guess, whether they are abreast of the research that alone can underpin the confidence a professional should have is left to chance. It will depend on the extent to which they as individuals pursue their professional development, and on the content of any training planned by the school as a whole. This clearly raises issues which go far wider than simply relations with parents: the theme of professionalism is picked up in Chapter 8. The point here is that professional knowledge and confidence is, in my view, an essential prerequisite of effective relationships between parents and teachers. Without it, parents are unlikely to have, in turn, the confidence in teachers on which a relationship of quality can be built.

Parental Choice

Parents are also involved in the education process in a rather different way. They are the consumers in the government's market model of the education service. The government's assumption is that, on the basis of information about school performance, parents will make decisions about which school their child should attend. Since under the funding arrangements money follows the child, successful schools will benefit and less successful schools will be forced either to improve or to go out of business. Criticism of this approach is explored in different ways in both Chapters 2 and 5 and it is not the intention to raise the general issues again here. However, it is important to point out that the evidence from the Keele survey suggests that, at least up until now, examination performance is not by any means the most important factor in influencing parental choice of secondary school. In the survey, parents are asked to tick any factor which strongly influenced them. Over 50 per cent of parents state that they chose the secondary school for their child because it was the nearest school to their home. Over 60 per cent chose a school because they believed their child would be happy there. By contrast, the school's examination performance was a factor for only 43 per cent of parents.

Many commentators have interpreted findings of this kind – of which there have been a number in recent years – as proving that the government's emphasis on performance data and choice driving up standards is misplaced. In my view, it is still too early to reach this conclusion. The steady publication of information about school performance may, over a period of time, change the culture and begin to influence parental attitudes. Already, over the three years of the Keele survey, the importance parents attach to exam results has risen markedly. Furthermore, there is no doubt that, whatever its impact on parental attitudes, it has caused headteachers and teachers to give higher priority than ever to both the analysis and the improvement of performance in schools. In any case, parental choice – the pivotal point of parental influence in the market model of education – is riddled with complexities and, in the major conurbations at least, provokes powerful emotions.

Of course, across large swathes of the country, parental choice raises barely a flicker of emotion. In Wem in Shropshire, for example, there is one very good comprehensive school – Adams College – and all the eleven-year-olds from the small market town and its hinterland transfer there. Handfuls of parents may opt for the private sector for reasons of tradition or elitism, but the gap in quality between them and the state schools is narrow or non-existent, and the individual choices of those parents do not disrupt the social equanimity of the district. Similar conditions apply in places such as Bicester in Oxfordshire, Diss in Norfolk and Windermere in Cumbria.

Parental choice in the large conurbations, where the quality of secondary education is markedly uneven, is an entirely different proposition, nowhere more so than in north London. Here it unleashes on an unsuspecting world the anxious but formidable north London parent. These are people who are absolutely committed to a good education for their children, but who do not expect to find it at their local comprehensive. Many of them begin with a general, principled commitment to state education, but find that in the quest for what they want for their own child this commitment is tested to and beyond destruction. Contrary to media opinion, such parents are by no means all middle class. The pressures of the six months or so between September and March of a child's last year in primary school age people years, cause huge stress and sometimes push marriages to the brink of destruction, as the state versus private school debate rages. I know from personal experience, but that is another story.

Overall, the evidence suggests that there are four defining characteristics of parental attitudes to school. Firstly, the vast majority of parents do want a good education for their children. Secondly, they are overwhelmingly happy with the schools their own children attend. Indeed, I would go so far as to say they are alarmingly happy. Schools are often not as good as they think they are, and their complacency is unlikely to encourage constructive change. Before the leaders of the teaching profession lynch me for reaching this conclusion, I should emphasise that this is not simply a mean personal interpretation of a positive finding. The evidence is in what the pupils say, which is analysed at length in Chapter 3. It is also to be found in the views of the government's school inspection agency (OFSTED), quite apart from the relatively objective evidence that, compared with those of a number of comparable western democracies, the education system in this country underperforms. Put bluntly, the evidence suggests that parents' expectations are too low.

Thirdly, if that is bad news, the good news is that the relationship between teachers and parents at school level is soundly based. In spite of the vilification teachers have taken from the media at times in the last decade, their contribution remains respected and appreciated by parents. Parents in turn feel welcomed by teachers, whom they find easy to approach. If schools were able to provide more information of a practical kind on both extra-curricular activities and on what young people should be learning, then it could bring about improvements in pupil performance. In short, there is room for a major policy initiative in this area, a point taken up in Chapter 9.

The fourth clear conclusion is that the views of parents – at least those revealed by the Keele survey and broadly confirmed by other research – are not what the government believe them to be. Nor are they what the government's opponents believe them to be. Nor are they always right, any more than anyone else's. Nevertheless, in a sea of subjectivity like education, where success depends so much on interactions between people and where a belief in success can assist in bringing it about, a much deeper understanding of parents' views is of central importance. A school that ignores them – like a national policy – is doomed to fail.

5 · Schools: Failure and Success

There's no success like failure and failure's no success at all.
Bob Dylan

The Downs

In the summer of 1995, Arsenal football club bought Denis Bergkamp, one of the best footballers in the world. That same summer, the government appointed the first education association in the country – to take over Hackney Downs, a secondary school for boys. In legal terms, this meant that Hackney Downs ceased to be maintained by Hackney Council and became the responsibility of a team of six people appointed by Gillian Shephard, the Secretary of State for Education and Employment. She gave the team – the education association – a brief to examine the state of affairs at the school and recommend either a programme of development and renewal, or closure. The team, of which I was a member, was given three months to reach its decision.

In the language of the press, this decision was described as 'a hit squad' being 'parachuted in' to 'sort out the worst school in the country'. Hackney Downs had arrived at this precarious point in its history by a circuitous route. It had been in decline for well over a decade. Extreme concern about its quality had been expressed in the late 1980s. A combination of changing social circumstances and the militancy of union extremists had undermined and worn out a long-serving head who had worked there since the days when the school was a proud boys' grammar school attended by the great, the good and the famous. Harold Pinter and Michael Caine had been there.

When that head finally retired, he was followed by a series of heads and acting heads who, for a variety of reasons, were unable to come to terms with the school's deep-seated problems. Hackney Council was unable to sort it out either. In 1993 it put forward a proposal for it to become a mixed school, as if the presence of some civilised girls might prove to be its salvation. The government rejected the idea: it was under-standably not convinced that girls would receive the education they deserved in a school where boys had underachieved for years and where behaviour was, to put it mildly, a matter of concern.

The following year, the school was inspected and, to no one's surprise, was found to be failing or, in legal terms, 'in need of special measures'. The school and the council drew up plans of action to improve the school, as the law requires them to do, but in the autumn of 1994 Hackney decided to cut its losses and close the place down. In effect, it concluded that the school's problems were intractable. Instead of throw-ing still more good money after bad, it would shut Hackney Downs, find places for the remaining boys elsewhere, and invest more in the other nine secondary schools in the borough, which were a great deal more successful.

This was eminently sensible, but in the politics of Hackney that is hardly relevant. As so often happens with poor schools, once the decision was taken to close Hackney Downs, people suddenly discovered they loved it. A combination of the local teachers' union, still a stronghold of the far left, the Socialist Workers Party and a faction of the local Labour Party which prioritised its own internal struggles above the needs of young people in the borough fought a long campaign to keep the school open. The teachers in the school, and the parents whose pupils attended it, obviously supported the campaign. The Director of Education, Gus John, on whose advice the closure decision had been based, was subjected to vitriolic attack. The leadership of the Labour council was overthrown by another group of Labour politicians only too happy to play at populist politics in order to begin their climb up the greasy pole.

In June 1995, a month after this new leadership group had taken control and just three weeks before the decision to close the school was due to take effect, the council reversed its decision in a vote which split the Labour group. It would, after all, keep the school open. The ostensible ground for this perverse decision was that a team of inspectors had looked at the school in March 1995 as a legally required follow-up to the previous year's inspection, and had found significant improvement in a number of areas.

This team has a lot to answer for. Its judgements were questionable. It found, for example, that financial management was satisfactory even though later evidence would reveal this to be palpably untrue. It also omitted to mention that, although the school's roll had now dropped, its staffing had not. It had thus become one of the most generously funded schools in the country. Some improvement was virtually inevitable: the issue was whether it could have been sustained in the long run if the school roll had doubled as it would have to have done for the school to become viable.

The council's decision adversely affected the budget of every other school in Hackney, an interesting example of politicians responding to a handful of activists rather than to the wider interests of the people to whom they were democratically accountable. Amazingly, such is the culture generated by the union locally that many teachers opposed the closure of the school in spite of the fact that keeping it open evidently damaged the reputation of education in the borough and cut funding for their own schools.

By now, within Hackney Council, the leading councillors were at war, not only with a large minority of their fellow Labour councillors, but also with the council's education officers, whose strongly worded advice they had ignored. The Chair of the Education Committee, David Phillips, argued that the government should have left Hackney Downs with the council, which had successfully improved other schools in the borough. While this had indeed been the case in the past, it was unthinkable in a council at war with itself and when the relationship between the school and the council had broken down completely.

These were the circumstances in which we, the 'hit squad', were 'parachuted in'. The parachutes were of poor quality. Our landing was rough. I first went to the school just before it reopened for pupils at the beginning of September, and walked round the dilapidated site. It was a depressing experience. The buildings were in a terrible state. Even the basics of ground maintenance had not been attended to, apparently for a long time. There were weeds growing between the paving stones and litter everywhere. One of my colleagues remarked: 'If I was one of the pupils here, I'd believe it was a moral imperative to misbehave.'

We spent that day thinking about the task ahead. Should we close the school as the council had originally decided? Or should we use our powers to give the school a fresh start, to create a really sparkling new school in the desert of central Hackney? The issue appeared to dominate not only our thinking, but also that of the teachers, the parents and the chastened local council. Perhaps it dominated the pupils' thinking too, but the evidence of that first day suggested otherwise, which is where Arsenal football club comes in. Among the many graffiti in the school was a bold one in black letters reading 'Bergkamp is Jesus'. It was refreshing to discover that this pupil, at least, was not looking to us for salvation.

Hackney Downs School may not have been, in September 1995 when just over 200 boys turned up to be educated, the worst school in the country. Even so, what we discovered as we prepared our report for the

Secretary of State was a school which was shabbily housed and in financial confusion. Above all, it was educationally short-changing its pupils. In blunt terms, the life chances of many of them were being ruined. As if to prove the point, the school's GCSE figures in 1995 showed that some of the best results were in Turkish, a subject in which the candidates *had received no teaching at all.*

In our report we describe the quality of education in the school. While every failing school is different, much of what we learnt about Hackney Downs does provide a basis for generalisation. Above all, it is an example of the state a school can end up in if it is mismanaged over years and fought over by petty politicians and lobby groups who have forgotten that schools exist for their pupils.

Hackney Downs also provides the clearest possible evidence that neither increasing funding nor reducing class sizes are, on their own, the solution to this country's educational problems. Unless the management is good and the teaching of high quality, even very large sums of money will change nothing. In the autumn of 1995, when the education association was preparing its report, Hackney Downs was spending at a rate of £6,489 per pupil per year. This is almost three times the national average expenditure per pupil in secondary education. It is, in fact, more than the fees of even some of London's most exclusive private schools such as St Paul's or City of London Boys' School. Its pupil:teacher ratio of 8:1 is one that most schools would not dare even dream of – the national ratio is around 18:1.

Despite these advantages, the quality of much of the education in the school was very poor. In our report we described the quality of teaching and learning in the following terms:

> The quality of lesson delivery was markedly uneven. In a small pro-
> portion of cases it was very good indeed, the teachers being focused,
> persistent and inventive. Memorable were a thoughtful and enriching
> lesson on *King Lear*, a drama class where the boys worked profitably
> throughout, much of the PE provision and some of the teaching for
> Information Technology. Most art classes were well conducted and
> productive.
>
> However, too often the lesson failed because the teacher did not
> engage the interest of the pupils, was unable to convey any personal
> interest in the subject, lacked initiative or seemed unwilling to deviate
> from planned material even when it was necessary. Often the teacher
> appeared to expect very little from the pupils except misbehaviour,
> and the pupils lived up to the expectation.
>
> It is noticeable that much of the marking of pupils' work is over
> generous. The teachers' intention is evidently to encourage, but, too

often, this laudable principle has been taken very much too far, with scrawled, inaccurate and obviously rushed work being labelled 'very good' or even 'excellent' and rewarded with high marks. This contributes to a lack of realism about standards . . .

Behaviour in general was poor and sometimes dreadful.

Most classes were subject to constant interruptions by a few disruptive boys whose often coarse and occasionally foul-mouthed comments addressed to one another and to the teacher ensured that little or no education took place. In such cases, the teacher's intention was overwhelmed by the need to gain some sort of control. In addition, there was a continual low level disturbance to which virtually all the boys contributed. In consequence, the quieter boys received scant attention.

Teachers often had great difficulty in getting lessons started. Boys often drifted in at various times during the first ten minutes, and it was not uncommon for the first 15–20 minutes to be spent gathering the group and establishing a sense of order.

The pace of progress, for all sorts of reasons was painstakingly slow.

Once order is established, it is standard practice to re-capitulate on the last lesson's work. Though this is helpful to some boys, it often takes too long and causes further bad behaviour. Overall, therefore, the pace of many lessons is painfully slow. In such lessons, low expectations, slow pace and poor behaviour seem to be locked together in a destructive spiral.

There is a low level of basic attainment in literacy and numeracy. This, in addition to the poor behaviour already mentioned, makes for acute difficulty in bringing the class along at a reasonable pace. The ability of many of the teachers to meet the needs of this diverse group of pupils appears to be limited. Many pupils find it hard to read even quite simple material with understanding and much of what is written and spoken by them shows inadequate language development. In relation to numeracy, the state of affairs is comparable. In Year 11 (age 16), for example, a significant number of boys struggled with simple arithmetic such as $168 \div 12$, while in another class several boys were unable to write two hundred and forty in numbers or say how many pence there are in £1.85 . . .

The dominant, overall impression is of a pervasively low standard of achievement, and, crucially, that some staff have come to accept that what each of them does in his or her own classroom is the norm.

Teacher expectations, teaching strategies, learning outcomes and classroom management are all in need of urgent attention.

The boys at HDS are being short-changed in terms of the quality of education provided and the school environment. One consequence of this is that even those boys who have reached a reasonable standard already and show some motivation to learn are constantly held back.

Many factors contributed to this state of affairs: the school's turbulent history; the cumulative effects of weak management; the disadvantaged circumstances of the school and many of its pupils; and the presence of some teachers who were very poor indeed at their jobs.

The chief cause of the school's problems was, in my view, the culture of the organisation. In good schools in disadvantaged areas there is a buzz, a sense of determination and an unshakeable belief among the staff both in the importance of their work and in their ability to make a difference for their pupils. In Hackney Downs, by contrast, the culture was fundamentally flawed, as we pointed out in our report.

The EA [education association] identified four disturbing features of the school's culture. First, too often we heard statements to the effect that, as one teacher put it, 'it is all very well talking about educational quality but this is a working class area'. While clearly the context of the school and the needs of its population must be taken into account, it is evident that at HDS both have been used to excuse under-performance. Many of the staff appear to believe that the school's circumstances are uniquely disadvantaged, though, objectively, this is not the case. There are many schools in similarly challenging circumstances, in the LBH [London Borough of Hackney] and elsewhere.

The second concern about the culture is the widespread belief among the staff that the school is under-resourced. While in terms of capital investment this is evidently true, in revenue terms it is the opposite of the truth. The roll stands at 202 and with the current staffing levels gives a very favourable pupil:teacher ratio. Since September 1995 the school has received funding on the same basis as a grant-maintained (GM) school. The annual expenditure per pupil in the financial year 1995–96 at HDS is £6,489, against a national average in GM schools of around £2,400. Nevertheless, if the school were to continue and to expand then, even on the most favourable imaginable estimates, funding per pupil would have to fall very substantially indeed, not rise, and the pervasive attitude of the staff to resources would be a major stumbling block to improvement.

The third disturbing feature of the culture is the generally held view that, after the turmoil of last year, the staff should simply be 'left alone to get on and teach'. In our view the school needs precisely the opposite. Partly because of the educational challenges and partly because of the 'politics' of the last 12 months, the staff appear isolated and insufficiently aware of classroom practice in other similar schools or even in other classrooms within HDS itself. It is as though, in at least some cases, they have forgotten what is possible in terms of standards in inner city education, a state of affairs which is a major contributory factor to the climate of low expectations.

A fourth strong element of the culture among the staff is the universal view that the school has improved markedly since the inspection of 1994 . . . We are prepared to take this on trust, but as the OFSTED report of 1994 indicates, the school was starting from a very low base. This view has contributed to a lack of awareness of just how far there is still to go and what the next steps in the strategy should be.

It is as if, in schools in these circumstances, there is a morbidity about them, as if the members of the school community begin, at least subconsciously, to will their own destruction. We recommended – and the Secretary of State agreed – that the school be closed as soon as possible and that the boys transfer to nearby Homerton House School. In July 1996, inspectors visited the boys in the new school and found that pupils has positive attitudes, teaching was good and that in integrating the Hackney Downs boys the staff had pulled off a 'remarkable achievement'.

In the absence of the leadership qualities that the school required, it had simply imploded. The school's circumstances were challenging. Many of its pupils had suffered the double blow of disadvantaged home circumstances and several years – often from the start of primary schooling onwards – of poor, demotivating education based on a destructive mixture of low expectations and patronising sympathy. Drugs were, and are, rife in the area. Inevitably this affects some of the pupils and therefore the school. Some of the most difficult pupils in the school came from homes where the parents were addicts or dealers.

It is possible, certainly, to sympathise with the teachers who were caught up in events often beyond their control. This cannot, and should never, be an argument for keeping the school open and continuing to provide an inadequate education to the pupils. Their needs are paramount. Precisely because of the disadvantaged circumstances in which many of them live, they desperately need a good education. The staff were not providing them with one. They were not making the most of the circumstances they could control (including that large budget). There are many other schools in similar circumstances in Britain's urban areas doing a far better job. The plain truth is that we would have been shirking our responsibilities had we done other than close down the school. Denis Bergkamp alone, however good, is not enough.

The Ups

The bleak picture painted in the previous section needs to be contrasted
with a bright and cheerful one. Port Vale are not nearly as good as Arsenal
and they don't have Denis Bergkamp, but just above their stadium (if
it can be described as such), with views out over the Potteries, is Haywood
High School. It is a mixed secondary comprehensive school sandwiched
between two council estates. It does not claim to be excellent or even
successful, but it is improving and it is going places. I described it in a
report for the National Commission on Education:

> The school serves two large housing estates, both of which are predomi-
> nantly council-owned and are representative of the more deprived parts
> of the Potteries. Behind the school a gloomy shopping street runs
> down the hill towards Burslem. The shops are of the small, local variety
> and each of them has its own one-armed bandits aimed, according to
> Yvonne Jeffries, the headteacher, to persuade pupils to part with their
> limited funds on their way home. Some years ago the fish-and-chip
> shop there did a roaring trade during the school lunch hour, and
> bought a row of game machines to exploit the pupils while they were
> in the queue. Yvonne Jeffries, who was appointed in 1989, decided,
> as part of her improvement strategy, to prevent pupils leaving the
> school at lunch-time. The chip shop owner was outraged. He said the
> school was putting him out of business. The school was unmoved and
> the chip shop is still there. The incident is a sharp reminder that
> 'being responsive to the local community' is not always plain sailing . . .

Everyone associated with the school recognised the qualities of the
headteacher.

> They shared her vision of an improving school with high standards
> and expectations, a positive reputation in the community and a staff
> who enjoyed being at work. They also believed that the headteacher
> had made a vital contribution in radically improving relations between
> pupils and staff. They mentioned repeatedly three particular character-
> istics of the headteacher's management style. First, she knew each of
> the staff well as a person, remembered to thank people for their special
> contributions and attended to those critical personal details which
> matter so much. We were told, for example, that whenever a member
> of staff moved to another school they would, on their first day in the
> new post, receive a personal note wishing them good luck.
>   Second, the headteacher was praised for her ability to delegate. She
> did so not only through the formal hierarchy but also through
> responding to the initiatives of individuals and through asking teams
> of volunteers to take responsibility for drawing up school policy on

important themes. We spoke, for example, to two teachers who had volunteered to draw up the school's anti-bullying policy though it was not formally part of their responsibility. They had taken the initiative to attend relevant courses, had led consultation with pupils and staff, and drafted a policy which had recently been approved by the whole staff. We encountered a number of similar examples.

Third, all the staff recognised that the headteacher was prepared to take responsibility for tough decisions, when they were necessary. These included decisions relating to staff performance and under-performance . . .

The positive atmosphere was also intoxicating.

Both pupils and teachers believed that the school had a positive and cheerful atmosphere. Certainly, in the classes we attended, we gained the impression of a warm and happy community.

In addition, there was a shared emphasis on high expectations. The pupils spoke of the consistent pressure from the headteacher and the staff to achieve. It has to be said that the same pressure was not present in the home environment of some of the pupils. The staff were convinced that during the five years in which they have made such significant progress the social problems of drugs, crime, unemployment and family breakdown confronting the school have intensified. For a significant minority of pupils this contrast clearly presented them with an almost irreconcilable conflict. The headteacher and many staff therefore often found themselves in counselling mode and believed that in the vast majority of cases the pupils trusted them sufficiently to share their personal dilemmas. Similarly, the evidence we gathered suggested that the pupils respected the teachers' contributions, both academic and pastoral . . .

A combination of sensitivity and attention to detail underpinned the school's progress.

The clear, firm, collaborative style that characterises Yvonne Jeffries' approach appears to have worked. It is worth noting in passing that the hard, lead-from-the-top, I'm-the-boss approach would have been unlikely to have been effective in the late 1980s when so many staff and pupils had been bruised by the process of reorganisation [which the school had recently gone through].

A further evident quality in the school is what might be termed a consistent striving. The staff we met were, as far as we could determine, seeking improvement at the level of detail as well as generality. In other words, it affected their approach to teaching, day-to-day interactions with pupils, and their planning. There was no sense of either complacency or hopelessness. To some extent this was a result of the headteacher's conscious effort to empower others, both staff and pupils.

The culture of the school encouraged people to make change happen rather than to wait for others to do so.

Finally, the school's culture was built upon excellent interpersonal relationships. Many schools state that they aim to achieve mutual respect, a sense of quiet purpose and positive relations between teachers and pupils. Haywood, even in its difficult social setting, has achieved this in reality. Educators have sometimes been criticised for putting 'caring' above 'achievement'. The Haywood experience suggests that not only is it possible to have both but also that the two can be formed in a virtuous circle.

Over the five years before I wrote this profile, Haywood High School had seen its performance improve significantly by whatever indicator you care to take. The process of improvement has continued since. In 1995, 28 per cent of pupils at Haywood gained five higher-grade GCSEs. This is below the national average, but also three times better than Haywood's own performance five years earlier. This represents a tremendous rate of improvement. Exam results are important, but they are not everything. At Haywood, other indicators pointed in the same direction. Attendance was up. Punctuality was up. Truancy was down. So was bullying. Yvonne Jeffries and her colleagues had managed, in challenging circumstances, to put in place a spiral of improvement which contrasts vividly with the spiral of despair into which Hackney Downs had descended.

The National Picture

The good news is that there are many more schools like Haywood High School than like Hackney Downs. As we have seen in Chapter 1, most of the indicators reveal, overall, significant improvement over the last decade. The bad news is that there are too many like Hackney Downs. Since the national four-year inspection cycle began, as of July 1996 over 170 schools have been found to be failing. Not all of these by any means are in the intractable state Hackney Downs was in. Nevertheless, this represents between 1 and 2 per cent of all schools. Thus, if the pattern continues throughout the cycle, we might anticipate that between 250 and 500 schools will be found to be failing nationally. Though this is a small proportion of all schools, it means that somewhere in the region of 10,000 pupils are being educated in schools which, by any civilised standards, are unacceptable. There are obvious consequences for the areas in which they live, for the jobs (if any) that they get, for the families they build and for their own children. Whatever else John Major wanted to cascade down the generations, it was surely not school failure.

Worse still, many more schools have been found to be not quite failing but nevertheless struggling to provide a decent education. The best estimate suggests that somewhere between 1,250 and 2,500 schools nationally are in this parlous state. If the high estimates of both categories are put together, we are faced with the terrifying statistic that one state school in eight is providing its pupils with an inadequate education. At the lowest estimate, it is one in fourteen.

Given the overwhelming case for high standards for everyone set out in Chapter 1, this level of failure is clearly intolerable. It is a damning indictment of the public education service and, indeed, of seventeen years of Tory government. Imagine this level of failure in other areas of service. Even at their worst, British Rail's trains are not late one time in ten. In medicine, failure rates are far lower too. To take another example, imagine the public outcry if an air traffic controller tried to justify a crash on the grounds that the other nine planes landed safely.

Something clearly needs to be done. Fortunately, in the last two years, the government, with the enthusiastic support of Her Majesty's Opposition, has begun to do it. After years of tolerating school failure at a phenomenal level, it is now possible to imagine its end. Until now, the slogan 'Successful Schools for All' has simply been empty rhetoric. For the first time, it could begin to describe reality. Achieving it will not be easy, but at least we can map out what needs to be done. Firstly, we need a means of evaluating the quality of every school in the country and a climate of openness. Secondly, we need to know what describes a good school. Thirdly, we need to know what a school should do to improve itself. Fourthly, we need to decide how best to intervene when a school proves incapable of improving itself. The chapter now turns to look at each of these issues.

The End of Privacy

In moving the second reading of his Education Bill in January 1944, R. A. Butler distinguished between 'the private life of the school and the public life of its district', by which he meant its LEA. He, and no doubt all his contemporaries, never questioned the notion that what went on inside a school was a private matter. If the system needed to be held to account, then voters could do so at the ballot box in local elections. Parents made the same assumption. Across the country there were lines drawn at school gates and notices stating firmly: 'No parents allowed beyond this line.'

Five decades later, it could not be more different. Every school is in the public eye. Parents are encouraged to come in: in some cases schools are pleading with them. Moreover, there is a mass of regulations requiring schools to publish information about their educational approach, their policies, their exam results and test performance, and their philosophy. The fact that schools' funding depends on the number of pupils they attract provides the pressure to ensure they attempt to market themselves. School prospectuses have become glossy documents which tread the fine line between positive projection and blatant marketing. Here is a typical example of a highly professional and responsible one:

> At Haggerston, learning is our priority. We have high standards and high expectations of all. We aim to provide a high quality education within a supportive pastoral system to ensure that our pupils achieve their full potential.
> (*Haggerston School Prospectus*, 1995)

Here is another:

> The school attempts to create a social and physical environment which combines security and care with challenge, stimulus and the highest expectations, where staff and pupils work together with the understanding and support of parents.
> (*Camden School for Girls Prospectus*, 1996–97)

Laudable and beyond reproach in every respect, but what is noticeable is the smooth-toned language of marketing. Both schools, in this case, are indeed providing a good education, but schools of half the quality are just as good at writing the marketing-speak.

It is not only the pressure of marketing which has opened up schools to the public gaze. There is also the pressure of performance tables. These were introduced by government for the first time for secondary examinations in 1993, and are due to be extended to primary schools in 1996. They are the central plank of what John Patten and his successor, Gillian Shephard, have described as the 'information revolution'. They set out in league-table form, neatly packaged for the press so that the results appear in most national newspapers, each school's public examination results. The rank ordering across the country and within each local education authority enables parents and the public to see how different schools compare in terms of the performance at GCSE and A Level. The Keele survey (see Chapter 4) suggests that parents are giving ever increasing attention to such data in their school choice decisions.

However, what the tables do not reveal is how effective schools have been. While research shows that schools do make a huge difference to how well their pupils do, an even bigger influence is the pupils' social background and prior achievement. Thus, in the current performance tables, a selective school which picks the most academically able children in an area or a school in an area where pupils have all the advantages of a wealthy and supportive home background are compared directly to schools which have less favoured intakes. Of course the more advantaged schools come higher up. The fact is, however, that this does not make them better schools. Their pupils, given the advantages they had when they joined the school, perhaps ought to have done better. By contrast, some schools with very disadvantaged intakes may have done remarkably well in the circumstances. Haggerston School, whose prospectus is quoted above, for example, enabled 36 per cent of its intake to gain five A–C grades at GCSE in 1995. Though this is much lower than many schools, it is a remarkable achievement for a school in which 70 per cent of the pupils come from homes on social security and many of them do not speak English as a first language. In terms of 'value-added' – as the jargon has it – Haggerston is a very good school indeed. Its teachers are giving the pupils a tremendous boost in their achievement.

Nevertheless, the published tables – in spite of their inadequacies – do put schools in the public eye. Schools that appear very low in the tables do experience pressure, and many have striven to improve themselves. Some headteachers claim the whole process is demoralising since, however much they try, they cannot progress all that far up the table. In public, this is what most headteachers say. In private, however, they sometimes say something different. They say that appearing at the bottom of the table has had a galvanising effect. They say it has enabled them to demand change from their staff and they often say that it had opened their eyes to the fact that they were indeed doing much less well than they should have been, compared to other schools in similar circumstances.

The pressure of published performance data is here to stay. Both the Conservative government and the Labour Opposition are pledged to extend them and to refine them. Research is under way in a number of universities to try to develop published indicators of the extent to which a school has added value. If it is successful, this will enable more effective comparisons of school performance. The complacent schools which have advantaged intakes and appear to do well in the present tables will find their fig leaves are stripped away.

If performance tables thrust schools firmly into the public eye, so too does the national inspection system. Under the 1992 Education Act, every school is due to be inspected every four years. The four-year cycle is not yet completed and, indeed, difficulty in recruiting sufficient inspectors means that for primary schools the schedule has slipped. Nevertheless, the impact of inspection has already been dramatic, not least because the reports are published. Indeed, the school is required to send a copy to every parent.

The evidence suggests that the threat of an upcoming inspection encourages most schools to review what they are doing and to try to improve themselves before the inspectors arrive. Since schools have nine months' notice or more, there is time for them to make changes. It is true, too, that in a minority of cases the threat of inspection has generated excessive tension and caused some heads and teachers to freeze like rabbits caught in the headlights.

What happens after inspection is, so far, less clear. It seems that in some schools there is a slump – a reaction to the exhaustion and stress the inspection has caused. Then the school begins to work on the action plan which they are required to put in place to address any problems the inspectors have uncovered. It is too early to say whether the action plans have resulted in steady improvement across the board, since even in the first schools inspected under the new system they have been in place only three years. Nevertheless, the evidence is cautiously encouraging.

What is certain is that inspection, like the performance tables, puts school quality firmly on the public agenda. In addition to parents, the local press usually takes a keen interest in a school's inspection report. Schools that have been praised usually seek press coverage because it is obviously in their interests. Those who fare badly usually find journalists only too keen to report the findings in any case. Some of the failures make it into the national press. Quite a number of schools have now been dubbed 'the worst school in Britain'. Both papers that want to urge the government to further reform and those that wish to attack the government for its inadequacies see benefits in publicising school failures. Those who have worked in schools that have been through this process of public humiliation talk of the stress it has caused. They talk of the damage it has done to morale, not only that of the teachers, but the pupils' also. In some cases, the whole community feels that it has been violated. In one place, for example, where inspectors were highly critical of the local schools, the local paper ran the front-page headline 'Dunce Town'.

The challenge for schools is to meet the demands of the twenty-first century, and the demands of the politicians and public for improvement, in this glare of publicity. They have to bring about change while knowing that their performance will be public knowledge and that there are journalists and politicians all too ready to condemn them if they fail. They know, too, that longing for a return to the privacy of the Butler era is futile. Public interest in the performance of public services – whether health, police, prisons or railways – is too great, and the pressure on politicians to open services up to accountability too strong to be resisted. They are probably becoming aware, too, that the pressure of public accountability, while requiring them to pay a heavy price, is nevertheless bringing, overall, greater improvement than the privacy of the previous era.

As if this were not a sufficiently demanding challenge on its own, schools also find themselves being asked to play a part in solving many of society's other profound problems. Schools are seen as having a crucial role in the fight against crime, drug abuse, child abuse, video pornography and the moral relativism of *fin de siècle* Britain. Even the ennui of many young people in the 1990s is blamed partly on the schools. Each time one of these subjects is debated publicly – which is most of the time – schools find themselves once again in the public spotlight. No wonder that every national newspaper, including the *Sun* – now has an education correspondent and that many have two or even three. For years, educators have yearned for education to be given higher priority. Now they are finding that it is a mixed blessing. On the whole, in my view, the gains far outweigh the losses. In any case, there is certainly no going back.

The Effectiveness of Schooling

Partly as a result of the information revolution, and partly as a result of an impressive body of research built up over the last twenty years, we know more now about the quality of this country's schools than we have ever done before. The published information shows that, in terms of GCSE passes, schools are, in general, improving. Recently, the Department for Education and Employment has pointed out that the rate of improvement is greatest among those schools which are in the bottom 25 per cent in terms of performance (*TES*, 6 October 1995). It should be observed in passing that this does not contradict the observation in Chapter 1 that standards may be falling for the bottom 25 per cent of *pupils*, since they are distributed across many schools. Nevertheless, it is a positive sign.

The research into school effectiveness over the last two decades has made an immense contribution to our understanding of school performance. Whereas in the 1960s and early 1970s the prevailing view of education and social researchers was that the effect of school on a pupil's performance was negligible in comparison to the impact of social class and upbringing, it is now demonstrable that schools make a significant difference to how well children do. This is welcome, not least because it confirms the common-sense view that parents down the ages have held. More importantly, it opens up the whole debate about school and teacher quality.

The old view fundamentally undermines teachers since it suggests that, however hard they work and however successful they are, it will make little difference to their pupils. The logic of this position drives any teachers who are concerned with improving the lot of their pupils – which includes most teachers – into demands for social and political change since, if schools make no difference, only this will change things.

The new view, now that we know schools make a difference, dictates a different logic. It requires teachers, individually and collectively, to review what they do and to try to improve it. The research on school effectiveness has thus contributed to a fundamental and wholly welcome change of climate. Teachers and schools now believe they can make a difference; they can work towards changes which are achievable and whose effects can be monitored. Change thus becomes an everyday reality, rather than something endlessly hoped for but never actually achieved.

This is not all. For, once schools begin to achieve real change which becomes noticed, they are actually enabled to advance some of the wider changes they might like to see. For example, by demonstrating their success, they can build up real support for increased school funding, whereas the old view that schools made no difference undermined the case for greater investment.

The research enables us to quantify just how much difference schools do make. In a recent study of ninety-four secondary schools in eight inner-city local education authorities, Pam Sammons, Sally Thomas and Peter Mortimore – one of the world's leading teams in this field – found that 'the difference between the most and the least effective schools was over 12 GCSE points for an average pupil'. (British Education Research Association paper, 1995.) This is the equivalent of achieving six grade B GCSEs as opposed to six grade D GCSEs. The same pupil would, at the most effective schools, have been, in the eyes of the world, a rip-roaring success with A Levels and university entrance beckoning and, at the least effective, a failure required to retake GCSEs or head down the low-status vocational route, no doubt with self-esteem in tatters.

The same study showed that even within schools there are large differences between different subject departments. This is hardly surprising to anyone who has been to school, but demonstrating it in research terms is overwhelmingly powerful. It points unmistakably towards the effectiveness or otherwise of each individual teacher. Recent studies in Australia and elsewhere point in the same direction.

Studies of primary schools show even greater differences in effectiveness. The most brilliant study in this field is *School Matters* by Mortimore, Stoll, Sammons and Ecob (Open Books, 1988). It measured not only effectiveness in terms of pupil performance in the three Rs, but also such crucial outcomes as pupil self-esteem, and revealed that schools with similar intakes performed very differently. Middle-class children in the least effective schools, for example, did noticeably worse than working-class children in the most effective. Moreover, Pam Sammons and others have shown that the effects of primary school have a long-term impact on pupil performance. Pupils who attended a more effective primary school do significantly better at GCSE than pupils of similar potential who attended a less effective one. The primary school effect indeed is at least as great as the secondary school effect. This is a powerful argument for giving primary schools more attention than they have been given traditionally. On the whole, both funding and reform efforts have been secondary-driven, yet ironically one of the best ways to improve the performance of secondary schools would be to improve the primary schools that feed them.

The research thus demonstrates that school really does matter. Parents are absolutely right to take the whole business of choosing schools for their children very seriously. The research does more than this. It also reveals the characteristics of the schools which are more effective. This in turn makes it possible to identify the effective school even in the absence of a value-added analysis of its examination or test results. It also establishes the goals that less effective schools should strive for as they seek to become more effective.

Recently, Pam Sammons and others examined school-effectiveness research from countries as diverse as Australia, America and the Netherlands as well as Britain. They drew together findings from a mass of studies and identified eleven characteristics common to effective schools. They are set out in Table 4. As Pam Sammons has written, it is an important feature of the list that 'the findings generally apply to different types of school: large and small; rural and urban; primary and secondary'.

Table 4: Characteristics of effective schools

Professional leadership	Firm and purposeful
	A participative approach
	The leading professional
Shared vision and goals	Unity of purpose
	Consistency of practice
	Collegiality and collaboration
A learning environment	An orderly atmosphere
	An attractive working environment
Concentration on teaching and learning	Maximisation of learning time
	Academic emphasis
	Focus on achievement

Purposeful teaching	Efficient organisation
	Clarity of purpose
	Structured lessons
	Adaptive practice
High expectations	High expectations all round
	Communicating expectations
	Providing intellectual challenge
Positive reinforcement	Clear and fair discipline
	Feedback
Monitoring progress	Monitoring pupil performance
	Evaluating school performance
Pupil rights and responsibilities	Raising pupil self-esteem
	Positions of responsibility
	Control of work
Home/school partnership	Parental involvement in their children's learning
A learning organisation	School-based staff development

[Sammons et al for OFSTED 1995]

Few people reading the list will find it surprising. Indeed, one of the chief criticisms of the twenty years of research into school effectiveness is that ultimately it only confirms what common sense tells us anyway. This is a view held most notably by Chris Woodhead, Her Majesty's Chief Inspector of Schools. In his view, school-effectiveness research is at best irrelevant and at worst dangerous nonsense which detracts from a need to change teaching approaches.

The British love to hate research. A hundred and fifty years of the myth of the practical man – I mean 'man' – has encouraged us to despise research as either irrelevant theory or a statement of the obvious. As a result, we not only fail to give research its due: we also fail to give it sufficient thought. Where in the common-sense view of schools, for example, is the idea of the learning organisation, in which teachers learn as well as pupils? The common-sense tradition suggests, on the contrary, that teachers know and children don't and that the job of the former is to pass on what they know to the latter. The research undermines this piece of 'common sense'. It suggests that schools are more successful when they take learning for teachers seriously, when they invest in professional development and provide a strategy for improving teachers' skills.

Similarly, common sense tells us that the only thing that really matters is the individual teacher's quality. We all remember good teachers with whom we made progress and poor ones with whom we did not. The research shows a more complicated picture. Of course the quality of the teacher is crucial, but in a school where the management has created a positive, constructive climate teachers who might struggle elsewhere perform effectively. In this sense, the school–effectiveness research echoes not common sense, but findings of research into business organisations, where the issue is, to put it in Sir John Harvey Jones' terms, getting extraordinary performance from ordinary people.

Furthermore, the effectiveness research requires teachers to face up to their own importance. They have awesome power and immense responsibility. What they do really does affect the life chances of the pupils they teach. Whereas under the old order there was a tendency to blame the system, society, the class structure – anyone other than schools themselves – for underperformance, now there is no escape.

The real power of the research, however, is even greater than this. It lies in the weight it gives to an argument, even where it simply confirms common sense. It provides overwhelming evidence on which to base suggestions to headteachers and teachers in schools, and policy proposals to politicians. For headteachers and teachers it is, for example, encouraging that research, in addition to suggesting the characteristics of effective schools, also indicates that, if schools attempt to put those characteristics in place, they will improve. In other words, what the research suggests should be done in theory works in practice.

For politicians, the research has provided convincing evidence on which to base some major policy and spending decisions. For example, the keen interest of both major parties in 1995 and 1996 in investing in headteachers' leadership skills results from the consistent research findings that improving leadership will raise standards. Common sense might have suggested this was true, but common sense without evidence would be unlikely to convince the Treasury to part with precious public money in an era of restraint. This is not to say that politicians will only spend money where research demonstrates it is likely to make a difference. The last decade is littered with examples of initiatives based on ideological prejudice rather than research evidence. To a greater or lesser degree, that is an inevitable outcome of democratic politics. Parties do have ideologies. The importance of research is that, where it is convincing, it can cause politicians to doubt their ideologies and to see that better results might come from more pragmatic approaches.

Partly as a result of growing awareness throughout the education service of the research on school effectiveness and partly because schools now have much more responsibility for their own management than in the past, there has been a growing tendency to seek the solution to our educational problems through changes within schools. If only, the argument runs, all schools could be as good as the best, our problems would be over. Critics, often but not always from the left, argue that this is a chimera, and that salvation will be found not within schools, but in changes to the system and society within which they operate.

Interestingly, a parallel argument is blazing in relation to this country's industrial performance. Arthur Francis, professor at the Glasgow Business School, argues that: 'national competitiveness is not the real issue . . . It is individual companies that become uncompetitive, and they do this because over time they get locked into management practices and organisational arrangements that become increasingly outmoded' (*RSA Journal*, October 1995). In other words, it is not the structure of the British economy that is the cause of our problems, but a lack of company effectiveness.

Arthur Francis explicitly rejects the arguments of those, such as Will Hutton, who point the finger at the failures of government economic policy, the relationship between finance and industry or national cultural values. These, he suggests, are simply a litany of excuses which let company managers off the hook. Challenged by a questioner at the end of the lecture quoted above, Arthur Francis refused to widen the argument and blame the system or culture. He agreed that government strategy was important but, he said, 'I do not think that is the key point. There are huge differences in the performance of companies within one country.'

This is precisely the argument of the school-effectiveness enthusiasts. The debate will no doubt continue to run in both the industrial and educational sectors. In fact, of course, neither side will win outright because, like most fierce academic disputes, it is a false dichotomy. The salvation of the education system depends on the subtle relationship between schools taking responsibility for their own improvement, and government (and other agencies) creating a climate and context within which they are encouraged to improve themselves. Neither on its own is sufficient.

It is not yet clear that the education service is psychologically ready to take full responsibility for its own improvement. It is still all too common for educators to blame government or society for the problems of schools. This is particularly the case in schools which are failing or struggling. In this country, the evidence suggests, there is a much wider gap between the best schools and the worst than in most western societies. Educators who argue for reforms of the whole educational structure are likely to find that their argument is fatally weakened by the serious failure of a significant minority of schools. They will, after all, be open to the charge that they are in no position to lecture anyone until they put their own house in order. For this reason, not to mention the serious damage failing schools do to the pupils that attend them, it is in the interests of educators, as well as everyone else, to attempt to reduce and, ultimately, eradicate school failure.

Improving Schools

The eradication of failure depends on the education system learning continuously from its attempts to improve schools and then using or refining these lessons in new circumstances. We have a growing body of experience of and research into how average schools can become good, and good schools better. We are also becoming experienced in the process of encouraging below-average schools to become average or better. Broadly, it seems that the same set of strategies will help each of these categories.

Our understanding is weakest in relation to schools that are complete failures. In these schools, the processes of school improvement that work in other schools do not succeed. In the cases of serious failure, a different, tougher and blunter approach is required. This section looks first at the approaches that appear to help most schools improve themselves and then at the policies necessary for the more intractable cases.

The most instantly evident feature of an improving school is that it is going places. It has a sense of direction. Some researchers describe this as a school 'moving' rather than being 'stuck'. Others talk in business-speak about mission statements and even visions. Indeed, the word 'vision' has become more popular in education than at any time since Joan of Arc was burnt at the stake. Michael Fullan reports a New York headteacher who is supposed to have said: 'Ten years ago if I'd had a vision they'd have locked me up; now I can't get a job without one.'

In improving schools, the head and the teachers are always telling you about their plans, their ideas for the future and their hopes for the school. In failing schools, by contrast, the talk is all about the external forces – the council, the government, parents – which are said to be responsible for the school's inadequacies. This does not mean that teachers in improving schools are necessarily enthusiasts for government policy or even sup-porters of it. It does mean that their prime focus is on the improvement of their school: government policy is seen as something that, whether it helps or hinders them, cannot be allowed to deflect them from the task. Certainly teachers in these schools are not simply going to lie down and let the latest policy announcement roll over them. To quote Michael

Fullan again, there is a sense in which these schools have become 'critical consumers of policy'.

Thus, for example, the government recently announced a Technology Schools initiative which offered schools £100,000 to become specialist technology schools on condition that they raise a matching £100,000 from the private sector. Some schools simply chose not to apply because they opposed the idea in principle. Others did not or could not get their act together. Many schools, however, saw this as an opportunity to access some new investment, to move the school forward, to improve their relationship with local employers and – above all – to provide their students with exciting new opportunities. In other words, they were making use of the government's political agenda to advance their own.

A second important aspect of many improving schools is that they set targets. In other words, they know not only where they are going, but also when they want to get there and how they will know that they have arrived. Schools set all kinds of targets: targets for the completion of a building or the implementation of a change in the curriculum; targets for overall pupil performance in public examinations or tests in the basics; targets for individual pupils.

In 1995, targets became fashionable. The Prime Minister made a speech about them. Gillian Shephard commissioned a report on them. Across the country, schools and LEAs adopted them and strove to hit them. They were enthusiastically advocated, too, by the Labour Party in its policy document *Excellence for Everyone*, not least because the best target-setting practice was in Labour's flagship local authority, Birmingham. Indeed, Labour leaders pointed out with some justification that the government appeared in this case to have stolen their policy. To its credit, even the government recognised the contribution of the second city. Birmingham schools feature in the target-setting report published by the government in 1996 and, at a drinks party recently, the education policy adviser from that bastion of ideological purity, the No. 10 policy unit, quoted Birmingham as the model authority. How times have changed.

The chief problem with targets is setting them at the right pitch. The natural tendency for those setting targets for themselves is to set them cautiously. If they are too cautious they will not have much impact. On the other hand, if the target is too ambitious, it can lead to demoralisation. In Birmingham they worked their way round this conundrum by encouraging schools to set two targets: one 'best case' target and one 'less optimistic' target. In this way, schools found themselves working towards a range rather than a point. The evidence suggests that, at the outset, schools will set targets that are too cautious, but that once they get the school improvement 'roll' going, they often exceed them by far, and their expectations of what is possible are raised.

The other danger with targets is that they are too all-embracing or too distant. On being appointed manager of Sheffield Wednesday, Jack Charlton was asked what the challenges were. 'We let in too many goals,' he is supposed to have said, 'and don't score enough.' This was no doubt true, but hardly provided a foundation for an improvement strategy. A similarly vague target was set by the United States government: 'The United States should be first in the world in science and maths by the year 2000.' Absurd: partly because it is hopelessly ambitious and partly because it depends on factors beyond America's control, such as how well they teach science and maths in Singapore, Japan or Germany.

Above all, targets need to generate the commitment of those whose job it is to attempt to meet them, be they schools, teachers or pupils. This is a challenge to policy-makers, leaders and managers at all levels. At school level, success in this respect often depends on the ability of a headteacher to maintain morale, confidence and self-belief even when progress appears to be slow. One hallmark of a great headteacher is this ability to keep their nerve through the time between changing the process and seeing the outcome. As T. S. Eliot describes it: 'Between the idea and the act . . . falls the shadow.' Following the performance of England's footballers in Euro '96, this ability to keep your nerve while waiting for results to improve might be called the Terry Venables syndrome. The following examples from a DfEE report on target-setting published in 1996 illustrate how effective they can be.

GROVE PRIMARY SCHOOL, BIRMINGHAM

Action

Each child in the school is expected to progress 'half a National Curriculum level per year', at the very least, and pupils falling below this are quickly identified in order to accelerate their progress. Pupils achieving above their expected rate of progress are encouraged to move forward as far as they can.

The school commissioned an IT package to provide an assessment database which could be used in a variety of ways. Assessment data is used, for example, *to identify and provide for differentiated groups of pupils*. Teachers log assessment data from the core subjects into the database every term. They use the information to select teaching groups for different purposes: 'fast track' English and mathematics groups, and to identify pupils with special educational needs. These pupils are assessed six times per year against English and mathematics criteria from within National Curriculum level 1 and 2. Teachers can then detect progress and redeploy resources in the most sensible way. For example, pupils' progress is formally recorded at six weekly intervals on letter sound, for instance, and on their ability to write to dictation and form letters. Meanwhile, teacher assessment of these skills and activities is ongoing. The formal recording of progress at regular intervals allows the class teacher and the Special Needs Co-ordinator to see how best to arrange the support of individuals and groups of pupils as well as giving a more finely tuned indication of progress than the National Curriculum levels alone.

Effect

The quality of teaching is very good in mathematics, and is well informed by effective assessment, which is used to constantly raise pupils' attainment in mathematics. 'Fast track' pupils in mathematics in Years 4 to 6 work confidently together; they enjoy and talk about their mathematics with each other, and are aware of the National Curriculum level at which they are working. *Last year four pupils achieved a higher grade GCSE pass in mathematics.*

Spelling was identified as a weakness and the teaching programme was changed to address the concern. Regular spelling homework, an award scheme and daily assessment were introduced. This action has led to measurable improvements in spelling. The school has now identified punctuation as an area for attention across parts of the school.

Teachers make effective use of the database to evaluate the quality of provision and to redeploy resources. The school produces graphs to show the progress of a year group in a core subject, to make comparisons between different intakes at the same point, to compare predicted and actual performance and to compare teacher assessment against National Curriculum test results. The database shows up imbalances between year groups which have implications for the organisation and the curriculum, for example if a class or group is performing significantly lower than expected.

Target-setting can be deployed to deal with the problems of a specific group of pupils or a specific subject area or, as in the case of Wakeman Secondary School in Shropshire, both.

Target-setting in the English department is one part of a wider concern to raise standards of achievement in this school. The school's inspection in 1994 had drawn attention to the relatively weak examination results of the boys compared to those of the girls. This confirmed the English department's already established concern with the matter following the publication of HMI's report *Boys and English*.

Action

The department's response took several forms. They used a questionnaire, followed up by more detailed individual interviews with some of the pupils to examine the differences in attitudes to, and views of, English of boys and girls. Using the information gained, the department made changes in teaching and curriculum to make the teaching as supportive of boys as it had been of girls. The teachers also revised their assessment procedures so as to focus more closely on specific aspects of attainment in English. They grouped the pupils into broader ability sets to improve the gender balance, girls having previously predominated in top sets.

Target-setting involves giving the pupils clear information about the progress they have made to date and the steps they need to take to improve their work. Initiatives are directed at both boys and girls although they arose out of a particular concern about under-achievement by boys. During the work the department has been supported by the LEA.

The first initiative was introduced on a trial basis last year and is to be extended to all pupils this year. As Year 11 pupils approach their GCSE examinations and after the pupils have been told the grades they are predicted to get, they are mentored. The pupils have detailed and specific discussions with the teachers about their progress and about what they must do to improve on their predicted grades.

Effect
In the trial last year, the pupils who had taken part in the mentoring system gained GCSE grades at C or above which were 25% better than the results which had been predicted before the mentoring took place.

Targets help to establish the sense of direction: they 'chunk' distant ambitions into achievable goals. The engine that makes their achievement possible is restless self-evaluation. Restless self-evaluation is the polar opposite of resting on your laurels. As Tom Peters has commented, the traditional saying 'If it ain't broke, don't fix it' has long since gone out of date. Improving schools constantly review what they are doing – not just those parts of the organisation that are a cause for concern, but every part. The essence of successful organisations in this post-modern world is the search for improvement, and effective self-evaluation is the key to it.

This is easy to assert, but the challenge of doing it well should not be underestimated. In any organisation, there is a temptation not to ask some of the most difficult questions: a headteacher may know in her heart of hearts that the reason performance is so poor in RE is that the teacher has not got the capability to teach it well. It is all too easy to buy new textbooks, reorganise the timetable or change the support mechanisms in order to avoid taking on the competence issue. For self-evaluation to be effective, the difficult questions must be asked. The other threat to effective self-evaluation is complacency: the 'we're all right really' syndrome. Self-evaluation that is shallow or confirmatory is unlikely to bring real change or improvement. Just as in high reliability organisations, such as airlines or chemical plants, any failure is rigorously investigated and lessons from it sought for the future, so schools can seek to examine underperformance. In one school they hold an inquiry each year into one or two typical cases of pupils who performed worse than expected in their exams.

Though the current system of externally imposed inspections is often contrasted, usually deprecatingly, with a self-examination model, the reality is that both are essential. The external system is a central part of holding a public service to account. Imagine, for example, the outcry if Michael Howard proposed that prisons would no longer be externally inspected.

On the other hand, rigorous self-evaluation is crucial to bringing about improvement. While no one would suggest that the present inspection system is perfect, the evidence points clearly to the conclusion that it has encouraged rather than replaced a culture of self-evaluation. In one secondary school I know well, the head and the deputies each attach themselves to a different department each term. They see everyone in that department teach twice during the term. They attend all the departmental meetings, examine pupils' work and then, at the end of the term, the department and the senior manager reflect together on what they have achieved and what the priorities for change and development should be. It is all part of a culture of restless self-evaluation.

The next stage in the development of this culture is for subject departments in turn to report on their evaluations to a committee of the governing body. When OFSTED inspectors arrive at this school – as they are due to in late 1996 – far from being a terrifying visit from the modern equivalent of the Spanish Inquisition, it will simply be a somewhat more formal step in an ongoing process of self-evaluation.

The success of restless self-evaluation depends upon evidence. There are many sources of evidence available to a school, some more obvious than others. The first, and perhaps the most important, is direct observation of what happens in classrooms and corridors. Indeed, many people outside a school judge it by the behaviour of the pupils as they go to and from schools. There is a school not too far from where I live into which the pupils drift in the morning. Adolescents clutch each other in uncomfortable embraces, not behind the bikesheds, but there on the pavement. Some of them are smoking. Others buy delicacies from a shop across the road which has realised the not entirely obvious truth that there is a market for meat pies, pasties and chips at 8.40 in the morning.

The wrapping from the pies is dropped between the shop and the school. It may be a good school – I've never been in – but the impression its pupils convey is not promising. If it has a sense of direction and purpose, the pupils certainly do not convey it on their way to school.

Inside a school there are similar sorts of evidence. In effective schools there is a sense of purpose everywhere. During lesson time the corridors are quiet apart from the occasional person striding in one direction or another, obviously on a mission. Even in buildings in need of repair – and there are plenty of them – the care with which the premises are kept is apparent: whether it be displays of work or an absence of litter, good schools cherish buildings and revere the learning space.

The central evidence of a school's performance, however, is what happens in classrooms. If the quality of a school is to be monitored, this is where it must be done. That is why the head mentioned earlier was right to insist that evaluation of departments must involve senior managers observing lessons; why any system of teacher appraisal must focus on classroom performance; and why the national inspection system – whatever its critics might say – rightly gives priority to inspectors watching teachers teach. If a school has no system for monitoring classroom performance, it will struggle to be good and, however good it may be, fail to change with the times.

For much of the post-war era, the prevailing attitude was that schools would decide what was taught and teachers would teach it – uninterfered with by 'management'. This was the culmination of the public school 'schoolmaster' tradition: an Englishman's classroom was his castle. Even as late as the 1980s, when a national scheme of school-teacher appraisal was introduced, systematic observation of teachers by each other was rare.

It is an immaculate irony that now, in the mid-1990s, the only remaining defenders of this 'schoolmaster' tradition are a few bastions of left-wing teacher unionism – a strand of thinking which perceives a headteacher observing a member of staff as a prime example of class oppression, regardless (incidentally) of whether the pupils (of whatever social class) are being short-changed or not. But the bizarre contradictions of a handful of left-wing teachers need not detain us. The fact is that one of the quiet transformations of the last decade is that systematic monitoring of classroom performance has become much more widespread. The benefits of this are not merely in terms of quality assurance: much more important is that it provides the shared evidence base for serious professional discussion among teachers about teaching techniques – about pedagogy.

In my first year of teaching, at the end of the 1970s, I was observed teaching by the headteacher. It was the first lesson after lunch and, almost as soon as the lesson began, I asked the group of eleven- and twelve-year-olds a question. To my delight, a forest of hands went up: the head would think they were mustard keen. I pointed to one of them, who kindly informed me that running in a viscous river down the blackboard was some of that lunchtime's school custard – not mustard but custard keen.

That lesson, which admittedly recovered slightly, was the only one he ever observed me teach and provided, apparently, the basis on which I passed my probationary year. I am not saying I did not deserve to pass; merely that the evidence base on which the decision was made was thin. Fortunately, times have changed and evidence of classroom performance figures ever more prominently in school improvement.

Other kinds of evidence are important too, especially those that relate to outcomes. Increasingly, schools have access to extremely valuable analyses of test and examination performance. Statistical techniques now enable schools to work out how much value they have added or, put differently, how much they have boosted pupils' performance. Often this data can be broken down to provide more detailed evidence. A school can see how well it does in relation to the more able or the less able, girls or boys, white pupils or black.

Increasingly, too, schools have access to data about pupil and parent attitudes and to comparative data about how they are using their budget. They can see, for example, whether they are spending more or less than comparable schools on books, equipment or support staff. This combination provides schools in the mid-1990s with a much higher-quality evidence base for decision-making than ever before. Of course, not all LEAs provide evidence of this quality and not all choose to access the data services provided by universities such as Newcastle, Keele and London. But the opportunity is there, and parents could legitimately ask what information schools do acquire. One of the potential benefits of a national inspection system, which has yet to be realised, is the creation at national level of a database of inspection evidence. Every lesson observed by inspectors – and there are many thousands of them – is faithfully stored on that database. If inspectors' judgements can be assumed to be valid and reliable – and admittedly this is a matter of controversy – this database is a gold mine. We will, over time, be able to find out which teaching strategies appear to result in the best outcomes. We shall be able to see which approaches appear to be associated with success among which groups of pupils, and so on. In Singapore and New South Wales, headteachers can access comparable databases from their desks and see how their school compares to all schools or to schools of similar type. It is only a matter of time before we make evidence of this quality available here.

Often evidence is even more immediately available to schools, except that they do not always think of it as evidence. All that boring filing, for example, can be a rich source of fascinating data. A primary headteacher I know in Nottingham persuaded City Challenge to fund a refurbishment of his drab, grey, inner-city playground. It became an attractive play area, zoned according to purpose: football at one end on astroturf, quiet sitting at outdoor tables at the other, and brightly coloured climbing frames in between.

Before they would invest, however, the City Challenge people wanted to know how he would monitor the impact of this change. He told them he had an office overlooking the playground so he would see for himself what difference it made. The prospective funders were not impressed by this argument. If there is one thing that defines the 1990s, it is that no one pays for anything unless the outcome can be measured. And by 'measured' they mean that the extent of success or failure must be summed up in a number. Words won't do – they are not 'hard data'; they do not have the spurious objectivity we attach to numbers.

My headteacher friend thought again. He could pay for an evaluation, of course, but that would mean reducing the scale of the development and, therefore, the children losing out. Then he remembered his filing cabinet. In there, as at every other primary school, would be the letters he wrote to parents. Among them would be letters he wrote to parents when their child had had a fall in the playground, warning them to look out for any signs of concussion. He told the City Challenge people he would count the 'headbang' letters and that he expected the number of them to fall once the improvements were made. They did – by half – and the City Challenge people were happy. They had a number to clutch at and the children had a playground that was *evidently* better.

A sense of direction, targets, self-evaluation, evidence: all crucial to school improvement, but how can they be given coherence? What is the means by which they are combined to form a strategy? The answer, to use jargon, is staff development. To use more jargon, it is the creation of a learning organisation in which every stakeholder – head, teachers, governors, as well as pupils – is learning all the time.

The first essential requirement, if a school is to become a learning organisation, is for it to plan its staff development well. A typical secondary school will have somewhere between £10,000 and £20,000 to spend each year on the development of its staff; a typical primary school between a quarter and a half of that. It is a substantial sum, but there are many competing demands on it. If the school is making a strategic switch – introducing a new IT network or a revised approach to behaviour and discipline – the necessary training and development must come from there. If a school is implementing a nationally mandated change – a new examination or test, for example – the training for that, too, must be paid for out of that sum. The same applies to, say, training in the use of a new syllabus in maths and to the countless training needs of individual teachers, such as courses in preparation for management, subject updating and competence issues. The £300 or so per teacher available to a school is hardly an extravagant sum. An improving school should make good use of this limited resource: a proportion, maybe 50 per cent, might be spent on overall school priorities; another 20 or so per cent on subject priorities; and the rest left to meet that myriad of individual demands.

In practice – the evidence suggests – the expenditure of this professional development resource is much more haphazard than it should be. It is not unknown for a school to find itself with a substantial underspend as the year end approaches and, at that point, to fritter it away because it all needs spending before the accounts are closed on 31 March. Often what is spent is used on a first-come-first-served basis in response to requests from individual teachers. The same kind of haphazard use of a precious resource applies to the five so-called 'Baker days'. When Kenneth Baker imposed a new contract of employment on teachers in 1987, it included a stipulation that, in addition to 190 pupil days, teachers would be required to work for five additional days. Given the climate of conflict and smouldering resentment at the time, it is hardly surprising that it was controversial. What is more surprising is that, all these years later, the days still unofficially bear Baker's name and are still resented by a significant number of teachers. Schools vary greatly in how they use them. In a well-led, well-planned, improving school, a programme of activities is prepared for them so that they are used, as they should be, as an important resource to help the school to implement its strategic priorities.

In many schools they are not used that way. Instead, people spend that valuable time, for example, cleaning the cupboards. In some schools – under the euphemistic title of 'departmental activity' – teachers simply drift away. This is a tragic waste of the biggest single investment that this country makes in the retraining and development of teachers. Every day that teachers work, we spend £40 million or so on their salaries: five days are worth £200 million. It is too much to spend on cleaning cupboards. Even the government itself has been pusillanimous about the issue. Recent guidance, approved by the Secretary of State, suggests that schools should use 'at least three' of the days for professional development purposes, thus raising the simple question: what are they supposed to be doing with the other two?

Planned and effective professional development is central to the creation of a learning organisation, but it is not enough. A learning organisation is as much a state of mind, a question of culture, as it is of planned use of scarce development resources. In a learning organisation, opportunities to learn and to develop are sought in all situations. At Haywood High School, for example, Yvonne Jeffries, the headteacher, takes great care to prepare the five-minute briefing for staff at the start of the day. It is not just an opportunity to pass on information: it is an opportunity to inspire, to have fun, to learn.

Staff meetings can be mind-numbing in schools, as in other organisations. I can remember, in my third year as a teacher, being elected to chair the staff meetings for the whole school year. I became very popular, solely because I kept them short. In the time we did spend meeting, we never debated anything of interest. I remember a long wrangle about how the chairs should be stacked at the end of assembly: it brought out people's most deep-seated anxieties. A head in a secondary school told me that she often attends meetings of the subject departments, more to see what they talk about than to intervene. Her patience gave way recently when, after forty-five precious minutes, the maths department had discussed nothing but on which shelves to stack the new set of textbooks. She intervened with a simple question: do you ever talk about teaching and learning? Silence. She suggested that they might consider, in future, holding their meetings in a classroom and start them with a ten-minute presentation from one of the team about a piece of work that had been taught: how had it been done? How well had it worked? And what kind of work had the pupils produced? Could it have been done differently or better? The pupils' work on the theme could be there, available for inspection and discussion. It was not, she argued, that the shelving of textbooks was completely irrelevant: rather that departmental meetings should be seen primarily as an opportunity to learn, and forty-five minutes spent on the textbooks were forty-five precious learning minutes wasted.

In improving schools, the culture values learning in all its forms and recognises that learning often takes place when least expected. If a school is to achieve true learning-organisation status, then its governors' meetings must rise above the minutiae of the agenda and become opportunities to learn too. Few governing bodies achieve this goal, although it is not hard to do. It simply requires the governors to decide that, rather than ploughing through the business agenda, they would prefer to start their meeting by examining pupils' work, watching pupils perform or hearing staff discuss their plans, for example, for improving literacy standards or improving examination performance in history. Half an hour on a real issue need not cause overworked governors to spend even more time at meetings: how many governors really believe that they could not fit a business discussion that took two hours in the past into an hour and a half, as long as the chairing was good and the governors kept to the point?

Another approach that I have seen work well is to use the money for governors' training not to send an occasional governor on an occasional course but, instead, to pay for an expert on a given theme to come and spend the meeting with the governors. The expert can talk about the chosen theme – say, special education – for fifteen minutes, answer questions and then, crucially, stay for the rest of the meeting and contribute right through the agenda from her or his perspective.

Turning a school into a learning organisation is partly a question of using resources well in order to make time for learning; and it is partly a question of exploiting the opportunities to learn that arise all the time in the course of a week at school. Oscar Wilde is supposed to have commented once that 'socialism will never come because there aren't enough evenings in the week'. If the creation of a learning organisation is seen as an extension of the existing and, no doubt, demanding schedule of a school, then it would go the way of socialism for the same reason. If, on the other hand, it becomes a different way of thinking about much of that drudgery, it can liven up the gloomy routine and be accomplished to the benefit of every learner, young or old, associated with the school.

This chapter began with one famous footballer. It is time to mention another. Glenn Hoddle may never have achieved the excellence that Denis Bergkamp achieves but, without doubt, he was one of the best British footballers of the 1980s. Now, in the 1990s, he is proving to be one of our most far-sighted managers, as his recent appointment as England coach indicates. Chelsea, under his direction, learnt how to play football again, after sleeping for a generation. Their 3–1 win over Wimbledon in an FA Cup quarter-final replay in 1996 followed two draws against them, one in the cup and one in a league match that happened to fall in the same week or two. Hoddle was asked why he thought Chelsea had won that night. He did not say because Ruud Gullit played a blinder (although he did); he did not say because the lads worked hard for ninety minutes (although they did); he said: 'We won because we learnt more about them over the previous two games than they learnt about us.' To cut a long story short, Hoddle has an inkling of what it means to be a learning organisation and, surely, anything Chelsea can do in this respect schools can do better. That is the challenge for schools in the mid-1990s. Many will rise to it, but what of those that don't? Are they destined to slide, like soccer teams, down through the divisions until they end up playing in front of a man and his dog in the Beazer Homes League?

The next section looks at the policy principles which can be derived from what we know about school effectiveness and improvement and suggests that we could aim, realistically, to eradicate school failure of the type which, until now, we have accepted as inevitable.

Imagining an End to Failure

During 1995, this country has seen the beginnings of a frank, open, serious debate about failure. In part this is because the education service appears to be increasingly successful. Examination results and participation rates have risen steadily for several years. OFSTED, the national inspection agency, has recorded an improvement in the proportion of lessons that are satisfactory or better. Meanwhile, at all levels in the education service – nationally, locally and in schools – there is a huge growth of interest in the research findings about school effectiveness and school improvement. In this respect, university-based researchers have made an important contribution to policy development. The debate about failure has also emerged because John Major's government has put in place means of inspecting every school and mechanisms for intervention in cases where a school is underperforming. It may not yet be perfect, but it is certainly a significant advance on what went before.

The growing interest in improvement is encouraging. It may be that, at last, cultural attitudes to failure in this country are changing. For too long, there has been a powerful strand of British culture which regarded failure in education as inevitable. Educators might have been expected to be in the vanguard of a campaign to challenge this poverty-stricken culture. In fact, teachers and their leaders have not taken the lead – they have been uncertain how to respond to the high-profile debate about failure and, in some cases, have been excessively defensive.

When the education service is accused of failure, the tendency among educators is to deny it or minimise it. When, for example, David Blunkett, Labour's Education Spokesperson, raised the issue of failing schools early in 1995, one union leader was quoted as saying that, if schools had sufficient support from government, they would never fail (*Guardian*, 12 April 1995). This view is untenable. Moreover, by suggesting that the only variable is government support it implies that the quality of teaching is insignificant. It therefore belittles, by implication, the entire profession.

Another union leader argued that 'dealing with a small number of schools in deep trouble is not the important agenda' (*Daily Telegraph*,

12 April 1995). For the pupils and parents concerned, it is surely the only agenda. More fundamentally, it needs to be recognised that a small number of failing schools undermines both the teaching profession and education as a public service. Their existence reinforces the negative cultural attitudes that so urgently need changing.

In the autumn of 1994, Chris Woodhead, Her Majesty's Chief Inspector, suggested that 30 per cent of teaching, according to OFSTED's data, was unsatisfactory or poor. Many teachers argued that he should instead have said that 70 per cent of teaching is satisfactory or better. This reaction is both defensive and complacent. Is it really appropriate for a profession to accept that 30 per cent of lessons are inadequate? Doesn't such a level of failure reinforce the cultural attitudes of those who believe that extensive educational failure is inevitable? Even if Chris Woodhead's figures proved to be exaggerated, surely a profession should be concerned about 10 or 20 per cent failure, never mind 30 per cent. The goal should be steadily to reduce the extent of failure. In the language of business, education should aim for ever higher reliability and, ideally, the teaching profession itself would lead the drive to achieve it. Yet at present, as the figures quoted earlier in the chapter suggest, there is a long way to go.

There is – because it is intrinsically difficult to do – insufficient research evidence on failing schools. The assumption tends to be that they are simply schools without the characteristics of effective schools. David Reynolds of Newcastle University suggests that this is too simplistic. Failing schools, he argues, have characteristics which actively militate against improvement. They have what Kate Myers calls 'antithetical characteristics'. Staff tend to blame pupils and the community for failure. They are fearful of outside intervention. There are feuds and cliques among staff. There is resistance to change. Good new ideas are met with cynicism. Effective staff in these circumstances often hide behind the norms of an ineffective group. Demoralisation is widespread, and teachers expect little from either the school as an organisation or from the pupils.

If Reynolds is right, then an improvement strategy which fails to take these 'psychological' problems into account is doomed to fail. There is no justification for allowing a school in this state to continue. It is a gross infringement of the entitlement of young people. Equally, the evidence suggests that traditional support and advice, even if it is accompanied by extra funding, will not be enough, as was true at Hackney Downs. The question is, then, what policy would enable pupils, including those in failing schools, to receive the education to which they are entitled?

In the reforms of the last few years, the underlying premise has been that schools should increasingly take responsibility for their own improvement. Through drawing on the school-effectiveness and -improvement research and the implementation of enlightened management strategies, most schools have welcomed this new responsibility and taken advantage of it. Their pupils have benefited as a result and this helps to explain the overall improvement in the performance of the education service over recent years.

The idea that school improvement is a job for schools seems blindingly obvious, but until the last decade it was not the basic premise of policy. It has implications for all those agencies, other than schools, that make up the education service. Instead of attempting to make schools improve or to 'do' improvement to them, their new role is to create a climate which encourages schools to improve themselves and enhances their ability to do so.

For local education authorities this has meant a profound psychological shift. After the 1988 Education Reform Act they ceased to have day-to-day management responsibility for schools and wondered what their *raison d'être* was. They had lost an empire but not yet found a role. For a while during the era of free-market Stalinism, it appeared that they might vanish altogether. If the government's goal of encouraging most, if not all, schools to opt out had been achieved, no doubt they would have done. During those demoralising months, some LEAs gave up any attempt to find a role and became little more than accounting mechanisms. Others, by contrast, began to create a new vision of a local education authority that would create the conditions in which schools could improve themselves. Birmingham and Lewisham, Nottinghamshire and Sussex, Shropshire and Newcastle began to define, through their actions, the notion of a school-improving LEA. Now that it has become apparent that LEAs have survived and that both parties envisage an important role for them, this new attitude has been adopted by more and more LEAs.

It is a role which has strong parallels in other fields, including business worldwide. Charles Handy defines it crisply in *The Empty Raincoat* (Hutchinson, 1994):

Small the centre should be, and partially dispersed, but it must be strong and well informed. The centre, after all, carries the ultimate responsibility for the whole. Its reserve powers typically include 'new money', i.e. the choice of strategic investments; 'new people', i.e. the right to make the key personnel decisions in the group; the design and management of the information system, which is the artery of the organisation; and, most controversially, the 'right of invasion' when things go wrong. Only those in the centre can have a view of the whole. They cannot run it, and should be too few in number to be tempted, but they can nudge, influence and, if they have to, interfere. The centre's principal task is to be the trustee of the future, but it needs to be sure that the present does not run out before the future arrives.

All the roles of the successful LEA of the mid-1990s are set out there. They are making strategic investments. They are helping to recruit good people. They are providing high-quality comparative information for schools and – controversially, as Handy says – they are intervening in schools which 'go wrong'.

It is difficult to imagine that all these things could be done well from Whitehall in a system with 25,000 schools, 400,000 teachers and 7.6 million pupils. This may explain why, even at the height of free-market Stalinism, the government shied away from abolishing LEAs.

Nevertheless, central government, too, has a vital role in promoting a climate of success. I return to this in more detail in Chapter 10, but three major responsibilities do need mentioning here. Central government sets the tone for the education service: it needs to combine encouragement with urgency, clarity about standards with advice; and it needs to encourage the wider society, not just educators, to take responsibility for educational improvement. Secondly, it sets the overall resource framework and needs to recognise that rapid fluctuations from year to year are inevitably disruptive of improvement strategies. Finally, it needs to create the kind of policy processes and networks that enable progress to be made. Whether or not government has played this part successfully in recent years is no doubt open to question. What is clear is that under Gillian Shephard it has come closer to achieving it than ever before.

A national policy to reduce the extent of school failure needs to be based on principles consistent with this approach to promotion of improvement. A national policy which promotes school improvement and provides steady investment is an important precondition. It is also essential to have in place an effective means of identifying failing schools. This demands the continuation and refinement of a national inspection system which is able to ensure the consistency of inspections across the country. It also requires clarity about the inspection criteria which define success. The central element of this definition should relate to the capacity of the school to improve itself.

The inspection process is not enough: it is also apparent that, over the next few years, further refined published performance indicators, based on value-added approaches, will need to be developed. These can be used not only as helpful additional data, but also as a means of checking on the consistency of inspectors' judgements.

As soon as more refined performance indicators had been developed,

OFSTED would be in a position to target its resources at schools which are less successful. For most schools – which performance indicators show to be functioning well – the inspection system could then consist of a self-review validated by an outsider. Its self-review could involve an external inspector and be checked against nationally accepted performance indicators. A full-scale inspection would then be necessary only in three circumstances: where the check revealed the self-review to have been carried out inadequately; where there was evidence that the school did not appear to have the capacity to drive its own improvement; or where its performance, as revealed through examination results, truancy figures, parental complaints or other hard data, appeared to be unacceptable. In order to achieve national consistency, to build up a good national database and to ensure a degree of pressure for improvement, it would, in addition, be wise to inspect at random about 10 per cent of all schools.

The reduced level of inspection for most schools would enable OFSTED to put more resources into in-depth inspection of less effective schools and into assisting these schools in the development of constructive post-inspection improvement strategies. These developments would help OFSTED achieve its stated goal of 'Improvement Through Inspection' and ensure that, over time, it was perceived as a central element of a national improvement strategy rather than as a kind of educational police.

In short, through a national programme of validated self-review for more successful schools and through external inspection and follow-up support for less successful schools, it should be possible to ensure that every school is either successful or improving, or both.

The policy principle underlying these proposals is that *intervention should be in inverse proportion to success*. The general assumption behind this principle is that most schools have within them the capacity to improve themselves steadily, as long as national government provides a sensible policy and funding framework. The precise nature of intervention in a school which is not succeeding should depend on the extent and character of its failure.

Any intervention needs to be carefully planned and based on knowledge of the school-effectiveness and school-improvement research. Its purpose needs to be clear: improvement cannot be imposed. The role of intervention should be to generate within a school the capacity for sustainable self-renewal, and to unblock the barriers to improvement or to offer the pupils learning opportunities at a more successful institution. This still leaves open the issue of whether local or central government should intervene. In general, though, surely intervention is likely to be more effective, credible and legitimate in the eyes of parents and the community if it comes from local level. Central government intervention should be the rare exception not the rule.

Struggling schools, by my definition, are those that, while they are not failing disastrously, are certainly not providing a good-quality education for their pupils and whose capacity for improvement, while not entirely absent, is limited. For them, the quality of the post-inspection action plan is more important than it is for more successful schools. Yet a struggling school, by definition, is less likely to be able to produce an effective plan. Each school in these circumstances should receive a limited sum of money specifically to purchase external expertise in the action-planning process. The government has recently made funds available to enable this to be done from 1996–97 onwards. If OFSTED's resources were redirected as suggested earlier, additional funding to allow effective implementation of action plans would become available.

As schools gain experience of planning their follow-up to inspection reports, there should be increasing research evidence of how best to develop and implement such plans. The strength of the British university sector in the fields of school effectiveness and school improvement provides an important springboard for further research and collaboration over policy issues such as this. The experience, both in this country and abroad, suggests that action plans need to be a judicious combination of the latest research evidence on school improvement with knowledge and detailed understanding of the school in question. For this reason, there can be no simple blueprint. It is vital that a school believes in, understands and is committed to the plan that emerges from the process and that the plan addresses the specific problems of that school in its community.

It is becoming evident from the inspection process that, in some struggling schools, poor performance is due to the significant underperformance of a relatively small number of members of staff. For this reason, there is a growing debate in policy and professional circles about the best means of identifying the teachers concerned and ensuring that they either improve or leave the profession. OFSTED has now developed a post-inspection process to ensure that this happens.

Failing schools differ from struggling schools, chiefly in that their capacity for self-improvement is very limited indeed. A failing school is therefore, by definition, one that is providing an inadequate education and is unable, without substantial external intervention, to improve.

One option to consider in these circumstances is closure and dispersal of the pupils. When David Blunkett suggested closing failing schools at the annual conference of the Association of Teachers and Lecturers in April 1995, he created a storm. In fact, what he said about closure (as opposed to 'Fresh Start') is nothing new. It is happening already in the case of a handful of schools which have been found to be failing. Furthermore, some LEAs have decided to close a school in advance of an inspection because they knew it would fail. If there are sufficient alternative places available in good schools within the area, it may be the most sensible option. This is what the education association at Hackney Downs School decided was the most practical means of improving education for the pupils who had been so poorly provided for there. Only a mile away was a boys' school which had spare capacity and was evidently improving. In British circumstances, at any rate, school closure, it seems, will always be controversial and the parents of pupils at the school can be expected to resist closure, however poor the school is. Their anxieties are also likely to be exploited by political activists of the far left for their own destructive political ends. A decision to close therefore needs considerable political will behind it at either local or national level, or preferably both.

A second option for a failing school is to develop an effective action plan, through a process of discussion between OFSTED, the school and the LEA; to make any necessary staffing changes; and, possibly, to invest some additional resources in specific aspects of the improvement strategy. This is the strategy used in a number of failing schools and appears, in some cases, such as Northicote School in Wolverhampton, to have been successful. The cost of such a strategy is likely to be very high and, in order to justify the demand for resources that would otherwise be available to other schools, it ought to be firmly established that the continued existence of the school is essential and that the improvement strategy is well founded on best practice and therefore likely to work. It is also important to note that the power of central government to intervene and take over a failing school provides it with important leverage over a local education authority. The threat of central government intervention has been an effective spur to local action in some cases. Actually, use of the power has been considered necessary only once, and then in unusual circumstances. It is likely that central government will use it sparingly and will usually prefer to leave the LEA in the frontline.

The progress of a failing school, once its improvement strategy is in place, needs to be monitored carefully. Schools need success criteria related not just to academic performance, which often takes some time to improve, but also to pupil behaviour, truancy, pupil and parent attitudes and staff development, which may be more amenable to short-term change.

In the case of some failing schools, this kind of approach worked successfully in the mid-1990s. There is, however, a small number of schools where the improvement strategy has not worked. In these circumstances, a school has been found to be failing and is still failing a year or more later. This is often the case after very extensive resources have been invested in it. If the needs of the pupils are to be the prime concern, this is a situation in which urgent action is needed.

Closure and dispersal might again be appropriate, but what if a school is necessary in that community? What if that would mean pupils making long, inconvenient journeys? Would they be likely to do so after their experience of education? Or would many of them join the ranks of the 'disappeared' – those teenagers, between 5 and 10 per cent of their peers in some urban areas, who cease to attend school and turn up next, if they turn up at all, in the criminal justice statistics?

In these specific circumstances, David Blunkett's 'Fresh Start' idea makes sense. The school would be closed and a new school opened on the same site. The change would have to be done quickly, perhaps over an extended summer break. It would also have to be more than cosmetic. It would need to be a new school with a new governing body. It would need professional leadership of the highest calibre. It would need the resources to attract new staff to what would inevitably be a risky venture. It would need to draw on the latest research and use innovative approaches to teaching and learning. It would need to be perceived by its staff and, above all, by pupils and the community as an ambitious and exciting attempt to create success and to make a clean break from the troubles of the past.

Some critics have already condemned this idea. It will not work, they say. But their case is fundamentally flawed. Firstly, it has been done successfully in America and, in effect, here too. In 1988, at Highbury Quadrant Primary School, the Inner London Education Authority intervened dramatically, controversially and, in the long run, successfully. Hammersmith and Fulham LEA has acted boldly in the case of Hammersmith School during 1995, and the evidence is that the new Phoenix School which has arisen in its place is making significant progress. Neither of these British examples was a fully fledged 'Fresh Start' (not least because the law in its present form makes 'Fresh Start' difficult), but they show it could be done.

The argument for a fresh start is not that it will always work. It will certainly be a major challenge wherever it is tried. Rather, it is that something must be attempted. Doing nothing can no longer be an option. In the late twentieth century, continued failure is simply unacceptable. Instead, there ought to be a restless determination to promote improvement. In this context, the two most encouraging developments of the mid-1990s are, firstly, the growing consensus at national level that addressing educational failure is an issue of the highest political and social priority; and, secondly, the increasingly apparent capability of the education service to learn continuously from the policy-implementation process about how to help good schools become better and poor schools become good.

The traditional response to those who raise the question of failure was to suggest that we should discuss the success of the many, not the failure of the few. This is a classic false dichotomy which the debates of 1995 and 1996 have begun to unmask. A serious debate about failure is, in fact, a precondition of success.

PART FOUR

As It Might Be

6 · A Brief Interlude Containing Two Paradoxes

The acceptance of paradox as a feature of our life is the first step towards living with it and managing it.

Charles Handy

Structure and Chaos

Over the last twenty-five years, scientists have become fascinated with chaos. The more they look for it the more they find. Indeed, it might not be an exaggeration to say that the burgeoning understanding of chaos has overthrown classical physics. From Isaac Newton onwards there was an assumption that the key to understanding the physical world was to work out the laws of nature. Once these were known and the initial conditions were established, it was argued, everything could be predicted. Nature would work *like clockwork*. As Richard Feynman put it: 'Physicists like to think that all you have to do is say, these are the conditions, now what happens next?' (Quoted in *Chaos*, Thomas Gleick, Abacus, 1987.)

In practice, of course, as everyone who has sat in a school science laboratory knows, it never turns out to be quite that simple. The experiments do not always seem to work out as they are supposed to. The failure of experiments is occasionally attributed to incompetence. More often it is attributed to some minor defect in the experiment which occurred because the experiment took place in the real world, rather than a perfect Newtonian world. We can all remember those maths questions that began 'Assume a perfectly smooth slope . . .'. Although we knew no slope in the real world was perfectly smooth, we suspended disbelief to satisfy the teacher, the examiner or the author of the textbook.

The point is that the failure of experiments for 300 years after Newton was put down to the absence of perfection or, to use a more recent term, to 'noise'. As Thomas Gleick put it:

Small non-linearities were easy to disregard. People who conduct experiments learn quickly that they live in an imperfect world. In the centuries since Galileo and Newton, the search for regularity in experiments has been fundamental. Any experimentalist looks for quantities that remain the same, or quantities that are zero. But that means disregarding bits of messiness that interfere with a neat picture.

Yet the bits of messiness or non-linearities are important. Not only that, they are everywhere. In the 1960s and 1970s a few pioneering scientists in fields as diverse as meteorology, fluid dynamics and economics began to focus not on the regularities but on the irregularities. What they discovered was chaos.

Thomas Gleick again:

> The modern study of chaos began with the creeping realisation in the 1960s that quite simple mathematical equations could model systems every bit as violent as a waterfall. Tiny differences in input quickly became overwhelming differences in output – a phenomenon given the name 'sensitive dependence on initial conditions'. In weather for example, this translates into what is known, only half jokingly, as the Butterfly Effect – the notion that a butterfly stirring the air today in Peking can transform storm systems next month in New York.

So much for the dramatic developments in science which I do not even pretend to understand. Oddly, though, there has been an astonishingly similar and unremarked intellectual development in the social sciences over the same period. In the 1960s and 1970s much of the writing of history was about competing systems, the conflict between social classes, underlying forces, economic determinism and all that. There were a few historians who wrote against the tide; in this country A. J. P. Taylor was pre-eminent among them. It was he who famously concluded his book, *The Origins of the Second World War* (Penguin, 1961), by saying: 'Hitler may have projected a great war all along; yet it seems from the record that he became involved in war through launching on 29 August a diplomatic manoeuvre which he ought to have launched on 28 August.' There has never been a sentence better designed to provoke the economic determinists and the class warriors, nor a better description of the Butterfly Effect in another context.

By now, of course, the tide has turned; chance and the individual have regained their rightful place in the explanation of historical events. As Simon Schama wrote in his magnificent study of the French Revolution, *Citizens* (Penguin, 1989):

> Nor does the Revolution seem any longer to conform to a grand historical design, preordained by inexorable forces of social change. Instead it seems a thing of contingencies and unforeseen consequences

... in fact, the Revolution was a haphazard and chaotic event and much more the product of human agency than structural conditioning.

Here, in all but name, is the Butterfly Effect again.

History is not alone among the social sciences, either. The study of management for much of the twentieth century was concerned with systems and structures. In the beginning there was the notion of the division of labour, and then of the separation of manufacturing into its constituent parts, a process which culminated in the conveyor belt. The era thus ushered in was christened the Fordist era, since the Ford Motor Company pioneered this approach and came to represent it in popular culture.

Now there is an academic debate about whether post-Fordism has arrived and what its defining characteristics are. For certain, the management hierarchies associated with the Fordist era are fast disappearing. Under the old hierarchies, decisions emanated from top managers gathered in vast corporate headquarters. Decisions were passed down a management pyramid. Each layer of the pyramid 'supervised' the layer below. At the bottom were the shop-floor workers: at the top was the magnate. In the 1960s, for example, the moderately large British company Metal Box built itself a state-of-the-art vast corporate headquarters on stilts near Reading station. Within little more than a decade, the whole building stood empty, and forlorn notices, eminently readable from any passing train, informed the travelling public that it was 'TO LET'. There were no takers. Metal Box built its corporate headquarters half a century too late to reap the value of its investment.

Management, by the 1980s, like science and history, was becoming chaotic. Hierarchies were broken up, layers of management done away with, responsibilities delegated and quality circles formed. Companies ceased to be hierarchies and became organisms. Tom Peters, the most successful management guru of the 1980s, called his third book *Thriving on Chaos*, and his fourth *Liberation Management: Necessary Disorganisation for the Nanosecond Nineties*. Even allowing for the hype, the similarities between his choice of words and the developments in science and history are striking.

Meanwhile, in a prison cell in communist Czechoslovakia in the mid-1970s, Václav Havel, then the leading dissident in the Stalinist republic, was arriving at a remarkably similar perception for completely different reasons. Stalinism was intolerable precisely because it was the ultimate system. He wrote, in a 1975 letter to Gustav Hašek:

For we never know when some inconspicuous spark of knowledge may suddenly light up the road for the whole of society, without society

ever realising perhaps how it came to see the road. But that is far
from being the whole story. Even those other innumerable flashes of
knowledge which never illuminate the path ahead . . . have their deep
social importance, if only through the mere fact that they happened:
that they might have cast light; that in their very occurrence they fulfil
a certain range of society's potentialities – either its creative powers
or simply its liberties; they too help to make and maintain the climate
of civilisation without which none of the more effective flashes could
ever occur.

The fact is that wherever we look – science, history, management, politics
– systems are giving way to chaos. Moreover, though the process is
unsettling, it is remarkably positive: individuals, informal teams and
creative energy matter again. As one American business magazine commented with stunning simplicity about the world's leading producer of
computer software: 'Microsoft's only . . . asset is the human imagination.'

Given this unstoppable intellectual surge towards chaos, one has to
ask why people in education in the late 1980s and early 1990s were so
obsessed with structures. It is time to recognise that reforming structures
alone will not bring about real change, least of all in education, where
quality depends so heavily on a chaotic myriad of personal interactions.
We need to understand that chaos matters too.

Equality and Diversity

Most people over thirty have read the Sellars and Yeatman classic, *1066
and All That*. For those with short memories or who are under thirty,
or both, it was a light-hearted romp through a thousand years of British
history. Among the many pearls of wisdom in their book, Sellars and
Yeatman invented an important classification. They defined the Cavaliers
as 'wrong but romantic' and the Roundheads as 'right but repulsive'.
The more one thinks about this classification, the more aspects of life it
seems to apply to. It is, in any case, the key to understanding the political
conflict over education in the post-war era.

Chapter 2 examined post-war educational history and attempted to
explain how we arrived where we are. If, instead of giving chapter and
verse, we generalised ruthlessly, we could argue that those fifty years
were dominated by an argument between two conflicting ideas. On the
political right were those who believed that the goal of education should
be diversity: diverse provision to meet diverse needs or demands. Hence
the right's defence of the grammar and secondary modern system and
its opposition to comprehensive schools. Hence its support for the almost

Figure 4

	INEQUALITY	EQUALITY
DIVERSITY	Wrong but Romantic	Right and Romantic
UNIFORMITY	Wrong and Repulsive	Right but Repulsive

forgotten direct grant schools. Hence, more recently, its support for city technology colleges, grant-maintained schools and a return to selection according to ability. An inevitable consequence of diversity, it argued, is inequality, which regrettably we will simply have to live with. There were those on the right who thought that inequality, like diversity, was a positive good. For example, the Senior Chief Inspector of Schools in 1941, F. R. G. Duckworth, argued: 'I confess that I am not much moved by what appears to sacrifice the interests of the few in favour of the many when one result is certain to be that the quality of persons required to fill posts of great importance and of a highly specialised nature is likely to be degraded.' These were the people, often few in number, but of a significance far beyond their numbers, whom political science describes as elitists.

On the political left, by contrast, the argument was that the overarching goal of education should be equality. If the consequence of the pursuit of equality was uniformity, then so be it. Hence the left's support for comprehensive education, its opposition to religious schools and its repeated demands for the abolition of private schools.

All of this can be summarised in a diagram (see Figure 4). The political right, it will be seen, are to be found in the top left-hand corner of the diagram, favouring a combination of inequality and diversity. In Sellars and Yeatman terms they are wrong about equality but romantic about diversity. The political left are to be found in the bottom right-hand corner, right in that they favour equality, but repulsive in their support for uniformity.

The diagram has two remaining corners. In the bottom left-hand corner we find the entirely objectionable combination of inequality and uniformity. No one, surely, would design a political programme which was both wrong and repulsive, at least not on purpose. This is the place where the education service might find itself if we had an over-prescriptive National Curriculum and a grossly unfair distribution of funds among schools. We came closer to achieving this detestable combination in the early 1990s than the government would care to admit. Sir Ron Dearing arrived, like all true heroes, in the nick of time.

The top right-hand corner of the diagram brings together equality with diversity. Even the phrase has a positive ring to it. It is my contention that education policy, as we approach the millennium, should aim to combine equality with diversity and should set out, at last, to create for the first time in history an education service which is both right and romantic.

The case for choosing this aspiration is not only that it has an obvious appeal. More importantly, the combination of equality and diversity would recognise two increasingly important social priorities which have made the stale conflicts of the post-war era simply inadequate. One is the need to develop an education system which provides every young person with the opportunity to succeed: in other words a system which provides equality, or as near as we can get to it, in terms of ensuring that virtually everyone reaches a much higher standard than, until recently, we believed was possible.

The other is the need to recognise the extent to which society has become more diverse over the last thirty years. It has, and will continue to do so. John Naisbitt talks of the global paradox. He argues that the globalisation of communications and economics paradoxically empowers the world's smallest players. Large companies have been able to succeed only by breaking up large bureaucracies and empowering small, flexible, but highly skilled teams. In a parallel shift, social homogeneity has broken down as each society is forced to come to terms with multi-racial, multi-cultural and multi-faith communities. A far greater range of lifestyles has been legitimised. Some bone-headed back-to-basics fanatics berate homosexuality from time to time, but even the ultra-Conservative British Parliament of 1994 agreed to lower the age of consent for gay men to eighteen. Over the last generation, the range of work and leisure options, especially for women, has multiplied. Women's soccer, for example, is said to be the fastest-growing sport in Britain. The message is that social diversity is here to stay. Just as our education system must strive to provide achievement for all, so too must it roll with the flow of diversity. Any attempt by a public service to impose uniformity on an increasingly diverse society would result in the service being blown apart.

If this argument is accepted, then equality with diversity is not just an interesting idea, but also a logical response to the changing nature of British society. It sounds attractive, perhaps, but what would it mean in practice? Some years ago I ran into a civil servant in a pub in north

London. My expectations of the conversation when it began were not high, particularly when he turned out to be a Treasury official. The subject that provided more hours of fruitless debate than any other in the 1980s emerged. Was it possible to imagine Labour ever again forming a government and, if it did, what would it do?

'Under the present government,' the official commented, referring to the seemingly immortal Thatcher regime, 'it doesn't really matter what the issue is, we know that the question we have to ask is, how do you create a market? The same question applies to issues as diverse as water, health, arms procurement and the inspection of schools. From our point of view this is very helpful because it means that we can get on with things without waiting for an instruction from ministers. They benefit too because it keeps up the momentum of reform.' He paused. 'What I want to know,' he asked, 'is what would be the equivalent question under Labour?'

I was unable to answer at the time, though the question was imprinted indelibly in my mind. An incoming Labour government – hoping to implement an agenda that lengthens with every passing year of Conservative rule – would certainly need to solve the puzzle. The alternative would be stagnation.

Two important political changes have taken place since the Treasury official surprised me with that insight in the mid-1980s. Firstly, the possibility of another Labour government has moved from the realms of fantasy, first to the realms of reality and then to the realms of likelihood. Secondly, Thatcherism has lost its way. 'How do you make a market?' was fine as a question while there were plenty of state-run monopolies to break up. When the question starts being applied to sub post-offices, prisons, railways and motorways, it looks like clutching at straws. As a result, both parties are looking for a new underlying policy question: Labour because they might win, and the Conservative because they might lose.

Equality with diversity might perhaps hold the key. The question to ask, at least about education policy, would be: 'What is the maximum amount of diversity consistent with equality?' This question is not quite as simple as the Thatcherite question, but then, as we discovered in the 1980s, excessive simplicity is not necessarily a virtue. Nevertheless, answering it, whether in relation to the National Curriculum, the nature of the teaching profession or the organisation of the education service, provides a rich and varied set of insights into policy.

The four remaining chapters in this part of the book examine each of these crucial aspects of education in the light of the structure–chaos paradox and the equality–diversity paradox. Taken together, they imply an education revolution, a revolution that, in my view, is necessary to prepare for the next millennium.

7 · The Millennium Curriculum: Redefining the Purpose of Education

A teacher, particularly the teacher dedicated to liberal education, must constantly try to look towards the goal of human completeness.

Alan Bloom

Three Blind Alleys

As a result of the education debate disappearing down three blind alleys during the last fifty years, there is a great deal of confusion about what schools are for.

The first blind alley was the idea of professional autonomy and control over what was taught in schools or, in lay person's language, the idea that teacher (and teacher alone) knows best. Essentially this was a legacy of the British reaction to fascism. Hitler and Mussolini decided the minutiae of what ought to be taught in schools, therefore it must be wrong in a democratic society. This kind of thinking was evident in the 1940s when the great 1944 Education Act was being constructed. Indeed it shines through in the description R. A. Butler gave of his interview with Churchill when the war leader appointed him President of the Board of Education in 1941. Churchill told Butler that he would have to oversee the complex administration of evacuating children from the cities and then changed the subject.

'I am now too old to think you can change people's natures,' he said. 'Everyone has to learn to defend himself. I should not object if you could introduce a note of patriotism into the schools. Tell the children that Wolfe won Quebec.'

Butler replied that though he would like to influence what was taught in schools this was frowned upon. Churchill turned serious and commented, 'Of course not by instruction or order, but by suggestion.'

Thus the Prime Minister of the most centralised government in twentieth-century British history, a government that had not the slightest qualms about fixing the price of hake daily, made clear he did not see a role for government in laying down what should be taught in schools.

This view was almost universal throughout the 1940s. When a back-woods Tory moved an amendment to the 1944 Education Bill which would have required 'part-time education for all male persons in the duties and obligations of citizenship', he was described by a fellow MP – who overwhelmingly won the day – as being 'very near Hitler'. And fifteen years after the war, the imposing General Secretary of the NUT, Ronald Gould, was arguing that the 'safeguard [of democracy] is the existence of a quarter of a million teachers who are free to decide what should be taught and how it should be taught'.

Even now, fifty years after the defeat of fascism, this view has signifi-cant support among teachers. Yet it is difficult to see in principle why in a democratic society the control of the curriculum should be left entirely to teachers. After all, through the democratic process decisions are taken to purchase people's land and houses compulsorily, to require them to insure their cars and to wear seatbelts and motorcycle helmets. The question of what should be taught in schools is of a great deal more importance than any of these almost universally accepted prescriptions. What is taught in schools not only helps to define the country's culture and democracy: it is also a critical element in building its future. Why should teachers alone decide matters which are clearly relevant to every citizen? In any case many other democratic countries – France, post-war Germany and numerous states in the USA for example – have never had the slightest concern about prescribing what is taught. In their view, teachers' professionalism lies chiefly in ensuring that young people learn what is in the curriculum, not in shaping the curriculum itself. Whatever else the fierce debate since 1988 over the National Curriculum has achieved, it has enabled us – and especially the teaching profession – to back out of the blind alley of professional control of the curriculum. However, this still leaves us in a maze with two other dead ends.

The second blind alley is the debate that ran through the 1970s and 1980s about whether the 'process' or the 'product' was more important. This was a debate more suited to medieval philosophers than twentieth-century education professionals and – had they heard it – one which would probably have left the mass of lay people absolutely cold. It went like this. The advocates of the 'process' model point out that the steps by which children and young people move towards learning something are themselves the most important part of learning. The fans of 'process' – and there are many in education – are those who believe that the journey is more important than the destination. This distils into an advocacy of giving primacy to the skills of learning and understanding, and correspondingly relegating 'facts'.

The advocates of 'product' take the counter-view that it does not matter how young people learn what they are supposed to learn as long as they learn it. For them the destination is everything. They therefore tended to emphasise the importance of 'facts' and 'content'. On the whole, over the last few decades 'product' fans have been heavily outnumbered among people who work in education and indeed have often become associated with a relatively small – but recently influential – group of right-wing pressure groups. There is however, in my view, no reason in principle why 'facts' and 'content' should be seen as intrinsically right-wing.

This is precisely the kind of blind alley that the debate about crime found itself in before Tony Blair took it by the scruff of the neck. The debate raged about whether the soaring crime rate would be reduced by being tough on criminals or by tackling the underlying social causes of crime. Blair finished it for good with his most famous aphorism (so far): 'Tough on crime, tough on the causes of crime'. Like many other crucial socio-political insights, this is what Tom Peters calls a 'blinding flash of the obvious'.

Exactly the same is true of the process–product blind alley. The equivalent Blairism might be 'keen on process; keen on product', for clearly both are important. In fact the debate on the National Curriculum since 1988 has helped us out of this blind alley since, without doing so consciously, it has indeed endorsed a Blair approach. Unfortunately, having extracted us from two blind alleys it has led us into a third.

Unlike the other two, this one is better imagined not as a long dark street with high walls down both sides and at the far end; but rather as a network of little pathways none of which really lead anywhere useful or as a series of false loops on the Norfolk Broads. We were drawn into this fruitless territory through a combination of poor curriculum design in 1988–90 with even worse curriculum implementation from 1990 to 1992. Thus, instead of looking at the National Curriculum as that which this democratic society believes every young person should learn by the age of sixteen, we have had a debate about whether it is over-prescriptive (which it was), whether it created teacher workload (which it did) and whether it included everything it should (which many lobby groups thought it did not). The debates have therefore been riddled with contradictions. The same people state that the curriculum is overloaded and prescriptive but complain that any given subject or theme is marginalised if it is left out. Thus the teacher unions have, for example, simultaneously advocated a reduction in prescription and leapt to the defence of those teachers who believe that the preparation of food should be part of the National Curriculum. They complained when the government wanted to recommend specific authors, and despaired when the whole of history was made optional for fourteen- to sixteen-year-olds.

Teacher workload is obviously important, but it is hardly an effective starting point for a debate about the National Curriculum. If its implementation had been better planned, then workload need not have been a curriculum issue at all. The government proved unable to distinguish the implementation process from the ultimate goal (a neat reminder incidentally that process and product both matter). Worse still, it failed to enlist teacher support for the National Curriculum in spite of the fact that unless teachers taught it with commitment it was not worth the endless reams of paper it was written on. Instead of actively involving teachers in the decision-making and implementation process, they were treated little better than the quarry workers in the *Flintstones* film. Furthermore, the same secrecy which infected Mr Slate's quarry affected the National Curriculum too. Thus, although the agencies were staffed with highly professional, dedicated, sometimes even noble people, the climate created by ministerial attitudes and the bitter relations between the then Department for Education and the agencies meant inevitably that they were always looking over their shoulders. In the old days before the National Curriculum, the Department of Education and Employment – then known as the Department for Education and Science – was staffed, or so it seemed, by serious, pragmatic, generally grey-haired, sober, career civil servants. But the civil servants involved in National Curriculum implementation were a new breed. They were young (or maybe I had just aged), and ideologically committed to the government agenda. At meetings they turned up and ended debates not through the quality of their argument, but by saying 'Ministers could not countenance' whatever it was. Sometimes they behaved like Millwall fans in suits.

By contrast, the staff of the agencies on the whole came out of schools and LEAs. From the point of view of ministers they were therefore part of that dreadful education establishment and not to be trusted. The National Curriculum Council (NCC) and the Schools Examination and Assessment Council (SEAC) could not even commission a small research project without permission from the Millwall lads.

Once research was commissioned it often struggled to find its way into the public domain. One usually assumed at the time that someone at the department, perhaps a minister, was unhappy with the findings, and that therefore they had been suppressed or delayed to such an extent that by the time they finally emerged the findings were irrelevant.

The most celebrated case was Warwick University's evaluation of

English in the National Curriculum. Ministers had decided on change
before the evaluation was complete. In the document it drew up to
support the ministerial view, the NCC quoted from the Warwick study,
but refused to publish it in full. As a result, everyone suspected that here
was a blatant case of selective quotation. The teacher unions clamoured to
be given the full text but the hands of the NCC officials were tied. The
researcher at Warwick was besieged with phone calls but honourably
refused to provide the document to anyone, in spite of her fury at the
suppression of her work.

Employed as an NUT official at the time, I worked on some covert
means of acquiring the document. Eventually, in the underground car
park of the NCC building in York (the same car park that floods every
time the Ouse rises in the spring), I was given the report in a plain
brown envelope. Deep Throat, it seemed, had made a reappearance. The
report inevitably turned out to be an innocuous affair. As A. J. P. Taylor
said of the speculation about the sexual practices of Bismarck's doctor,
it is often more interesting not to inquire. However, it did enable one
to conclude that the NCC had indeed been guilty of selective quotation.

At any rate, such were the small and ultimately meaningless channels
into which the first round of National Curriculum implementation led
us.

For reasons examined in Chapter 2, Sir Ron Dearing was appointed
in May 1993 to try to steer the curriculum debate out of this third and
most confusing blind alley. He did so with some aplomb. His approach
was the essence of pragmatism. The absurd secrecy was swept away,
teachers were consulted until they became tired of it and pragmatic
compromises were reached on teacher workload, prescription and the
extent of professional discretion. What we are left with after Dearing is
a curriculum that will do. It is the equivalent of an F-reg Ford Escort
with a reconditioned engine which will no doubt travel reasonably well
to the end of the century as long as it is driven with care and serviced
regularly. It is much better than the over-complex, unreliable and
undriveable vehicle that preceded it, but hardly the kind of vehicle in
which one would choose to cross the threshold of a new millennium.

The teacher unions, finding themselves, to their surprise, in the driving seat in the summer of 1993, proposed to Sir Ron Dearing that once
his process of revision was complete there should be no further major
curriculum change for five years. Teachers, they said, were tired of
change. They were becoming cynical about implementing any given
curriculum change because, like London buses, another would be along
in a minute. Thus, they reasoned, if the government wanted to implement
the revised National Curriculum effectively it should concede this five-

year moratorium. There was an unspoken rationale behind the proposal too. If there were high-profile ministerial commitments to the moratorium it would make it much harder for succeeding ministers to succumb to the temptation to impose their own enthusiasms on schools. To everyone's surprise, Sir Ron and then John Patten accepted this proposal and made it their own. One or two teacher leaders, startled by the extent of their success, then began to try to wriggle out of it, since it dawned on them that some of their members might not like Dearing's F-reg Ford Escort. Most sensibly recognised that a roadworthy Ford Escort was better than any vehicle that spent most of its time at the garage.

Thus, it now seems probable that the Dearing curriculum will survive broadly intact until the end of the century. It is possible that an incoming Labour government might start to alter it in its first year. More probably, it would see the wisdom of resisting the temptation to tinker straight away. It would, after all, have a tremendous range of educational changes to pursue quite apart from the curriculum. If so, we can surely, as a society, seize the opportunity to have a serious, considered debate about the purposes of schools in the twenty-first century. We can prepare ourselves – after fifty years in blind alleys – to set out down the broad highway into the century ahead. We can have a curriculum of quality ready for the year 2000. Surely we learnt something on the road from Churchill's office to the underground car park in York. The rest of this chapter is intended to outline the possible shape of the millennium curriculum. It should be emphasised at this stage that the omission of something should be taken to mean not that it is not important, but that it need not necessarily be compulsory in schools. Many possible elements of the curriculum – technology in general and aspects of the arts – omitted here would be central to the infinitely wider curriculum of secondary education, which the proposals in the final chapter would make possible.

Seven Different Ways of Knowing the World

The central message of Chapter 3 is that far too many young people are simply not motivated by what secondary school has to offer. Therefore, when the curriculum is redesigned in the year 2000 the motivation of young people needs to be a consideration of the highest priority. Sir Ron Dearing, to his credit, identified the issue in his review in 1993 and argued forcefully that if schools failed to attract pupils then, like a business that failed to attract customers, they needed to consider altering the product. However, his review took place within the constraint that both government and the teacher unions were totally opposed to radical change. He has further advanced this case with his proposals, in 1996, to bring greater flexibility and coherence to the post-sixteen school and college curriculum, but this exercise, too, was constrained by the government's unshakeable commitment to A Levels. In the year 2000 there need be no such constraints. Indeed to shy away from necessary change in that critical year would be unforgivable.

Motivation, though important, is not the sole concern. One could imagine, for example, designing a curriculum around modern music, sport, computer games and soap operas which might pull in the crowds but would hardly fulfil the purposes of society, or justify the existence of the school system. In redesigning the National Curriculum, therefore, it is also necessary to anticipate the changing needs of democratic society in the early twenty-first century as well as to motivate young people.

It is my contention that, perhaps for the first time in educational history, it is possible to arrive at a curriculum which can fulfil both these purposes magnificently. The economy and democratic society demand increasing levels of educational achievement from everyone, while the multiple threats to the continued existence of the planet give that drive the ultimate justification. The agenda for education, therefore, could hardly be more motivating. Meanwhile, information technology will provide new and exciting ways of teaching and learning. Moreover we have, at last, a theoretical understanding of children and young people that will assist teachers in their task.

For this last piece in the jigsaw we are indebted to the widely recognised contribution of Howard Gardner, the Professor of Education at Harvard. Chapter 2 described the attack in the 1960s on Cyril Burt's idea that intelligence was general, inherited and fixed. Howard Gardner is perhaps best viewed as the man who finally drove the stake through Cyril Burt's heart. His contention is that intelligence is specific, affected by upbringing and schooling as well as inheritance, and potentially unlimited. In his groundbreaking book *Frames of Mind* (Basic Books, 1983) he set out to describe a radically different view of intelligence. His critical argument was that intelligence does not develop uniformly in each individual. Rather, it is better to view each individual as possessing seven intelligences, in each of which each individual progresses at different rates. He summarises his view in his more recent book *The Unschooled Mind* (Fontana, 1993).

> I have posited that all human beings are capable of at least seven different ways of knowing the world – ways that I have elsewhere labelled the seven human intelligences. According to this analysis, we are all able to know the world through language, logical–mathematical

analysis, spatial representation, musical thinking, the use of the body to solve problems or to make things, an understanding of other individuals and an understanding of ourselves. Where individuals differ is in the strength of these intelligences – the so-called profile of intelligences – and in the ways in which such intelligences are invoked and combined to carry out different tasks, solve diverse problems and progress in various domains . . . these differences challenge an educational system that assumes that everyone can learn the same materials in the same way . . . Indeed, as currently constituted, our educational system is heavily biased toward linguistic modes of instruction and assessment and, to a somewhat lesser degree, toward logical–quantitative modes as well.

Howard Gardner's conclusion from this line of analysis coincides with that drawn from the analysis in Chapter 3 of pupil attitudes to school. 'One consequence of the current system', he argues, 'is that many people unjustifiably deemed successes, as well as many needless casualties, emerge from contemporary educational systems.'

This aspect of Gardner's work is often interpreted in a very shallow way. People assume that his argument would support the view that 'It's OK if Brian isn't very clever at sums because he gets on well with people,' or, in Gardner terms, 'What he lacks in intelligence two he recovers through intelligence six.' This kind of interpretation, prevalent among many educators who come across Gardner for the first time, is dangerously patronising to Brian and an insult to Gardner. The point, surely, is to think about each individual's profile of intelligences and to encourage the development of a profile which is rounded and will enable them to play a full part in a democratic society.

Even more importantly, Gardner's point relates to how things are taught: what the jargon calls pedagogy. Gardner goes on to argue:

While educators have always noted differences among learners, they have always been strongly inclined to believe that all students learn in similar ways. This assumption works out well . . . for those whose background and learning styles happen to be compatible with the teaching styles of their teachers, and for those who can learn in the way in which materials have traditionally been taught (say, from lecturing or from textbooks). But there are also casualties: students who are motivated to learn but whose own learning styles or profiles of intelligence are not in tune with prevailing instructional practices.

So the profile of intelligences is a starting point for changing the approaches to teaching and learning. Gardner goes on: 'Schools can exert efforts to match teaching and learning styles . . . [they] can deliberately collect and make available resources – human and technological – that fit comfortably with the disparate learning styles and cultural back-grounds that exist in any student body.' He suggests that, for any given aspect of the curriculum worth teaching, there are at least five different ways to approach it and that they 'map onto the multiple intelligences'.

'We might think of the topic,' he proposes, 'as a room with at least five doors . . . students vary as to which entry point is most appropriate for them . . . Awareness of these entry points can help the teacher intro-duce new materials in ways in which they can easily be grasped by a range of students.' The five entry points he puts forward are: the narrational or story-telling approach (the one, by far, that I personally respond to best!); the logical–quantitative approach; the foundational or philosophical approach; the aesthetic approach; and the experiential approach.

A skilled teacher in this scheme of things is one who is able to open each of these five doors and knows which will be most appropriate for each of her or his students. One goal of policy would then be to ensure that each teacher had mastered the full repertoire necessary to open the room of learning, not just for an elite, but for everyone. In short, if we are to design a curriculum that can motivate and make possible success for all young people, it will need to recognise the full breadth of Gardner's seven intelligences and the importance of his five doors. This is the starting point for the proposals in the rest of this chapter.

The Basics of the Twenty-first Century

'Back to basics' disappeared from the front pages into the seedy bedrooms of a handful of careless and perhaps unfortunate Conservative MPs. As a political theme, it is unlikely to see the light of day ever again. However, before its shabby dissolution, it had a significant impact as a slogan – above all in education.

Paradoxically, by the time Dearing had arrived on the scene there was consensus about the importance of the basics. The only disagreement was about whether we should go back or forward to them. The teacher unions urged Dearing to commit himself to 'the basics of the twenty-first century'. This meant those elements of learning which are essential to learning everything else: such as reading, writing, numeracy and com-petence in information technology. Dearing agreed and so did everyone except a handful of right-wingers who wished that the second half of the twentieth century had never happened.

There were debates about some details of the curriculum in the basics. In mathematics, for example, the issue was whether to merge the idea of 'using and applying mathematics' into the rest of the subject or leave it as a free-standing element. In terms of classroom reality this is little more than a technicality. In English the chief debate was about standard English and how it should be defined. Away from the frontlines of this conflict, here, too, it is hard to see what all the sound and fury are about. Everyone agrees that every child needs, in addition to whatever dialect they speak every day, access to what used to be called BBC English. Without it so many things in life – job interviews for example – become extremely difficult. The same is true of grammar and spelling. The idea that these should not be considered important is absurd: knowledge of the structure of something as important as the national language is crucial. It is also an important element of learning a foreign language. It should not be beyond the wit of man or woman to put these things into suitable words for a statutory order (the delegated legislation that lays down the school curriculum). In any case, the day-to-day experience of the classroom will be influenced much more by the extent to which teachers are committed to the general principle I have described than by the words of the legal text.

There is little controversy about information technology. Here the issue is whether teachers have the knowledge and skills to integrate information technology into the teaching of every subject and whether government is prepared to invest in them.

In the year 2000 there may need to be a greater clarity in describing the curriculum in the basics associated with the use of national model schemes of work: the British tradition of expecting every teacher to invent her own wheel may be fading and not before time. These are relatively minor modifications of the Dearing curriculum however.

Another Language

Living in a country whose first language has become the universal language is both a blessing and a curse. It is a blessing because 60 per cent of the world's radio broadcasts are in English, 70 per cent of the world's mail is addressed in English, 85 per cent of all international telephone conversations are in English and 80 per cent of the data in the world's computers is in English. People to whom it is the mother tongue therefore have an immense advantage.

It is a curse because it encourages a lack of motivation to understand other languages and because it means that this country's national language, far from being treasured, is taken for granted. There is no sense in this country of the need to nurture the national language in the way that the Icelandic, the Russian or the French languages are collectively nurtured. This contributes to the ambivalence about English culture examined in the next section of this chapter.

If English is becoming the universal language of the global market place, then the argument that the British economy depends on the compulsory learning of another language in school is weak. However, the case remains strong for other reasons. For a start, the learning of a second language undoubtedly teaches one a great deal about one's own language. I remember a conversation between an Englishman and his German friend in Friedrich Wilhelmstrasse in Berlin that went like this:

English person: 'In England we call Friedrich Wilhelm, Frederick William.'

German person: 'That's absurd.'

English person: 'What do you call Henry VIII?'

German person: 'Heinrich der Achte.'

More than this, learning another language is essential in developing an understanding of the importance of languages in the creation and development of culture. Finally, learning another language contributes to learning about the structure of language in general.

All of these are important considerations regardless of the commercial arguments, and seem to me to establish the learning of a foreign language as a basic of the twenty-first century. It is not clear that the present post-Dearing arrangements are right in this particular respect. Under them, a language is compulsory for all young people from eleven to sixteen. This has two flaws. Firstly, if the resources, especially teachers, were in place, it would be better to make the learning of a second language compulsory from seven to fourteen, not eleven to sixteen. This would enable us to take advantage of the facility for language learning children have before they enter their teens. Secondly, if the case for a second language is the one made here, it is hard to justify it being compulsory for those who, as a result of family background or experience, already speak a language other than English, though of course they should be entitled to learn a third or fourth language if they choose to.

Cultural Inheritance

If agreement about the basic skills – the tools of further learning – is likely, agreement about what aspects of this country's culture should be passed on, and how, is much less likely.

One aspect of the process–product debate was that the advocates of process were not interested in transmitting the culture from one generation to the next through the curriculum since they did not see knowledge as all that important. Among the advocates of process were many who went beyond this position. They were fiercely opposed to transmission of the culture because they rejected it. They believed that it was either a capitalist culture, an imperialist culture, a patriarchal culture or a Eurocentric culture, or that it was all four. Far from transmitting it, therefore, the task of schools – these people would argue – was to critique (to use their favoured term) the culture, to reject it and perhaps ultimately to overthrow it. Under this kind of attack from the left it was inevitable that the transmission of culture would be defended by the far right. The problem for the rest of us was that these defenders sometimes gave the transmission of culture a bad name because they defended it on the grounds that imperialism, patriarchy and so on were of intrinsic merit. As a result, the fundamental point about whether or not young people had an entitlement to the culture of the country in which they had been brought up – warts and all – was missed.

The idea of the transmission of culture is, however, eminently defensible on a number of grounds. One is the argument put by the brilliant conservative academic, Allan Bloom. His book *The Closing of the American Mind* (Penguin, 1987) is perhaps the most important contribution to the debate about the purposes of education in the last decade. His book is long and philosophical. It is also a *cri de coeur* against the prevailing youth culture. Young people, he argues, are drowning in a sea of cultural mediocrity and moral relativism. The students he sees in the universities where he works, students he assumes are among the brightest Americans of their generation, are, in his view, no longer able to discriminate what is good from what is bad, what is true from what is untrue and what is beautiful from what is trash.

He blames this state of affairs to some extent on the university authorities which yielded to the passing and shallow demands of students in the late 1960s instead of standing up for the philosophical tradition of the west, which universities were created to maintain and extend. What is more, he argues, democracy, certainly in its late-twentieth-century guise, has a tendency towards relativism. After all, its crucial characteristic is that the majority decides. This is, however, no way to approach absolutes such as truth. The market economy has a comparable flaw. The role of the university in a democracy, he concludes, is to maintain and extend that philosophic tradition which began with Socrates and Plato and entered two centuries of crisis with the Enlightenment. Students need to be inducted into this tradition and to understand the masters before presuming to pass academic judgement themselves.

One does not have to follow Allan Bloom all the way to his corner of despairing elitism to recognise the critical importance of his line of argument for the education system. Surely, he seems to say, as inheritors of a remarkable and precious tradition of thought, we have an obligation to pass it on (perhaps refined a little) to the generations yet to come. If we do not, how can we expect every individual from his or her own experience to develop an ability to think through the central puzzles of humanity to a level which has taken all mankind 2,000 years? The idea is absurd. Not passing on the tradition, therefore, implies raising a generation less able to distinguish goodness, truth and beauty than its predecessors.

Cultural transmission's other supporters are much more down to earth metaphorically and closer to home literally. The Welsh and the Scots have never been in any doubt that it is part of the task of schools to transmit elements of their culture to the next generation. The French share this certainty. Doubts about transmitting the national culture appear to be a peculiarly English phenomenon.

I was struck by this when, as the then Education Officer, I was responsible for preparing the NUT's response to the original National Curriculum history proposals. There were two sets of proposals: one for England, the other for Wales. The NUT, therefore, had a working party in each country. Whereas the NUT members in Wales urged the inclusion of all the defining moments in Welsh history, the English working party questioned the government's suggestion that the history curriculum should emphasise national history, and urged a much greater emphasis on an international perspective.

The contradiction runs not only through the NUT, but through British society as a whole. English culture lacks any clarity: the English are confused and sometimes apologetic about their heritage. Like all national histories, that of the English is a mixture of glory and brutality, success and failure, triumph and disaster, war and peace, oppression and liberation. It runs all the way from Bobby Charlton and Ian Botham to Graham Taylor and Ted Dexter. And, like any other national history, it is not one but many. The history of the English landed aristocracy is different from that of its working class. Even from a distance any given individual wants to take sides according to preference. ('Which side were you on at Naseby?' Cromwell once shouted to a crowd. 'And which were you on at Burford?' came the reply.) National histories are like that: messy and controversial. That is no reason to run away from them nor to apologise for them. They need to be debated and understood. It seems to me, therefore, that some central elements of British culture, including English culture, ought to be a significant part of the curriculum entitlement of young people in the year 2000.

It may be argued that this is narrow and nationalistic since Britain has not only become multi-racial and multi-cultural, but also part of Europe. Any transmission of British culture must reflect these momentous developments along with others. The mistake, however, is to assume that because, for example, some young people in British schools have parents or grandparents from the Indian sub-continent, British culture is not relevant to them. Of course, if they are in good schools they will learn to recognise and have pride in both mother tongue and fatherland, but they need also to understand the society of which they are a part and in which, in all probability, they will live their adult lives. Without that understanding, any disadvantage they suffer from racism, which is still endemic in British society, will simply be reinforced.

The Ability to Reason

In 1858, with the impending crisis that would sweep the United States into civil war only two years away, Abraham Lincoln and Stephen Douglas contested one of the two Illinois seats in the United States Senate. Lincoln was anti-slavery: at least he opposed the extension of slavery into any new states that might be established west of the Mississippi and in particular in Kansas and Nebraska, which were the focus of attention that year. Douglas was no friend of slavery. Brought up in Vermont, he had never owned slaves. However, he believed strongly that it was for each individual state to determine its own attitude to slavery, rather than a matter for the Federal government in Washington. (Perhaps John Major should look up Stephen Douglas' arguments as he seeks to defend the British opt-out from the European Union's social chapter, but let that pass.)

Both were well-known figures in Illinois, though Douglas had the more substantial political career behind him. Perhaps this is why Lincoln was more enthusiastic about the *Chicago Tribune*'s suggestion that there should be a series of debates between the two in each of the main towns in the state. Douglas, reluctantly at first, agreed to participate, and the two camps met to establish the ground rules for the debates and to arrange the schedule. Robert Johannsen, who later edited the texts of the seven debates (*The Lincoln Douglas Debates of 1858*, OUP, 1965), describes the atmosphere in which they took place:

> Thousands of people gathered to hear the two leaders in the heat, dust, humidity and rain showers of late Summer and early Fall. The campaign was not without its pageantry. Parades and rallies complete

with brass bands and glee clubs greeted candidates as they moved from one town to another. Douglas travelled in style, riding in a special train . . . his vivacious young wife accompanied him and did much for his campaign by charming his constituents. Lincoln's mode of transport was much more modest . . .

Electioneering, it seems, changes little: the debate, the parades and, if possible, the vivacious young wife are, of course, still ingredients today, whether we like it or not. But in one way it has changed dramatically. In his speech at Freeport, Illinois, Lincoln explained what the thousands who had turned out would hear by way of entertainment: 'I am to speak for an hour, he [Douglas] for an hour and a half and then I am to reply for half an hour.' The massive audience was going to listen for *three hours*. This is a flavour of what they heard. First, Stephen Douglas in Ottawa, Illinois:

> Now you see that upon these very points I am as far bringing Mr Lincoln up to the line as I ever was before. He does not want to avow his principles. I do want to avow mine, as clear as sunlight in mid-day. Democracy is founded upon the eternal principle of right. The plainer these principles are avowed before the people, the stronger will be the support which they will receive. I only wish I had the power to make them so clear that they would shine in the heavens for every man, woman, and child to read. The first of those principles that I would proclaim would be in opposition to Mr Lincoln's doctrine of uniformity between the different States, and I would declare instead the sovereign right of each State to decide the slavery question as well as all other domestic questions for themselves, without interference from any other State or power whatsoever.

And now from Abraham Lincoln at Jonesboro:

> While I am upon this subject, I will make some answers briefly to certain propositions that Judge Douglas has put. He says, 'Why can't this Union endure permanently, half slave and half free?' I have said that I supposed it could not, and I will try, before this new audience, to give briefly some of the reasons for entertaining that opinion. Another form of his question is, 'Why can't we let it stand as our fathers placed it?' That is the exact difficulty between us. I say, that Judge Douglas and his friends have changed them from the position in which our fathers originally placed it. I say, in the way our fathers originally left the slavery question, the institution was in the course of ultimate extinction, and the public mind rested in the belief that it *was* in the course of ultimate extinction. I say when this Government was first established, it was the policy of its founders to prohibit the spread of slavery into the new Territories of the United States, where

it had not existed. But Judge Douglas and his friends have broken up that policy, and placed it upon a new basis by which it is to become national and perpetual. All I have asked or desired anywhere is that it should be placed back again upon the basis that the fathers of our Government originally placed it upon. I have no doubt that it *would* become extinct, for all time to come, if we but readopted the policy of the fathers by restricting it to the limits it has already covered – restricting it from the new Territories.

Following Lincoln in the Freeport debate Douglas began by congratulating the audience:

The silence with which you have listened to Mr Lincoln during this hour is creditable to this vast audience . . . Nothing is more honorable to any large mass of people assembled for the purpose of a fair discussion, than that kind and respectful attention that is yielded not only to your political friends, but to those who are opposed to you.

They certainly deserve congratulations for that and, with hindsight, for something else too. They followed three hours of closely argued debate which involved a wide range of references to American history and to the principles of political theory. When I read the Lincoln–Douglas debates as a student and, as I read them again to prepare this book, I was astonished that argument of that quality and intricacy was presumably followed and understood by a mass audience.

A lengthy excursion into American history may have its fascination, but it is not what this book is about. I simply want to make one observation: the standard of public argument about the great issues of the day has fallen catastrophically. This is the era in which political debate is conducted through the soundbite and the tabloid. The quote detached from its context has become the chief weapon of political argument. Perhaps this is unavoidable, but our education system does not need to pander to it. It ought surely to be a central purpose of schools that young people learn the ability to reason. They should be able to spot a *non-sequitur*, identify the moments when facts and opinion are elided and treat with caution the weighty conclusion based on flimsy evidence. We cannot guarantee that they will learn these skills from television, popular music, the tabloid press or the now ubiquitous computer games. Since they are a critical element of humanity and a central factor in all learning at the highest levels it would be fatal to neglect them or leave them to chance.

Reasoning is perhaps the pure core of thinking. Thinking, too, is grossly underestimated in school learning. Once, after I had raised this issue in a brief piece in *Education* magazine, I received a letter from a former colleague whom I know to have been a brilliant teacher. She said she remembered a conversation in one of her lessons that went like this.

Teacher to pupil: 'What are you doing?'

Pupil to teacher: 'I'm thinking.'

Teacher to pupil: 'Well, stop it and get on with your work.'

Whenever I tell this story to groups of teachers it never fails to raise a smile. That is because all of us who are or have been teachers recognise that we, too, have been that absurd.

The tendency in schools is to teach whatever has to be taught and to assume that pupils will learn to think as a matter of course. Yet thinking, like other processes, is something we can learn to do and get better at. This is one of the few things that has been proved conclusively by education research. Researchers at King's College, London, conducted a controlled experiment in which two similar groups of young people were taught science between the ages of eleven and fourteen. One group was taught conventionally, the other was taught to think and to reflect on their thinking as well as their science. It is important to note that they were not taught 'thinking' as a separate 'process' activity, but through learning science. The 'thinking' group did dramatically better in GCSE science. Not only that, they did dramatically better in English and mathematics too. The results are shown in Table 5. (It is taken from the report of the National Commission on Education (1993) and is based on the work of Philip Adey and Michael Shayer.)

Table 5: Percentage of pupils obtaining GCSE grade C or above, comparing a special teaching approach (CASE) with a control group

	Boys 1989		Girls 1990	
Subject	*CASE pupils*	*Control group*	*CASE pupils*	*Control group*
Science	41.7	12.8	50.0	33.3
Mathematics	49.1	16.4	55.2	42.4
English	44.6	16.1	85.2	58.1

Yet, in spite of this dramatic result, which is reinforced by evidence from across the globe, there has been no national initiative to follow it up. Handfuls of schools, to their credit, have tried to make use of it of their own accord, but learning to think has not featured at all in the National Curriculum debate. Like reasoning, this should not be left to chance. It, too, can be put right in the year 2000.

This is not a minor issue. We are told repeatedly that we live in an information society. This is true. There has never been a society which generated so much information. The moment Michael Atherton scores a run, the screen can reveal what his test batting average is and how he is placed in the world rankings. The *Sunday Times* is enormous, even allowing for advertisements, and that is only Sunday. Soon, through the merging of television, telephone and computer technology, we will have a stunning array of means to access information. Everyone, in every home, will be able to look things up, not just in the homes that have hundreds of books on the shelves. At Keele University, as recently as 1994, I was introduced to the 'gopher'. This is a neat little computer device which you can instruct to search the world's databases for anything you choose to mention, and will come back and tell you what is available. Type in 'earthquake', and in seconds it tells you that the UN in New York has a database on this topic and it asks you if you would like to see it. If you indicate 'yes', the UN database appears on your screen in the Potteries. When I first saw this, I thought it was a miracle, but actually it is commonplace. The information society has indeed arrived – even in Stoke-on-Trent. Access to the Internet is becoming ubiquitous, and Tony Blair has promised that, in partnership with BT, Labour, if elected, will network every school and hospital in the country.

Mention this theme in polite society and, sure enough, someone soon says 'information is power'. Does it therefore follow that the democratisation of information achieves what idealist dreamers have sought for centuries: the ultimate democratisation of power? It might follow, if the premise was true, but the premise is not true. Information on its own is nothing. Information only provides access to power when it is linked to reason and thought. For information to be useful, people must be able to make selections from it, to connect diverse strands of it together, to ask intelligent questions of it and to reject parts of it which, though they are there on the screen, in the book or on the paper, appear to be inaccurate. Even then, thought and information need to be linked in a chain of reasoned argument. It would be an irony if, at the very moment in history when information has become universally accessible, we lost the capacity to think about it intelligently.

Self-Esteem and Expectations

If all young people learnt how to reason and how to think, it would be a tremendous step forward, but it would not be enough. As the pace of social, technological and economic change has increased, so too has the pace of decision-making. The rapid decision-making required in many workplaces, or in national or local political debate, demands, in addition to the ability to construct an argument, the self-confidence to put it when it matters. All of us know the feeling of having left a conversation or a meeting with the most brilliant argument constructed in our heads, but with the frustration of knowing that the courage to put it failed us. Then, in the car park or the coffee bar afterwards, we tell our close friends what we would have said, but by then it is too late. Information is not power. Even information with thought is not power. Information with thought and self-confidence is irresistible. Conversely, a lack of self-confidence is often at the core of the sense of powerlessness that so many people feel when they ponder how they might change their circumstances.

For these reasons, schools ought consciously to promote young people's self-confidence and self-esteem. This can be done, of course, through praise and encouragement. Here, the danger is that, particularly for the young person who is having difficulty learning, the teacher is so keen to praise and encourage that he or she rewards what is shoddy work. Here we enter the complex relationship between pupil self-esteem and teacher expectations. This is the realm at the heart of teacher professionalism. The central challenge is how to raise pupils' self-esteem while simultaneously maintaining, or even raising, expectations. The issue can perhaps be best explained in a diagram (see Figure 5).

The pupil who expects little of her or himself and of whom little is expected is, very likely, headed for failure. The government has, over recent years, rightly identified high expectations as a critical aspect of educational achievement. Hence its repeated accusations that too many teachers have expectations which are too low. The evidence from inside failing schools bears out the destructive impact that low expectations can have. The problem, which teachers often sense rather than articulate, is that if expectations are raised without improving pupil self-esteem, then the outcome can be that pupils who already felt incapable are now having even more demanded of them. The result? Demoralisation.

Similarly, there is little point in promoting self-esteem by lowering expectations. I remember a conversation with one of my daughters in her early teens. Imagine a scene, perhaps replicated in countless living rooms across the country. *Neighbours* is on, well into its second half. My

Figure 5

SELF-ESTEEM

		Low	High
EXPECTATIONS	Low	Failure	Complacency
	High	Demoralisation	Success

daughter has been sitting in front of it with a school exercise book in her lap. From time to time she has written in it. Now she casts it aside and fixes her eyes all the more firmly on the screen. She gives 100 per cent of her attention to the soap, even though the 40 per cent she had given it up to that point had been perfectly adequate to follow the plot. 'Shouldn't you get your homework done?' I ask tentatively. 'I've finished it,' comes the reply. 'How do you know?' 'The teacher said to do a side and a half and I've done a side and a half.'

The debate is over barely before it has begun. Take a similar conversation in another living room at a different end of the country:

'Why did you stop there?' asks a parent of a twelve-year-old boy.

'Because I'll get 10 out of 10. If I stopped sooner, I wouldn't.'

'But you've hardly spent any time on it. Why don't you go on?'

'Mum,' eyes raised fleetingly to heaven in irritation with this persistent adult. 'In our school it's very hard to get more than 10 out of 10.'

Another conversation ends abruptly. Another example of high self-esteem and low teacher expectation breeding complacency.

The goal should be to promote self-esteem and high expectations simultaneously. It is easy to write this, but achieving it is a remarkably demanding professional task. It requires teachers who have an extraordinary combination of personal qualities and professional skills. In our 1992 publication for the IPPR, Tim Brighouse and I tried to summarise these in a list:

GOOD TEACHERS
Qualities and characteristics
- Good understanding of self and of interpersonal relationships
- Generosity of spirit
- Sense of humour
- Sharp observational powers
- Interest in and concern for others

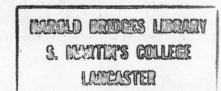

- Infectious enthusiasm for what is taught
- Imagination
- Energy
- Intellectual curiosity
- Professional training and understanding of how children learn
- Ability to plan programmes of learning appropriate to the particular groups of children and/or individual pupils
- Understanding of their curriculum in the context of the school as a whole

Meeting this specification is, by any standards, demanding. It might be observed in passing that, if this is what we as a society want from teachers, we are not asking for the teaching profession to be a cross-section of society: we are asking for them to represent all that is best within it. Chapter 8 concentrates on the reforms that would be necessary to ensure that we have that kind of teaching profession in the twenty-first century.

In the context of this chapter, three points need to be made. Firstly, only if we offer a range of opportunities to succeed, spanning all seven of Howard Gardner's intelligences, can we guarantee to offer every young person the chance to shine, which is so important to everyone's self-esteem. And teachers need the skills to open all five of Gardner's doors to learning.

Secondly, there are teaching and learning strategies which can enable high expectations and high self-esteem to be pursued simultaneously. These involve, for example, being clear when it is improvement rather than an absolute standard which is being rewarded. They involve actively seeking opportunities to give young people opportunities to succeed. For example, at a school I visited in San Diego, it was a requirement that every pupil in the school should show at least two visitors round it every year. Visitors reported on the performance of the pupil in showing them round. Here the school was assessing Gardner's sixth and seventh intelligences as well as encouraging pupils to take pride in their school.

Achieving this task also involves ensuring that no pupil feels anonymous, for there is nothing more crushing to self-esteem than anonymity. Yet we all know – and most teachers will admit – that, especially in large schools, many pupils drift through without anyone ever really getting to know them. This poem (by the American Michael Buscemi and quoted at the 1979 American National Parent-Teacher Association Convention) has become one of the hallmarks of Tim Brighouse's brilliant lectures. It captures what being one of the invisible children feels like:

The Average Child

I don't cause teachers trouble
My grades have been OK
I listen to my classes
And I'm in school every day
My parents think I'm average
My teachers think so too
I wish I didn't know that
Cause there's lots I'd like to do
I'd like to build a rocket
I've a book that shows you how
Or start a stamp collection
Well no use starting now
Cause since I've found I'm average
I'm just smart enough you see
To know there's nothing special
That I should expect of me
I'm part of that majority
That hump part of the bell
Who spends his life unnoticed
In an average kind of hell

Schools have developed strategies designed to avoid this pitfall too. A secondary school in Sheffield, for example, has a different 'Child of the Week' every week in each of its first two years. The Child of the Week has a report card each day on which every teacher must make a positive comment and each evening the parents must read and sign it and comment if they want. Parents and pupils love the week they are special, but most important is the constant hammering home to the teachers that no one should be left to feel anonymous. Part of the justification for the proposals in the final chapter is that they would make the average child a thing of the past. Even car manufacturers appear to have realised this: there is, as they say in the advertisement for a Peugeot, no such thing as an average person. These are brief examples of the strategies schools can and do use to promote self-esteem, but they raise one further issue.

If we want teachers capable of promoting high expectations and high self-esteem throughout their careers, then they must be seen not only as servants of the system, but also as beneficiaries. They must become learners too: learning because in a changing world teachers always have learning needs; and learning because they must set an example to young people.

A Moral Community

Secondary school pupils have a talent similar to that of the great cartoonists. In producing nicknames for teachers, they have an unerring eye for some inner truth. Like cartoonists, their sharpness in this respect depends on careful, and possibly instinctive, observation and close textual analysis of the spoken word. When I was a pupil at a Quaker secondary school in the late 1960s, the word we picked out when we acted out our impressions of our headteacher was 'community'. The fact that we were all members of a community, as well as individuals, was his constant theme, and we mocked him for it. He was a good and humane man and, I am sure, looking back, probably thought that to be mocked for the use of the word 'community' meant he was succeeding. It is also evident, looking back, that he was successful in establishing a sense of community, underpinned by the school's non-violent, open-minded Quaker philosophy.

Perhaps, too, he was ahead of his time. In the twenty-five years since then, there has been increasing concern at the collapse of notions of community. As Richard Hoggart observed in a lecture at the Royal Society of Arts in March 1994, there has been:

> [a] loss of any sustaining sense of community. This is an irony. On the BBC, and everywhere in broadcasting, if anything happens in any town, they begin by saying: 'This small, well-knit community'. It is the cliché of the age. They should stop saying that and simply say 'This place' . . . The sense of community has gone in many working-class districts, partly because the terraced houses have been cleared away (as they should have been) and partly because of the period when tower blocks were substituted . . . The big works have now gone in favour of labour intensive works on the outskirts of towns and cities . . . What tends to happen is that the people who are still there are those who cannot get out.

The loss of community in this sense has been paralleled by a loss of faith in the family and the decline of the Church as stable organisations to which the mass of people necessarily belong. Hoggart again:

> the biggest agent of change in societies such as ours proved to be that we have lost the external authorities. They no longer exist or are merely shadows. Whether it was the church or chapel there was always a group which we thought of in Hunslet as 'Them' – Us and Them. The sense that there are powers that be outside has gone and with it, as part of it, has gone the sense of religion.

Educators have a tendency to discuss the community in which a school is situated as if it were an ideal of the motherhood and apple-pie variety. Hearing them talk sometimes conjures up those images of old ladies on bicycles, and cricket on village greens of which John Major is so fond. The reality is different. Villages are increasingly populated by commuters who rarely speak to each other, while city communities include such features as people lying dead in their flats for three years without being found, youths beating to death a man who had gently reprimanded them for vandalising a bollard, and the robbing and fatal mugging of a man who stopped to ask the way.

The truth is that the communities of inner cities are extraordinarily diverse, in terms not only of race and class, but also of aspiration. Indeed, the inner city is better perceived as several communities inhabiting the same space but rarely, if ever, relating to one another. In a small park I know well in Hackney, the benches are inhabited in the daylight by elderly people walking their dogs. At night they are inhabited by the youth, often smoking dope. The only thing they have in common is a lack of respect for the law, since dogs are not allowed there any more than drugs are. Otherwise, it is reminiscent of those schools in the bush during Zimbabwe's liberation struggle: one army controlled them during daylight, another in the hours of darkness.

Amitai Etzioni, the leader of the American Communitarian movement, much favoured by politicians of the right and left, and certainly a major influence on new Labour in this country, describes a state of affairs in the United States several degrees worse than here (*The Spirit of Community*, Fontana, 1995):

> Youngsters are enrolled in many public schools – and quite a few private ones – with their characters under-developed and without a firm commitment to values. The basic reason is that their families have been dismembered or the parents are overworked or consumed by other concerns and ambitions. As a result, the children tend to be poor students. Moreover, if their lack of character and moral values are not attended to while at school, they will graduate to become deficient workers, citizens and fellow community members . . . Nationwide one out of 20 pupils carries a gun . . . the number of young Americans killed by firearms was more than twice as high in 1990 as it was in 1970 . . .

The only moral community to which all young people are entitled – indeed compelled – to belong to is the school. This is the late-twentieth-century reality. If we want young people to learn the rules of living and working in communities – how to solve differences of opinion, how to respect a variety of beliefs, how to make collective decisions in a democratic society, and so on – then these must feature in the curriculum of schools. It is fortunate that many schools already make a magnificent contribution in this respect. Many schools are well-ordered places in which young people treat each other and their teachers with respect. Sometimes they seem like islands of civilisation trapped behind barbarian lines.

Indeed, for some young people, schools are the only places where they see the more noble aspirations of humanity – truth, justice, beauty, fairness – being consistently demanded and displayed. As Etzioni puts it: 'To the extent that the family no longer provides these values, the community turns to schools to teach the young to tell right from wrong.' Many achieve this in spite of the fact that they are sited in areas which have been devastated by poverty and unemployment. In its sobering report on urban education in 1993, the government inspection agency, OFSTED, commented that 'schools varied in their degree of success in establishing an ethos which embraced explicitly moral values. Relations among pupils, including those of different ethnic heritage, and between pupils and teachers were generally characterised by mutual respect.' Thus, even in schools which OFSTED severely criticised from the academic angle, there was evidence of success in generating a sense of community. In some areas this is no small achievement.

Part of Tony Blair's appeal has been his assertion that the community is important, not instead of, but as well as, the individual. In his campaign to become Labour leader, he defined the party's essential purpose as 'using the power of society to advance the individual, based on a belief that it is within a strong and active society that an individual can flourish'.

To restore society and local communities sufficiently to play this part of advancing, rather than restraining (or even terrifying), the individual requires a coherent set of social policies dealing with employment, the family, crime and education. At present, the only area in which there is evidence of success in this direction is education. Whether Tony Blair leads the Labour Party to victory or not, the next government will need to build on the contribution of education to enhance the sense among young people of what it is to belong to a moral community. The curriculum of the twenty-first century must take this into account. My former headteacher, it turns out, was absolutely right. I hope we did not give him too hard a time.

The Hour Is Getting Late

There remains only one further purpose of education to mention. By comparison, all the rest of this chapter fades into insignificance. Education must have a role in ensuring the continued existence of human life on this planet.

The generation which currently has its hands on the levers of power is the first generation to have grown up knowing that it could destroy life on the planet. From 6 August 1945 – the date of the Hiroshima bomb – this potential has been evident. Since the Cuban Missile Crisis in 1962, people have been conscious that a false move or two in the diplomatic game could have catastrophic consequences. Throughout the latter decade of the Cold War, there were all too many moments when diplomacy appeared to be lurching towards the brink. Then, when the Cold War ended in the late 1980s, after an initial euphoria, we discovered that the world had become more dangerous, not less. The two armed camps had, after all, established lines of communication and ways of working which minimised the risks. This, I suppose, is what Elliott Richardson, the then US Ambassador to London, meant when he entitled an extremely dull lecture to Oxford students in 1975, 'The Dynamics of Stability'. (I remember only the title and the dullness because I fell asleep, along with three other people in the back row.) Since the Cold War ended, by contrast, we have faced plain old instability. The nuclear danger from North Korea or Pakistan is no less threatening and a great deal harder to predict. You can almost hear the diplomats thinking that, in the language of *Coronation Street*, at least you knew where you were with Brezhnev.

Nuclear weapons, however, are only a fraction of the problem. Humanity's insistent urge to dominate nature, which for the last 200 years has been all-conquering, no longer appears to be such a wise project after all. In Werner Herzog's brilliant film, *Aguirre, the Wrath of God*, the hero sets out to conquer the New World and ends up floating helplessly down the Amazon accompanied only by a tribe of monkeys. The madness of his search for power still leaves him imagining that he rules all he surveys. 'I am Aguirre, the Wrath of God,' he cries, ignorant of his utter powerlessness. It is a metaphor for all tyrants, and for humanity as a whole unless we can replace the drive for mastery with a recognition of interdependence.

In a memorable lecture delivered to commemorate the fiftieth anniversary of the United Nations, Sir Shridath Ramphal recollected Clement Attlee's words at the opening assembly of the UN at Westminster Central

Hall in January 1946: 'we have to bring to the task of creating permanent conditions of peace, the same sense of urgency, the same self-sacrifice and the same willingness to subordinate sectional interest to the common good as brought us through the crisis of war'. Ramphal advances, surely rightly, the case that what was important then has become essential now:

> As we have seen, both the vision and the values were there briefly in 1945. We have to return to values, we have to develop a vision of and values for the world of our inseparable humanity. We cannot face the 21st century inured in those values of the 20th century that failed to serve us well as a global neighbourhood; the values or lack of them that will yet make this century remembered as both the best of times and the worst of times – and all too distressingly the best of times for a few, the worst of times for many.

Perhaps there is already a growing recognition that a radical change of direction is necessary. The growth of consumerism – with companies vying to demonstrate their eco-awareness – is a sign that we are all environmentalists now. There have been major shifts in the attitudes of governments and populations across the globe, but the old juggernaut, though its speed may have been marginally reduced, still thunders on. If identifying the need for a new agenda is this generation's achievement, then bringing it about and solving the problems that currently surround us are tasks for the next.

As Professor David Orr argued in his prophetic Shumacher lecture in October 1992:

> there are . . . reasons to rethink education that have to do with issues of human survival, which will dominate the 21st century. The generation now being educated will have to do what we, the present generation, have been unable to do: stabilise a world population which is growing at a rate of a quarter of a million each day; stabilise and then reduce the emission of greenhouse gases, which threaten to change the climate – perhaps disastrously; protect biological diversity, now declining at an estimated rate of 100 to 200 species per day; reverse the destruction of rainforests (both tropical and temperate), now being lost at the rate of 116 square miles or more each day; and conserve soils, now being eroded at the rate of 65 million tons per day.
>
> The future generations must learn to use energy and materials with great efficiency. They must learn how to utilise solar energy in all its forms. They must rebuild the economy in order to eliminate waste and pollution. They must learn how to manage renewable resources for the long term . . . for the most part, however, we are still educating the young as if there were no planetary emergency.

It is difficult to disagree with Orr's relentless argument. It can be pointed out, however, that there are an increasing number of examples of schools advancing this agenda in spite of the mountain of government-regulated change inflicted upon them during the cultural revolution. Many schools are involved in recycling now (even if motivated partly by money), but some go further. For example, at an awards evening I attended recently in the urban Midlands, there was a gardening prize as well as the standard fare of academic and sporting awards. A primary school I know in Islington uses the nearby Regent's Canal as a resource to teach about erosion and ecology, rubbish and regeneration. The children, whose classroom windows look out over the water, are rewarded from time to time when a graceful heron fishes before their eyes.

These are the beginnings of a global consciousness which will, early in the next century, need to pervade the curriculum. Orr makes an impassioned plea for precisely this:

> We need a new ecological imagination with which we can envision restored landscapes, renewed ecosystems and whole people living in a whole biosphere. Yet in a technological age it should come as no surprise that our imagination is increasingly confined to technological possibilities: faster and more powerful computers, televisions, virtual reality generators and genetic engineering. George Orwell once warned that the 'logical end' of technological progress 'is to reduce the human being to something resembling a brain in a bottle'. Orwell's dream is coming true . . . we need decent communities, good work to do, loving relationships, stable families and a way to transcend our inherent self-centredness . . . yet our imagination and creativity are overwhelmingly aimed at things.

It is interesting that Orr's ecological argument leads back to the notion of a moral community and Gardner's seven intelligences. He explains that 'the modern curriculum teaches a great deal about individualism and rights, but teaches little about citizenship and responsibility'. His words echo Etzioni's Communitarian agenda (and indeed the new Clause Four of the Labour Party). Some schools are already advancing down this path. In the year 2000, when we bring forward, after five years of vigorous debate, the new National Curriculum, it will have to build on the work of these pioneers since, as Bob Dylan put it, 'the hour is getting late'.

The curriculum I have attempted to describe is rich, varied and ambitious, and has immense motivational potential, drawing as it would on all of Howard Gardner's seven intelligences. I do not believe it is unrealistic. Already there are schools excelling in each of these areas, and some across many of them. To achieve it across the country – as an entitlement for the citizens of the twenty-first century – would require that education in general, and a revision of the National Curriculum in the year 2000 in particular, be given high priority. Its success would depend on a reconstruction of the teaching profession and a radical change in both the structure and culture of the education system. These are the subjects of the next two chapters. If we succeed, then, at the end of the century, we will be able to trade in our F-reg Ford Escort (which would be recycled) and drive away in a Rolls-Royce (which would run, of course, on a renewable source of energy).

A Stakeholder Curriculum

Deciding broad curriculum content involves, as we have seen, cutting through the thickets of cultural and historic controversy. There is much more to the creation of a National Curriculum, however, than deciding what it should include. It requires reaching conclusions, too, on how those decisions should be made. The chaos of the decision-making process which made the present National Curriculum has already been described.

Though a complicated machinery was established for making curriculum decisions under the 1988 legislation, the answer to the question 'Who decides?' was 'Ministers do.' Take this extract from Kenneth Baker's autobiography (Faber and Faber, 1993), for example: 'I also wanted to ensure that as regards history our children would leave school with real knowledge of what has happened in our country over the last thousand years.' Few would argue with the view Kenneth Baker had expressed, but his close personal interest in the detail of history, on his own admission, arose from the fact that 'History had been the subject of my degree, and I had produced an anthology of poetry which told the history of England from Boadicea to Elizabeth II . . .'

In the end, Baker moved on to another Cabinet post before the history curriculum was concluded and disagreed with what his successors eventually did. In an interview he gave the author in 1996, he suggested that ministerial decisions on these important questions actually had their origins in chance conversations. He described how: 'On the curriculum . . . [Margaret Thatcher] did have views, she certainly had views. She always had views, actually, which as far as I could see came from her hairdresser who lived in Lambeth and the hairdresser was very worried that her children . . . were going to be educated by a lot of Trots . . .' This is fascinating, but hardly comforting. Hairdressers from Lambeth surely have no more right to shape the curriculum than any other interest group, and perhaps a little less than some.

If we want a stable but flexible, accepted but forward-looking, National Curriculum in the next century, we shall have to do better than this. Even if we could guarantee a stream of able, honest and conscientious education ministers – which, if the last fifty years is anything to go by, we can't – leaving the shaping of the curriculum to the whim of individual ministers is clearly unacceptable in what ought to be a widening and deepening democracy. On the other hand, it is proper in a democracy for the elected government to establish the broad thrust of policy for the curriculum, as for other areas of policy. It is also true that one cause of the centrally directed approach to shaping the curriculum was that the education establishment seemed, from the ministers' point of view, to be intent on delay, postponement or even inactivity, while ministers rightly sensed an urgent need for change. The challenge is to combine that justifiable impatience for change with a serious consultative approach.

Sir Ron Dearing has many achievements to his name. The least remarked upon, but in the long run the most important, is that he has met this challenge. His simple, common-sense touch has resolved the paradox that almost destroyed the National Curriculum in the early 1990s. The approach he has developed is, of course, applicable across other areas of policy too. He begins, on the basis of the instructions given him by ministers, by seeking views on the theme from everyone who might have a view. He attends meetings at which he raises a few issues, asks a few sharp questions seeking information or clarification, but mostly he sits there in alert listening mode.

After a few months, he is in a position to publish a consultation document which clarifies the terms of the debate, sets out the areas of emerging consensus and asks questions about the areas of controversy. It is launched, with verve, to the press and media, and a more formal consultation phase ensues. Here the key has been consultation, not just with representatives of organisations, but also directly with real teachers, parents and governors. Simply making sure this happens gives everyone a better view of reality and reduces the room for 'bullshit' in the system. Behind the scenes, Dearing is trying out possible solutions with trusted colleagues, floating the possible solutions in meetings with ministers and officials and, at the same time, seeking new angles on tired debates. He knows that from polarised debate deep division or shabby compromise are the likely outcomes. Only by changing the context and by opening up the long term can creative solutions be found. Once he has done that, he begins to write. The drafting focuses his mind, but does not bring the consultation phase to an end. The draft is on the word processor and can be changed at any time. When I read the first Dearing report, I was sure I could pick out one or two sentences which had been changed right at the last minute, following discussion with union general secretaries.

Then the draft is shared with the other key players, especially ministers, altered again if necessary, and published. Unlike Sir Richard Scott, Sir Ron Dearing insists on a clear, concise, executive summary, and his staff have a flair for publicity. It all seems so simple and straightforward. It surely provides us with a model process through which we can achieve a millennium curriculum next time round. The simplicity, however, is deceptive. In fact, Dearing's achievement is astonishingly skilful.

In their great days in the late 1980s, Liverpool scored goals of breathtaking simplicity sometimes. I remember one vividly in the 5–0 defeat of Nottingham Forest in 1988. Beardsley picked up the ball deep in his own half, surged past one tackle, looked up and saw Aldridge starting a run. He struck a fifty- or sixty-yard pass which threaded its way through the Forest defenders and into the path of Aldridge. With one gentle nudge, the striker ensured that it rolled past the advancing goalkeeper and into the net. John Motson described the goal as one of 'stupendous simplicity'.

Dearing's achievement is of that character. As we begin to think about the preparation of the millennium curriculum, it is worth thinking about what lies behind the success of the Dearing process. First, there is diplomatic skill of the highest order: working out what the central issues are, what the principles behind them are, and what among the many things that pressure groups say are fundamental issues and what are froth. In addition, there is calculation about what is politically possible, and what, imaginatively, can be done to create room for manoeuvre. Second, and even more important, is the ability to generate trust. Dearing has done this consistently: his predecessors palpably did not. They did not even try. This is not just a question of Dearing's personal qualities, it is also that he has no axe to grind: as he puts it, referring to his former career in the Post Office, 'I'm just a simple postman.'

If the curriculum is to be refined and made fit for the twenty-first century, then appointments to the curriculum authority will have to be people of similar stature and integrity. If the authority is packed with political friends of the Minister, or filled with second-rate placemen or women, it will fail, with dire consequences for us all. In addition, we need education ministers who take their responsibilities seriously, as Gillian Shephard does, and Kenneth Clarke did not: and ministers of obvious competence as Gillian Shephard is, and John Patten was not. Labour shadows, in recent years, have generally been competent but short of vision or real stature. Only Neil Kinnock in the early 1980s, Jack Straw periodically in the late 1980s and David Blunkett in the mid-1990s have risen above the mediocrity. If Labour is elected, we must hope that Tony Blair will do what no other Labour leader has done, and appoint his Shadow Education Spokesperson as Secretary of State for Education.

The success of curriculum decision-making also depends, however, on the response of others to the official process. However effective Dearing's successors might be, if those who represent teachers or parents, employers or school governors, are obsessed with short-term considerations or their own petty, internecine strife, then we shall fail again. An effective government could, to use Fisher and Ury's evocative phrase, build these groups 'a golden bridge', but they cannot make them cross it.

The effectiveness of a curriculum depends ultimately on the extent of teacher commitment to it and its legitimacy and credibility among other education interest groups. To use the most fashionable phrase of 1996, everyone, including, as they get older, young people themselves, must have a stake in it.

Teachers' representatives, especially, must see the reopening of the curriculum debate as an opportunity not to pursue short-term goals, whether in relation to pay or conditions, but instead to build an effective working partnership with government and society in general. They must see it as an opportunity to extend ambition across society, to build commitment to learning, and to put behind them (and us) the narrow, self-defeating anti-educational culture which has characterised this country for most of the twentieth century. In doing so, they may see it as an act of idealism if they wish: ultimately, however, the status and pay of teachers depends on the importance that society places on their work. Thus, teacher unions could legitimately argue that the achievement of a genuinely ambitious curriculum would help them achieve their long-term goals for salaries and conditions too, whatever happened in the short-term. Representatives of other interested groups – universities and employers included – need to take a similarly strategic view. The next revision of the National Curriculum provides us all with a moment of truth.

Making It Happen

Suppose for a moment we were able to agree on how to decide about the future of the curriculum. Suppose too that we had, through that process, reached agreement on what its contents should be. We would still need to decide how to put it into effect.

The present National Curriculum is 'statutory' with a capital S. People outside of schools who examined it – if they were foolish enough to do so – would be shocked. The law lays down programmes of study (content), statements of attainment (outcomes) and assessment arrangements (tests). Many other countries have a national curriculum: some lay down one of these aspects, and a few two: no others define, statutorily, all three. Kenneth Baker and his successors did not adopt a belt-and-braces approach to the National Curriculum: they went to two belts and two pairs of braces. Of course, writing something into law does not make it happen, otherwise no one would drive at over 30 mph in built-up areas. Just as the traffic and parking regulations require an enforcement system of police and traffic wardens, so there need to be mechanisms in place to enforce the curriculum.

In this respect, too, ministers left – almost – nothing to chance. The law imposed a duty on school governors and headteachers to implement the National Curriculum, including its assessment arrangements. It also gave parents a right to complain if they believed their children were not receiving their entitlement. Then, externally designed tests – which tested the core of the National Curriculum – were put into place. The results of these were to be reported to parents and, in some cases, published. Finally, the government created an inspection system, the central plank of which was designed to find out how effectively the National Curriculum was being taught.

The only chink in this armoury of enforcement powers was that individual teachers had no duty to implement the National Curriculum, although of course they were – and are – contractually required to carry out reasonable instructions from the headteacher, who did – and does. It was this chink that made it possible for the unions to boycott the National Curriculum tests successfully in 1993. Without it, they could have been brought to book for advising their members to break the law.

The question for the future is whether curriculum enforcement needs to be quite so draconian. The present regime is hardly designed, after all, to build teachers' loyalty to the curriculum, still less to excite their enthusiasm. On the contrary, it is more likely to induce sullen acceptance. As Tacitus put it, in a different context, 'they made a wilderness and called it peace'.

Sir Ron himself realised this during his first dark months in office in 1993. That, no doubt, explains why, in the letter to the Secretary of State that accompanied his first report, he argued: '. . . I have been deeply impressed – at times moved – by the strong commitment of everyone concerned in education to serve our children well.' This was a new tone, symbolising a new era. Nevertheless, his consultations had impressed on him that there were 'some hard lessons' to learn. The hardest of all was how to achieve the balance between ensuring that the curriculum was implemented on the one hand, and the need to generate professional commitment on the other. Baker had argued: 'Vagueness and lack of detail will allow an inadequate or lazy teacher to skip the important parts.' When I interviewed him in 1996, he was unrepentant about this approach. Indeed, he asserted that his only serious mistake was not to legislate to lengthen the school day: then, he claimed, his prescriptive curriculum could have been fitted in, and its problems would have vanished.

Dearing rejected this line of argument, not only because it was even more draconian, but also because it misses the point. The problem with excessive prescription is that it destroys teachers' commitment and undermines their image of themselves. In any case, if there are lazy and inadequate teachers – and no doubt there are a few – the solution is surely not to set down in detail what they should teach lazily and inadequately, but to remove them from the profession altogether. It is no coincidence that the relaxation of the curriculum prescription that followed Dearing's report has been followed by a focus on the effectiveness or ineffectiveness of teachers. It was inevitable and right that it should be.

The problem is that, as yet, teachers have not begun sufficiently to reassert their professional judgement in the new context. The scars and bruises of the early 1990s have given way to the anxieties and tensions of the mid-1990s. Though Sir Ron and others in influential positions have urged teachers to use their discretion in implementing his revised curriculum, many are still too anxious to do so. Teachers still often ask when the curriculum agency or inspectors will clarify exactly what it is they want. Ultimately, teachers must answer these questions for themselves. It is what being professional demands. Teachers should not have the power to determine education policy: nor should they be slaves to it. Success depends on them making sense of it for themselves.

If that is the goal, how then should the curriculum be enforced? This issue, in my view, is in need of further debate, but tentatively I would argue as follows. There should be a clearly argued document of between ten and twenty pages, stating this society's curriculum aspirations. A first draft of this should be published for consultation two years in advance of the date for implementation of the revised curriculum. It should be consulted on widely, and then finalised.

This text – which should be entitled *The Millennium Curriculum: Aspirations for the Twenty-First Century* – should then form one of the working texts for the detailed task of revising the current statutory order.

The early sections of this chapter might be seen as my attempt at an early draft of it. It should be established at the outset that one goal of the revision would be a further reduction in the extent of prescription. The essential knowledge, skills and attitudes across all curriculum subjects should be established, both those that are in the curriculum and those that would flow from the *Millennium Curriculum* text. This would be the compulsory core. Indeed, within the compulsory core greater prescription in relation to the teaching of the basics might be considered. Otherwise, the text should be considered sufficient to inform revision of the remainder of the existing subjects, which should be treated as advisory.

Standards should be clearly set in the compulsory core. They should be derived partly from the existing curriculum and the tests that have been based upon it. More importantly, however, they would be established by reference to international comparisons. A series of research studies of the best education systems on earth would be commissioned and used by those redrafting our curriculum to ensure that what we expect of children and young people in Britain, especially in mathematics, science and the national language, more than matched expectations elsewhere in the world. One consequence of this approach would certainly be a raising of expectations in mathematics, where standards in this country fall far behind those among our competitors.

As David Reynolds put it in a study entitled 'Worlds Apart' (OFSTED, 1996): 'England had two to three times as many low achievers as several other countries including France, Germany, The Netherlands, and Japan, in the 13 year old sample [in one major study of mathematics] . . .' Moreover, Reynolds concludes:

> that performance in mathematics in England is relatively poor overall . . . that this performance has deteriorated relative to other countries over the last 20 years; [and] that English children have a very wide range [from very good to very poor] of achievement and a particular excess of numbers of low achieving pupils . . .

Worse still, as he drives home the bad news, 'the historic advantages of the English system with its high achieving pupils have disappeared'.

However depressing this might be, approaching curriculum revision with this kind of research at our fingertips would be a giant advantage over the process used for the first National Curriculum. Then, not only was there no attempt to research the international state of play systematically, there was not even any attempt to achieve consistency of standards across subjects within the National Curriculum. There was nothing but guesswork. This explains why, in the summer of 1995, eleven-year-olds did far better in science tests than in maths or English. It is certainly not true that primary school standards in science are higher than in the other core subjects, simply that the expectations built into the curriculum and the tests are not consistent.

The end result of this detailed work would be, in addition to the *Millennium Curriculum*, the following:

- a defined compulsory core, which would be statutorily required and would include everything in whatever subject we believe everyone in school should be expected – definitely – to know, understand and be able to do; and
- a series of documents for each subject, setting out what are believed to be nationally desirable content and skills.

We would know, too, that as far as possible the expectations at each stage of the curriculum would be consistent with the best in the world. We would have a curriculum which was ambitious, both in what it encompassed and in the standards it set. Policing it would not need the current enforcement system. Schools would be expected to ensure that the compulsory core was provided. For the desirable remainder, they would be held accountable by inspectors for either providing it for all their pupils or for explaining rationally, and on the basis of sound educational argument, what they are doing instead.

Beyond that, all that is necessary is to ensure that the public, and especially parents, are much better informed than they are currently about the learning they can expect for their child. In successive studies, parents say that this is information they want. The proposals in the final chapter explain how it can be provided.

Testing Without Destruction

All that still leaves us with strategic decisions to make about assessment and testing. Reams have been written on the subject in the last decade or so. Often the measured and thoughtful research has been drowned out by the storm of political controversy. It should soon be possible to cut through the tangles of the controversy and reach a settlement fit for the twenty-first century. Here I want to set out, briefly, what its principles might be.

The root of the controversy of the last decade was an elision of two separate potential purposes of testing children. They need to be tested by teachers so that teachers can find out how well they are doing and to decide what they should learn next. This is called 'formative assessment' in the jargon. In addition the government argued, from 1988 onwards, that they should also be tested at different ages in order to check that schools were performing satisfactorily. This second purpose was a matter of accountability.

Of course, there is an area of overlap between these two roots of assessment. If the formative assessment a child undergoes is one that has national standards built into it, it enables the teacher to understand more about the pupil in relation to others than if the test does not. However, the areas of tension between the purposes are more powerful than the overlap. If the primary purpose of a test is to hold the school accountable then, inevitably, teachers will resent it if it takes up too much time and it will – in fact – damage children's education if it drags them away from teaching what the children are supposed to be learning.

Furthermore, if this accountability measure depends on the teachers themselves carrying out the assessment, then the temptation for them to ensure, at the very least, that their pupils do as well as possible will be great. This is why, in the United States, over 80 per cent of school districts claim that their pupils are performing above average and why, in one LEA that introduced testing for accountability purposes before the National Curriculum, some schools registered over 100 per cent.

A test designed for accountability purposes will also lead to teachers teaching to the test: boning up on past papers, question-spotting and drilling in the techniques appropriate to the test. We all remember the advice our teachers gave us as our public examinations approached and we sought desperately for means of clutching at straws. Educators tend to frown on the idea of teaching to the test. They talk disapprovingly of 'assessment leading the curriculum'. While it has obvious disadvantages – especially if it leads to people beating the system rather than learning things – it has advantages too. It is actually part of the purpose of tests to lead the curriculum. There is no surer way of ensuring people teach, say, basic arithmetic than requiring that all children be tested in it. The downside of this process can be avoided if the test is changed regularly: beating the system is avoided because the system changes. In other words, there are positive advantages – rarely mentioned – of shifting the goalposts. Management consultants realised this long ago: quality assurance, they argue, requires constantly changing the performance measures.

On the other hand, it is evident that a teacher needs to assess pupils regularly in order to monitor progress and to shape the next phase of teaching. For these purposes, national tests at the end of, say, infant or junior education are clearly hopeless. Much more regular assessment is required. Teachers need to be skilful in designing and using their own assessments, and they need access, too, to a range of assessments based on the national standards established in the National Curriculum.

Given this context, it is possible to lay down sensible principles for a national assessment and testing system. We need, firstly, a clearly established national testing system at the ages of seven, eleven and fourteen. The government has made tortuous, but ultimately substantial, progress towards putting this in place. The tests should be simple, focused on the basics of the twenty-first century, changed from time to time and either marked externally or properly 'moderated' (or checked) by independent examiners. It might not be necessary for all pupils to take these tests since their aim is to establish accountability and to provide information on changes in national standards. In larger schools, a sample of pupils might be sufficient.

Secondly, in order to encourage pupils to move ahead where they are able to, we need to make it possible for pupils to be assessed at the different levels of the National Curriculum when their teacher thinks they are ready, rather than having to wait until the end of the stage of education. This sounds odd to people in school education because we have traditionally linked assessment to age (hence the eleven-plus, for example). But in music education we have long since realised that to do so was absurd and, of course, young people enter the grade examinations when they are ready. The same applies to the driving test and many other forms of assessment.

As Sir Geoffrey Holland argued at the 1996 North of England Conference, this is crucial to opening up opportunity and to freeing our school system from the rigid industrial model of mass education in age-related groups. In the final chapter of this book, I argue for each young person to be in a position to pursue her or his own educational plan. To make this possible, the assessment system needs to be detached from its rigid relationship to the age of pupils. Each time a pupil moves to a higher level in the National Curriculum, this should not only be recorded at school, but also reported to parents. All too often, letters are only written home when pupils are in trouble: this would provide an excellent opportunity for a letter of congratulation and a moment of celebration.

Thirdly, in order to ensure that these assessments have public credibility and are broadly comparable across all schools, a system needs to be established for validating the assessments of different schools. It would be prohibitively expensive for all these assessments to be marked outside the school. Instead, each time a school is inspected, its assessment procedures should be examined thoroughly and, if they are found to be rigorous, they should be given a licence to assess until the next inspection. If not, then an external regime would have to be imposed. In between inspections, the school would be left to get on with it although, like a season-ticket holder on the train, it could anticipate the possibility of a random check-up. These proposals would provide a system of National Curriculum assessment which matched rigour with flexibility and accountability with professional discretion.

Much more would be necessary, however, if assessment is to make its full contribution towards higher standards. The real driving force of improvement is teachers' pedagogical skill, and at the core of that is the ability to assess pupil progress in a refined way. Some teachers excel at this, and it shows in all that they do. Others are less successful. In the Keele survey, one of the commonest complaints that pupils make is that their work is marked shoddily. In any case, even when work is well marked, it is not always apparent either that the marking is consistent with standards in other schools or that the information derived from marking informs the teacher's plans for the future.

Some of this unevenness of standards of assessment competence among teachers results from differences in what might be called their aptitude. It is also, however, a strategic issue for the education service as a whole. The evidence suggests that the investment made in the assessment skills of infant teachers in the early 1990s as part of National Curriculum implementation really did improve competence across the board for that group of teachers. No such investment was forthcoming for junior teachers, and the announcement of a relatively paltry sum for this purpose in 1996 is a classic case of too little, too late. Similarly, there was a substantial investment in teachers' assessment skills when the GCSE examination was introduced in 1987, but this was never followed up, not even when tests for fourteen-year-olds were introduced five years later.

Unless we invest in teachers' assessment skills, we shall not be able to achieve the standards we want. Nor shall we be able to achieve the tailoring of education to the specific learning needs of the endlessly diverse young people in our schools that is essential to success. Some of the investment should go into direct training; some should go into enabling teachers to see children's work from other schools and to learn from their peers in other schools. At the moment, this crucial cross-fertilisation often does not even take place between different teachers in the same school, never mind between schools.

And some of the investment should be directed into making use of information technology to assist with assessment. Already a number of schools have experimented with Integrated Learning Systems. These are computer packages designed chiefly to teach young people numeracy and literacy, and other subjects as well. They have already demonstrated a clear potential to raise standards, especially in mathematics. They have problems too. They are prohibitively expensive (though they will become cheaper), and they are inflexible and difficult to link to the overall learning programme planned by the teacher. Their ability to assess pupils' performance, by offering them a range of tasks in a short space of time and the speed and efficiency with which they can reach conclusions and diagnoses is, however, unquestioned. I have been involved in researching the use of Integrated Learning Systems in prison education. I have learnt a lot about prisons, implementation of change and my own prejudices from doing this work, but much the most interesting outcome of the research was the admission of one of the teachers in the project that the computer was better equipped to diagnose a new prisoner's learning needs than she was. Before the ILS was installed, diagnosis had been carried out through an interview and some tests. The ILS was more objective, not influenced by the prisoner's criminal record, regional accent or personal manner: it was also able to offer a far wider range of test questions in a given time than any traditional paper-based test could do.

This has immense implications for teachers, suggesting that they will need to concentrate increasingly on higher-order assessment tasks – above all, balancing motivation and standards – while leaving lower- and middle-order tasks to machines, supported occasionally by administrators. The computer can make this possible because it is also a brilliantly quick marker of work and recorder of achievement. Machines will not replace teachers, but they can support them both in providing further evidence on which to base diagnosis and planning and in relieving them of drudgery. Especially in relation to assessment, they could be the key to a much higher degree of professionalism.

Coming of Age

One more curriculum issue remains. Originally, the National Curriculum covered the age range five to sixteen. After the age of sixteen, there were A Levels and a motley range of vocational qualifications for those young people who stayed on in school.

Even as Kenneth Baker and his colleagues began to implement the National Curriculum in the late 1980s and early 1990s, the ground was shifting beneath their feet. The numbers staying on in education after the age of sixteen increased rapidly. At the same time, the new General National Vocational Qualifications (GNVQ) became increasingly popular. Meanwhile, the National Curriculum for fourteen- to sixteen-year-olds proved incompatible with the GCSE, with giving young people choice and with the constraints of school timetabling. Kenneth Clarke, in a rare outburst of rationality, acknowledged this in January 1991. Then, in the Dearing reports of 1993 and 1994, the idea of extending vocational options to fourteen- to sixteen-year-olds was proposed, not least as a means of motivating those who remained uninspired by traditional fare. Dearing also recommended that the choice for fourteen- to sixteen-year-olds should be widened, partly to offer school flexibility, and partly to acknowledge that young people of that age are effectively adult and, if they are not treated that way, are all too likely to vote with their feet.

The Dearing Report of 1996 took all this a stage further and brought us a step closer to a coherent range of options for fourteen- to nineteen-year-olds. It did so by providing a common framework to include all the qualifications which are available after the age of fourteen. A diagram from the report (see Figure 6) shows how. In effect, therefore, the National Curriculum has never covered the five to sixteen age range. It has been extended 'downwards' to include four-year-olds, but at the top end it has lost fourteen- to sixteen-year-olds, whose curriculum fate is increasingly tied up – rightly – with that of sixteen- to nineteen-year-olds.

For the *Millennium Curriculum* we need to formalise what has happened by default. The school curriculum should cover ages four to fourteen and be shaped around the plans set out earlier in this chapter. When pupils reach age fourteen it should be seen as a coming of age. Young people should play an increasing part, from then on, in shaping their own future. With clear advice and guidance, they would be able to make their way through a fourteen-to-nineteen curriculum which was based on the assumption that they would remain in education beyond the age of sixteen. This arrangement would also need to ensure that they continue to develop their skills in the basics and study a balance of academic and vocational options. Young people could build up credits over the years between fourteen and nineteen. Examinations at sixteen should cease to be – as they still are, both in design and in cultural impact – a school-leaving examination, and become instead a staging post on the route to lifetime learning.

Sir Ron Dearing's 1996 report has helped us in this direction, but the political constraints provided by a government obsession with A Levels as the 'gold standard' and a right-wing suspicion of anything but assessment by examination prevented him from thoroughgoing modernisation. We must hope that the next government – whatever its political complexion – is less interested in reinventing the mid-twentieth century and more interested in discovering the new millennium.

Just as we need to redefine the purposes of education, we need to redefine the purposes of qualifications. Instead of being seen solely as a recognition of the completion of a course of study, each qualification

Figure 6: Proposed framework of national awards

National Award: Advanced Level		
AS and A Level	GNVQ Advanced Level	NVQ Level 3†
National Award: intermediate Level		
GCSE Grades A*–C	GNVQ Intermediate Level	NVQ Level 2‡
National Award: Foundation Level		
GCSE Grades D–G	GNVQ Foundation Level	NVQ Level 1‡
National Award: Entry Level*		
Common to all pathways: Three grades A/B/C		

† NVQ Level 3 obtained by young people primarily through Modern Apprenticeship/Employment.
‡ NVQ Levels 1 and 2 obtained by young people primarily through Youth Training/Employment.
* Entry Level at grades A, B, C equivalent in demands to Levels 3, 2 and 1 of the National
  Curriculum, but contextualised for the post-16 age group.

should be seen as the start of another. They should be a floor, not a ceiling; a beginning, not an end. If the notion of lifetime learning is to become a reality, then education should have a beginning and a middle, but no end: less a good story and more an unfinished symphony.

8 · New Teachers for a New Century

'I do not know anything about boat races,' Sam says, 'and the Yales may figure as you say, but nothing between human beings is one to three. In fact . . . I long ago came to the conclusion that all life is six to five against.'

Damon Runyon

The Present Reality

The last decade has been an immensely difficult one for teachers. In the mid-1980s there was the depressing guerilla conflict over teachers' pay and conditions which culminated in the imposition of a national contract and the establishment of a review body which fixed pay rates without recourse to negotiation. There followed years of free-market reform and turmoil in schools caused as much by the government's abysmally inadequate approach to the implementation of reform as by the reforms themselves. This phase culminated in the 1993 test boycott and the subsequent calming of the waters by, first, Sir Ron Dearing, and then Gillian Shephard.

The end of the test boycott, however, only opened the way for the central issues of the decade, quality and standards, to rise to the top of the agenda and stay there. While this opened up potentially wonderful opportunities to improve the status and image of teachers, it also – inevitably – meant a public focus on the small but significant percentage of teachers who are not up to the job and the similar proportion of schools which are failing. Whatever the intentions of the leading politicians and Chris Woodhead, the Chief Inspector, to many teachers it felt as if they were all being tarred with the brush of failure.

One primary teacher writing in the *Sunday Times* on 14 April 1996 expressed how many of his colleagues felt by suggesting that he expected shortly to see a newspaper headline reading 'HITLER A NAZI: TEACHERS RESPONSIBLE'.

Add to that sequence of high-profile pressures from the political arena a steady escalation in the negative consequences of a dividing society, a firm restraint on public expenditure, class sizes which have risen for five consecutive years and a steady decline in the state of school buildings, and it is hardly surprising that many teachers are demoralised, and believe that the inherent stresses and strains of their work are not given sufficient recognition. If teachers and their leaders sometimes sound defensive and even defeated, it is surely understandable.

The problem is that the demand for ever-higher standards and for reform has not finished yet. On the contrary, in spite of all that the education service has been through, it has only just begun. For teachers to attempt to revive their fortunes by turning the clock back is therefore unthinkable. In any case, the comfortable inadequacy of the late 1970s and early 1980s would hardly be an improvement on the decade of conflict and controversy which followed.

The only sensible way in which teachers can revive their sense of self-worth, rebuild their professional respect and begin to take control once again of their destiny is to take education reform by the scruff of the neck and lead it. They can sign up for the crusade for higher standards or they can allow it to trample over them. After all, the last fifteen years is littered with trades and professions which sought, like King Canute, to turn back the tide, only to find that it not only wet their feet, but swept them away altogether: Fleet Street printers and Welsh miners spring to mind.

The teaching profession has an unparalleled opportunity to promote its own reconstruction in preparation for the learning society. If it is to do so it will need bold, visionary leadership. The only alternative is for it to find itself being reconstructed by others. The second option requires less courage, but probably involves more hardship and demoralisation: no one, least of all members of a noble profession, enjoys the sense of powerlessness that results from being tossed and washed up on a flood tide.

This chapter first of all sets out the formidable barriers to reconstruction and then outlines the features such a reconstruction might have.

The Barriers to Reconstruction

While most of the education system has been radically reorganised over the last decade, what stands out about the teaching profession is how little it has changed. This is not to say that the profession has not changed at all; simply that, relative to the rest of the system, changes in its structure and formation are limited.

A series of measures between 1984 and 1995 did increase central government direction of how teachers are trained. Courses of teacher training must now follow a series of criteria laid down in government circulars which set out the competencies aspirant teachers are meant to gain during their training. The government is considering in 1996 establishing a National Curriculum for teacher education to ensure greater emphasis on the teaching of the basics. In 1994, responsibility for funding of these courses was separated from the rest of higher education and given to a new agency, the Teacher Training Agency, which had power to fund courses based either in universities as they traditionally have been, or wholly in schools as the government's informal free-market advisers would like. Even so, training remains largely based in universities, and the government requirement that trainee teachers should spend two-thirds of their time in schools has widespread acceptance. Schools and universities have established broadly successful partnerships which oversee this training. The old days when the schools which offered teaching practice places to students were, frankly, patronised by university colleagues have largely gone. The partnerships, in which schools have much more influence than they ever did in the past, are also more firmly grounded in reality than some of what passed for training was in the past.

There have also been changes to the training of teachers during their careers. Until 1987, most of the funding available for teachers' professional development was haphazardly distributed to teachers who wanted to do long courses on secondment. Since then, two shifts have taken place. After 1987, the funding was distributed more equitably among local authorities, mainly to assist in preparing teachers for the changes, such as the National Curriculum, which resulted from the government's reform programme. Then, from the early 1990s, increasing quantities of this budget for professional development – between £300 million and £400 million per annum – were devolved to schools for them to spend as they chose, to meet their own school development priorities. Over a decade, the onus of investment had thus passed from the individual teacher to central government and from there to school management.

Over the same period, two other changes affected teachers' professional development. The five non-pupil days had been introduced into teachers' contracts. Given the context within which they were introduced, these extra days were bitterly resented and an element of the resentment lingers still. But the imposition was not foolish. It provided a vital resource for teacher development which some, but not all, schools use well.

Finally, there was the introduction in 1991 of teacher appraisal. The idea was controversial in the profession and feared by many teachers. In the end, in spite of resistance, the scheme was introduced with the backing of all the teacher unions. They even, almost uniquely, agreed a joint statement commending it to their members. The appraisal process involved each teacher being appraised every two years, and focused on their growth and development rather than assessing their performance to decide their pay or promotion prospects. By the end of the four years over which it was phased in, far from posing the threat to teachers that some had anticipated, it had slid so far down the list of priorities in most schools that it was in danger of becoming an irrelevance. In 1995, the government announced that it would review the scheme, with the aim of making it more 'rigorous'. One might have expected, given the investment of commitment union leaders had made in the original scheme, that they would protest at this decision. In fact, they gave it a cautious welcome, more because it had ceased to be a priority than because they had shifted their ground.

In another era, this programme of reforms affecting the teaching profession might have been considered radical and substantial. In fact – comparatively speaking – it looks modest. Teacher leaders can take some modest satisfaction from the fact that the professional landscape is still recognisable. Meanwhile, advocates of radical reform such as Chris Woodhead, the Chief Inspector, have begun to regret publicly that the government's revolution did not begin with the training and development of teachers rather than leaving it to last.

That time has now certainly come. It is not only that the reform programme has arrived at that point; the state of the teaching profession in terms of morale as well as the growing impact of school-improvement strategies and information technology also make it necessary. Strong though the case is, there is a sense of hesitation. Reform of the structure and content of education has been important and controversial, but the nature of the teaching profession is the crystalline heart of it all. In the end, education is nothing more than a myriad of interactions between learners and teachers. We simply cannot afford to make a mistake, hence the pause for breath. Hence too the relatively modest pace of change in the profession over the last ten to fifteen years.

Awareness of what is at stake is not the only factor damming back the potential flood of change. There are also four substantial barriers standing in its way. The first is that politicians, who are relatively confident when dealing with structure, funding and, these days, accountability, are markedly reluctant to become embroiled in the classroom itself. They have been happy to prescribe the curriculum – what should be taught – but not how it should be taught. Even in the 'what' they have retreated

from the highly prescriptive approach favoured by Baker and have urged
teachers to use their professional judgement. In relation to the 'how',
they have sometimes pontificated about whole-class teaching or the
importance of 'phonics' in the teaching of reading, and it is surely legitimate for them to do so, but they have shrunk from any attempt at
imposition for the very good, pragmatic reason that they know it will
not work. Chris Woodhead, who is known for his advocacy of whole-class
teaching and getting back to basics, often remarks that he and the politicians can say what they like, but unless teachers have the will to change,
nothing will happen. At the start of 1992, Woodhead was one of three
so-called 'wise men' who reported on primary school teaching and recommended a mixture of approaches, including greater emphasis on whole-
class teaching. Everyone remembers the report, but few can point to any
significant classroom change that resulted from it. 'Real change', as one
American teacher union leader put it, 'is real hard.'

This sense of impotence ought to lead government to the realisation
that, if it wants to alter the shape and character of the teaching profession,
then it will need to find a means of collaborating successfully with teachers
in order to do so. Any major reconstruction will depend upon government
and teachers finding a new partnership in which, unlike the old post-war
partnership, there is a real sense of urgency. This is the challenge facing
any politician who wants to raise standards significantly. So far, however,
it has proved elusive.

This is partly because of the bizarre arrangements that have been put
in place to govern the profession. These form the second substantial
barrier to radical change. Though teachers have sought it for over a
century, no government has been willing to cede self-government to
teachers. Instead, the DfEE and its predecessor departments have regulated it with the help, from time to time, of a range of advisory committees
or quangos. Although the Conservatives were elected in 1979 to roll back
the frontiers of the state and, specifically, to reduce the number of
quangos, in fact the state apparatus has grown, and the number of
quangos has proliferated, not least in education. Each of the new educational quangos has a partial responsibility for the governance of the
teaching profession.

The Teacher Training Agency, set up by Act of Parliament in 1994,
has responsibility for funding and shaping how teachers are trained; the
School Curriculum and Assessment Authority, set up by Act of Parliament in 1993, decides what they should teach; OFSTED, the inspection
agency, set up by Act of Parliament in 1992, decides how well they are
teaching it; and the School Teachers Review Body, set up by Act of
Parliament in 1991, decides how much they should be paid and the terms

and conditions under which they should work. In each of four consecutive years, therefore, the government established a new educational quango with major responsibilities in relation to teachers. Each of these quangos is answerable to ministers and is therefore shadowed by the DfEE.

This division of labour between a number of agencies, not one of which has reached what might be called maturity, creates a number of problems for teachers. One is that there is rivalry between them. At times it seems as if they compete with each other for newspaper headlines, with the exception of the Review Body, which keeps a low profile. In 1995, it seemed that if it was not Nick Tate intoning on the twin themes of morality and cultural relativism, then it was Chris Woodhead drawing attention to the extent of failure among teachers. This is not to say that the themes are not important, but it is to question whether repeated headline-grabbing is the route to progress.

The uneasy relationships are reflected not merely in rivalry for the headlines, but also in the execution of duties. OFSTED and the TTA, for example, manage, most of the time, to suppress their conflicts, but only just. No wonder the DfEE has become anxious about all the quangos to which it has, in effect, given birth. In some parts of the public service, quangos result from the hiving off of some activity. This is the purpose of the thrust towards so-called 'next steps agencies'. In education, the picture is much less clear. Often a quango – like the National Curriculum Council, the short-lived forerunner of SCAA – has been created and then been carefully shadowed by an army of civil servants, who clearly do not sign up to the maxim about having dogs and barking yourself. Tensions between the DfEE and the agencies, particularly OFSTED, thus bedevil the picture too. There is a minor element of personality here. Chris Woodhead was Chief Executive at SCAA before he became Chief Inspector, while Anthea Millett was Director of Inspections at OFSTED before taking over the Teacher Training Agency, but the real tension is institutional, and it is hard to imagine that it would disappear even if all the agencies changed hands.

Responsibilities do overlap, and quango chiefs will always find it in their interests to make an impact on either ministers or the public, or both. Gillian Shephard, to her credit, has tried to encourage effective collaboration, with some success. The establishment of her Consultative Group on School Standards in 1995, on which all the quangos are represented, was a helpful step towards co-ordination. She has also given the quangos tasks to do in collaboration. The TTA and OFSTED are jointly reviewing teacher appraisal, for example, and both are working with SCAA to promote national debate about changes in pedagogy.

Even so, none of them has responsibility for the teaching profession as a whole. Governance is thus, at best, splintered. To compound the difficulties, there is little sense of the long term. So far, I have mentioned only the full-time paid staff of the quangos but, with the exception of OFSTED, all have lay members on a governing council or committee, and all of these are appointments of the Secretary of State. Though some of the appointments, particularly in the pre-Shephard era were, to put it politely, unusual, none of them is so lacking in perception as to miss the fact that there is an election looming. Many of them expect it to bring their days in the sun to an end. Their eyes are therefore fixed firmly on the short term. Many of the more right-wing among them have become restive in the Shephard era because there is not the same sense of helter-skelter change (before it is too late) that existed under John Patten.

Overall, while OFSTED, the TTA, SCAA and the DfEE under Gillian Shephard have, on some important themes, begun to take responsibility seriously and push their horizons well beyond the election, the pervasive sense of short-termism, particularly when it is linked to the divisions among them, has prevented any radical rethink of the nature of teaching and learning or of the scope and character of the teaching profession.

In these circumstances, the obvious place to look for radical rethinking is to the representatives of the teaching profession itself. Disappointingly, the search reveals only that the representatives of the teaching profession are as splintered and short-termist as those who govern it.

The one pure market in the entire education sector is the competition among unions for members. There are six of them competing for the membership subscriptions of just over 400,000 teachers and headteachers. Two of them are solely for headteachers and deputy headteachers. The other four fight over the rest of the profession. One of them, the Professional Association of Teachers, is marginal and much smaller than the others. It is committed to a no-strike clause and has only been influential at all because it has had close, informal working relationships with some Conservative leaders.

The other three – the National Union of Teachers; the clumsily titled National Association of Schoolmasters, Union of Women Teachers; and the Association of Teachers and Lecturers – are roughly equal in size (the NUT has around 180,000, the NASUWT 155,000 and the ATL 140,000 members).

Though the original distinctions between them are now lost in the mists of time, rivalry between them is intense. Paradoxically, the solvency and robustness of each one of them contributes to the weakness of the profession as a whole, since none of them sees any real incentive to merge with the others. Markets, of course, have their positive side. Subscription rates are kept low (they are half those of American unions and substantially less than rates among university teachers in this country, though the latter are less well paid), and the unions tumble over each other to support members in trouble. The downside of the market is the need it creates to emphasise their differences.

The NASUWT made its name and recruited most of its membership by being different from the NUT. It was founded as a reaction to an NUT ballot in favour of equal pay for men and women teachers just after the First World War, and made its major spurt in growth through developing what might be described as a low-brow, militant stance in the 1960s – a philosophy which it has retained to this day. This is in conscious contrast to the NUT's sometimes tortuous attempts to balance traditional trade unionism and a strong professional stance. On the journey back after a speech I had given in January 1996, the bullish General Secretary of the NASUWT, Nigel de Gruchy, described me as a 'mad professor'. I replied that he was an old cynic. 'That's what I'm paid to be,' he replied, as the train pulled in. Though we were both joking, we were both right too.

The ATL, meanwhile, with its origins in the old grammar school sector is playing – in recruitment terms – the long game. Moderate in the extreme, it has grown steadily in the last ten years, especially among primary teachers, by steady advocacy and by presenting itself as the voice of the ordinary teacher.

The NUT, by contrast, is still coming to terms with the loss of the overwhelming influence it had only thirty years ago, when almost 70 per cent of all teachers belonged to it. Now its market share is a little over 40 per cent. It retains a sense of ambition about the role it could play in changing education, but it still appears to assume that it might, one day within the foreseeable future, recover its lost strength, if only everyone else, including the government and the Labour Party, would behave properly. Moreover, it is increasingly hampered, both in policy development and in public image, by a large minority of left-wing activists. Sometimes one has the impression that the entire ragbag of daft activists who were expelled from the Labour Party during the Kinnock era have found their way into the membership of the NUT. In 1995 a small group of these militants outrageously jostled and heckled the Shadow Education Secretary, David Blunkett. In 1996, the radical and strategic attempt of Doug McAvoy, the General Secretary, to weaken the union's annual conference by offering 'one person, one vote' democracy to the entire membership was defeated by the left-wing activists who dominate conference. New Labour has evidently arrived: the arrival of a new NUT appears to have been postponed indefinitely.

From time to time, the divisions between the unions, intense though they are, can temporarily be overcome. I know this from indelible personal experience. I drafted, in the early 1990s, as an NUT official, more statements on behalf of all six unions than – I guess – any official in the history of education. It was a tortuous business, and depended, above all, on careful drafting and phoning the various general secretaries in the right order. The key was to leave the most doubtful of the six to last, and then shame them into signing by informing them that the other five had signed up. Sometimes one had to stretch the facts slightly and suggest to two general secretaries that the other five had signed up. The most secure way of reaching an agreement of all six was to give staff below the level of general secretary the opportunity to work together before bringing a joint text to their bosses. These two techniques together helped to establish the test boycott in 1993, and the break-up of that temporary alliance reveals their limitations.

Mostly, the divisions of history and the logic of the market prevent agreement. All that is left then is a series of temporary alliances between two or three of the unions. The result is that the teaching profession is weakened by its divisions and its public image is damaged by the accurate impression of divided leadership that is presented through the media.

The damage this pure market does is, however, much worse than this. Its most profound effect is that it makes it difficult, if not impossible, for union leaderships to speculate boldly about the long-term future of the teaching profession without risking membership loss. In 1991, for example, David Hart, the thoughtful and far-sighted General Secretary of the National Association of Head Teachers, suggested in a widely reported speech that a greater degree of subject specialism in the upper years of primary school needed considering. Among the primary heads who make up his membership, this is akin to a bishop speculating whether the Ten Commandments still have any relevance. There was uproar, quelled only when the union's President wrote to every member playing down the remarks and asserting that what the General Secretary had said was certainly not official policy. Yet the incident undoubtedly cost the NAHT members. I know that for a fact because I was at the NUT – which includes headteachers among its members – receiving phone calls from erstwhile NAHT members.

Thus, any union leader who speculates controversially risks coming under attack from his (amazingly in a profession which is 70 per cent women, they are all men) rivals. The competitive market, therefore, drives union leaderships in the direction of caution and the lowest common denominator. This, in turn, affects the public image of the profession. During Easter week – the week of the teacher conferences –

the unions, with the NUT in the forefront, convey a traditional union image with an emphasis on pay, conditions and expenditure and a critique of any attempt to measure performance or hold teachers to account. While these clearly are the legitimate issues for union conferences, the profession would benefit hugely if there was also an emphasis on raising standards, on improving teachers' professional development and on bringing teaching and learning approaches into the twenty-first century.

Furthermore, during the year between conferences, union leaders – in the soundbites they manage – again tend to focus on the narrow, traditional agenda. Thus the impression created is of a profession which seeks only more investment and less accountability. In fact, the unions often publish thoughtful pamphlets, intelligently exploring issues such as accountability, but sadly these rarely make an impact on the public image of teachers.

Their image is further undermined by the blockheaded militancy favoured by the NUT's left-wing minority, which dominates its annual conference. It is difficult to know which is worse for the profession's image: threatening industrial action over virtually anything or not carrying out the threats with similar monotony. Probably worse than either are the television pictures, repeated year after year, of the Socialist Workers Rent-A-Mob selling their papers outside the conference and reading them inside it. Whatever else one might say about the state of the profession, it is clear that its public relations are, to say the least, inadequate. The old trade union quip comes back to me: it often seems as if teachers are lions led by donkeys.

A Professional Council

The endemic divisions and short-termism which result from the arrangements for the governance and the representation of teachers mean that there is no national forum in which the profession's long-term future can be debated. There is, for example, little or no debate nationally about the relationship between teachers and the growing number of support staff working in schools. There is little or no debate either about the implications for teaching methodology of all that has been discovered over the last generation about how children learn. The implications of these and other important changes for the structure and funding of teachers' professional development are barely debated either. While the Teacher Training Agency is beginning to raise these crucial questions, in the eyes of many teachers, however good its work may be, it has been pigeonholed as yet another of those agencies which 'does things to us'.

Truly radical change on the central questions about the future of the profession depends on debate in a forum which has legitimacy among teachers too.

This is the case for a professional advisory body for educators which advises government and the profession as a whole on teacher training and development, on teaching and learning, and which thinks in visionary terms about the profession five, ten or fifteen years into the future. The traditional demand for a General Teaching Council similar to the General Medical Council or the Law Society might conceivably fit the bill. It would certainly help to enhance the status of the profession, particularly if it established professional standards and enforced them. On the other hand, neither the GMC nor the Law Society, nor for that matter the General Teaching Council which Scottish teachers enjoy, has shown any great inclination to think boldly about the future. Indeed, the risk with any such professional body is that it becomes hidebound by tradition and a force for conservatism. It would be a supreme irony if, at the moment when radical thinking about the future of teaching is most needed, a new organisation for the defence of the status quo was established.

In any case, although the teacher unions have all subscribed to an agreement to promote a General Teaching Council, the commitment to it among some of them is superficial. It is something that they agree about only because it has seemed unlikely to occur. The Labour and Liberal Democratic parties, however, are committed to creating one. If they come to power and put forward specific proposals, the precarious alliance of unions may well fall apart. Although no one believes such a council should take on traditional union functions, at least some among their leaderships will fear a loss of influence.

There are thus two questions to answer before the right forum in which to begin the reconstruction of the profession can be established. What form of governance is appropriate for the twenty-first century? And how do we get from here to there? The rest of this section attempts to answer these questions in reverse order.

During the Thatcher years, committees of inquiry went out of fashion. Kenneth Baker expressed the attitude to them of the governments of those years in his autobiography when he talked about how best to proceed to the establishment of a National Curriculum:

> In former days, the Department would have set up a Working Group to proceed at the leisurely tempo of a Royal Commission, consulting widely and reporting in three years. But the decline of educational standards in Britain demanded swift action . . . This was never going to be easy but I was determined to drive it through . . .

John Major has occasionally made use of inquiries, but only reluctantly in order to dig himself and his colleagues out of the holes they tend to dig themselves into. It is doubtful whether the experience of the Nolan and Scott reports has done anything to revive the government's enthusiasm for major inquiries.

Nevertheless, in education, Dearing has done the idea a power of good. He has been chairing at least one inquiry, and sometimes two, on a rolling programme since 1993. It seems to me that the future of the teaching profession is precisely the kind of issue on which a substantial, thoughtful inquiry would make sense. It could examine the longer-term future and think imaginatively about how the teaching profession ought to develop. It could bring a long-term, coherent perspective of the future to a profession dogged by its splintered, short-termist present. There is time for an inquiry too, for though there ought to be a sense of urgency there is no immediate deadline. It should be established with a view to developing some more effective means of self-government than the teaching profession has now or has ever had in the past, though otherwise its agenda should be wide-ranging.

Governments are always cautious about establishing inquiries with any degree of independence because, by definition, they tend to think for themselves. On the other hand, a new government of either party after the forthcoming election of 1996 or 1997 may find that the idea has much to commend it. After elections, government always have too many fronts on which to advance; prioritisation and timetabling become essential. By setting up a major inquiry into the scope and character of the profession of teaching, a new government could enable itself to advance in the short term with the inevitable structural changes while simultaneously establishing a substantial and possibly radical agenda for the second half of its period in office. It certainly seems to me the most sensible way to proceed on an issue which demands a substantial degree of consensus, or at least consent, which requires much more than superficial analysis and which is of fundamental importance to the future of this country.

If such an inquiry were established, it would have a logic of its own and predicting where it might lead would be difficult. Nevertheless, for the sake of a sense of completeness, I want to suggest the kind of conclusion it might reach and thus to answer the other question I posed at the outset of this section.

I imagine the establishment of a Learning Council rather than a General Teaching Council. The latter suggests a body designed to defend the interests of teachers. The former name, by contrast, would be consistent with the development of a learning society and emphasises that the goal would be to promote learning generally, and among teachers in particular, rather than to defend the status quo.

Its responsibilities would include the development of a Code of Ethics for the teaching profession (see the last section of the chapter for ideas on what the Code might cover), and offering advice to government on the supply of teachers, the entry requirements for teaching and the training, induction and professional development of teachers. Most important of all, it would establish and enforce professional standards of behaviour and competence. It would be able to do so because it would hold a register of those entitled to teach and would be able to strike off those who fell below the expected standards. Beyond these responsibilities, it would clearly have a role, too, for projecting the teaching profession both to itself and to the wider world. If all it did was to get teachers to feel more proud of their work and persuade others to be more respectful of it, it would have made a major contribution.

Its governing council should comprise three equal parts: a group elected from among teachers, not only in schools, but also from institutions which provide teacher education; a second group representing parents, governors, local education authorities and other partners in the education process including the end-users (as it were), employers; and a third group of government appointees, among whom at least half would have to be experienced of and knowledgeable about education in general and teaching in particular. This would ensure that a majority of those on the council were, or had been, directly involved in the provision of education. The government would bring its power to appoint into disrepute if it used it to put political placepeople on the council. It should aim not to use them to run a political line, but to ensure that there were substantial numbers on the council who would be imaginative, visionary and able to question the status quo. The chair of the council, who should also be a government appointee, should be a figure of undoubted stature and credibility, known for her or his independence of mind.

The rest of this chapter is an imaginary programme of work for the Learning Council. What it amounts to is a complete reconstruction of the teaching profession in preparation for the role it is destined to play in the creation of the learning society.

A Reconstruction of the Teaching Profession

Teachers teach, but unless they learn constantly, they will be unable to perform their central role in a rapidly changing society. There is so much for them to learn. They need to be able to develop new skills and understandings consistent with the latest research in education and psychology. Information technology impacts ever more profoundly on learning: they need to understand its impact and potential. They need to keep up to date with their subject or subjects. They need also to understand the changing society in which we live so that they can guide or signpost their students into the inevitable uncertainties of the future. As schools and other centres of learning become more permeable and woven into the fabric of a learning society, teachers will also need to build relationships with a wide range of other professional and social groups and they will, especially, need to become more effective in building partnerships with parents. Increasingly, therefore, what will characterise teachers is their understanding of learning and their commitment to it. What follows is an agenda for reconstruction which would enable teaching to become a learning profession fit for a learning society. I think of it as an agenda rather than a set of prescriptions because, ideally, a programme of change should emanate from teachers themselves rather than being imposed upon them. The proposals here are, therefore, a starting point.

A New Respect for Research

The Teacher Training Agency recently published a short leaflet – a statement of aspiration – about teaching becoming a 'research-based' profession. This, in a nutshell, is what is required. It is not what exists at present. Many teachers are suspicious of research and theory and doubtful about its relevance to them 'at the chalkface'. Research, it seems to many teachers, does not help them get through the day.

This focus on the practical is hardly surprising given the logistics of a teacher's day and given the fact that it is a way of thinking that teachers share with much of British society. Moreover, much of the research and writing about education in the last two decades does appear to be either irrelevant or turgid or both. There is no reason at all why university sociologists should not write neo-Marxist or post-modernist tracts, but if they do, teachers – with so much to do – can hardly be expected to rush home and read their words of wisdom. Too much of the research of the last two decades has been of little use to teachers or those with decisions to make about the future of education.

Nevertheless, there has also been much that is excellent and valuable. By far the most influential and useful to both teachers and policy-makers has been the work on school effectiveness and school improvement examined in Chapter 5, but there is also much more. For example, work on how teachers can successfully assess pupils' work, on the impact of different types of assessment on boys' and girls' achievement, on planning procedures, on involving parents, and on effective self-evaluation and appraisal, is all of direct potential benefit to teachers and schools.

It is also important to recognise that, increasingly, the research community is international. Work in Australia on teacher effectiveness, in America on the nature of intelligence, and in Canada on the implementation of change – to mention just three examples – is all of immense value to educators here.

The trouble is that too little of the research actually results in real change. Part of the cause of this difficulty is that many teachers simply do not get to know either what the research says or what its implications are. Some are suspicious, but most simply suffer from the absence of systematic arrangements for ensuring research findings are disseminated. There is no obligation on teachers, as there is on doctors, to keep abreast of the latest research. There is no equivalent of the *British Medical Journal* or the *Lancet*. Whether teachers find out about research depends upon the initiative of those individuals who have the energy to find out for themselves and on the plans schools make for training their own staff. This set of arrangements is, putting it as politely as possible, haphazard, and it has to change.

If the demand side needs overhauling, so too does the supply side. Though the quality of educational research in the UK is improving, and international connections are helpfully strengthening, there is no sense anywhere of a research strategy in education: where are the frontiers of our knowledge about education? Where would we like to push out across them into the unknown? What do we need to know most? What do we need to know first? What can we find out from abroad, and what must we test in British circumstances? What are the strengths of British research, and how can they best be built upon?

There are handfuls of people who could begin to answer some of these questions and hazard guesses at others. There is absolutely no sense of consensus about answers to them and little evidence of an attempt to seek one. The Teacher Training Agency, the most far-sighted of our quangos, is beginning to ask questions but, as we know, they influence only part of the agenda. The DfEE has a shameful record of research which compares unfavourably with those of other government departments, such as Health. It has realised the need to rethink its role in developing and promoting research but, to date, has done little or nothing about it. Meanwhile, researchers themselves are increasingly focused on winning contracts – any contracts – and the teaching profession's leaders have shown no inclination to engage in a debate that has barely begun when they have so much else on their plates.

If we want a research-based profession, it needs a concerted effort from all these participants. Government needs to promote research in priority areas – such as in the impact of information technology on learning – and it needs to purchase directly more research in these priority areas. Researchers themselves need to concentrate not just on winning contracts and completing them, but also on writing about them in plain English and disseminating findings in usable form. And teacher leaders – aided and abetted by all the national agencies – need to articulate the research priorities of teachers and to encourage teachers to seek out research. Teachers need pressure to do so – an obligation laid down by a professional council, for example – and support too: above all they need more time for their own learning. Much of the agenda that follows is designed to create this balance of pressure and support.

An MOT for Teachers

Let us imagine that there is a governing council for the teaching profession established in the way I described earlier in the chapter. Imagine that one of its chief goals is to promote higher professional standards: expecting all teachers to keep up with research and training on teaching methodology; demanding that teachers' performance achieves certain minimum levels; and insisting that, over time, the performance of every teacher improves as he/she gains experience and benefits from the lessons of research and the application of technology.

The question is, how would it make this happen? Let us assume for a moment that teachers had more time at their disposal as a result of some of the practical developments set out later in the chapter and that the council controlled the register of all those allowed to teach so that it could establish re-registration requirements. One such requirement could be that, every five years, all teachers should undergo a thorough professional review. This would involve a trained peer interrogating them about the extent to which they had developed and refined their skills and applied the lessons of research: it would involve the reviewer consulting colleagues, parents and pupils about the teacher's performance and checking that the minimum requirements of a member of the teaching profession had been met. These might include, over a five-year period, a requirement to participate in professional development activities, to watch other teachers teach and to spend time working in, or visiting, a variety of educational institutions. There might be an obligation, too, to work outside teaching, on full pay, for a term in the five-year period. I read a novel years ago – I have forgotten its title and its plot, but I have remembered one sentence from it. 'The best teachers', it said, 'are the ones who might have been something else.' It rings true and, if it is, then we must ensure that teachers have the opportunity to be something else as well as being a teacher. In short, we are talking about an MOT for teachers. The benefits of an MOT are surely obvious in terms of improving performance, but how could teachers ever be persuaded it would be in their best interests?

For a start, it would vastly enhance their status in the community. It would demonstrate a new commitment to standards. It would demonstrate that teachers were taking the quality bull by the horns. At the moment, the bull is on the loose. Of more direct benefit would be the gains teachers would make in terms of entitlements to professional development. It is a late-twentieth-century fact that if you want to persuade government to give you a right, the best way of doing so is to ask it to impose a duty. Finally, the procedure could be established only as part of a wider set of changes which involved relieving teachers of some of their administrative chores.

A number of outcomes of an MOT are imaginable. A teacher might be given clearance to re-register. Presumably, this would be the outcome for the majority of teachers. Another tranche might find that certain conditions had to be met before their registration could be completed: they might, for example, need to participate in some skills training with computer technology.

There would also, no doubt, be a small percentage of cases who would not come through their review. Poor performance is never an easy subject to discuss, particularly in teaching where, until recently, it almost had the status of a taboo. Now, as a result of rigorous inspection, the debate over schools like Hackney Downs and the growing concern among all politicians, the taboo has been broken. Teachers and their leaders have been flailing helplessly in the storms that have resulted. They have been reluctant to approve the one concrete measure that has emerged: that inspectors should inform headteachers of the names of those teachers whose lessons were graded 6 and 7 on a seven-point scale. At the NUT conference, a motion was passed supporting strike action in schools where teachers were thus 'victimised'. This defensive response is the route to disaster. The public would be unlikely to understand, still less support, a strike aimed at maintaining the job of an inadequate teacher. The teaching profession desperately needs a strategy, consistent with its aspirations, for addressing the question of teacher failure. A system of five-yearly MOTs, overseen by the profession itself, would fit the bill.

It is also worth pointing out that the proposal would benefit the inadequate teachers themselves. Such teachers, at present, often drift through year after year in teaching, mocked and derided by many of their colleagues, suffering acutely from the damage to their self-worth that teaching poorly inevitably inflicts and achieving nothing in terms of career satisfaction. The approach of the five-yearly MOT would provide the necessary prompt to seek career guidance and counselling and a route out of the profession which would do the least possible damage to their dignity.

These brief paragraphs leave much detail to be resolved. There are practical issues about how the MOT would be organised and funded, for example. I am convinced, though, that tolerance of inadequacy is fading rapidly as higher standards are sought and that if teachers put no proposals forward for improving standards within the profession they should not be surprised if others do. Finally, it needs to be emphasised that the main purpose of the MOT proposal is not to deal with the incompetence of the few; it is much more than that. It is the key to a new professionalism.

Attracting the Best

The MOT would raise professional standards and reduce the number of failing teachers. If it is to succeed, however, it needs to be linked to reforms designed to ensure that recruits to teaching are well prepared, well motivated and highly capable from the outset. Teacher unions have rightly emphasised the risk of a teacher shortage within two or three years, perhaps on the scale of the one that did so much damage in the late 1980s. They point out that, as the recession ends, the demand for graduates from business and elsewhere will rise, and teaching, which has recruited reasonably strongly in the early 1990s, will become increasingly unattractive because its pay levels are relatively poor. The shortage is likely to be particularly acute in the crucial subjects of science and mathematics, where this country's performance is already unacceptably low. Already recruitment to teacher training is becoming more difficult than it was in the early 1990s.

The unions highlight the risk of shortage because they believe it assists them in their campaigns for higher pay. Of course, pay is part of the answer. The market operates in teacher recruitment just as it does elsewhere. Teachers' pay compares poorly with business, commerce, law and medicine, but favourably with other aspects of the public service such as nursing, social work or university teaching. The worst defect in the present pay arrangements is not so much starting salaries as the lack of opportunities for really significant rises in pay five or so years into the profession. Increased pay would help recruit more and better teachers: so would a change in the structure of the pay system designed to reward successful teachers who have stayed in teaching for five years or more.

It would be foolish to believe, however, that the attraction of teaching is simply a matter of pay levels. In any case, substantial increases in teachers' pay – which forms a large part of public expenditure – are unlikely to be achievable without other major changes. Whatever government is in power, it will have many competing demands on its resources which will remain strictly limited by the obvious reluctance of people to pay higher taxes. In this context, other means of attracting the brightest and best of each generation into teaching will have to be found. Many of the proposals in this chapter are designed to assist in bringing about that outcome.

Before examining the other proposals, it is necessary to look at how best to project the teaching profession. Much of the argument in this chapter has dealt with the poor public image that the profession tends to project of itself. Often its own leaders convey a sense of a profession which is battered by reform, has lost control of its own destiny and is only able to complain from the sidelines while begging hopelessly for additional funds. This may be slightly exaggerated, but it is all too close to the truth.

The truth in schools is substantially different. I have described in Chapter 5 the positive culture inside Haywood High School, a culture which is replicated across many schools in disadvantaged and other areas. The first step towards making teaching attractive should therefore be an attempt to convey the reality more accurately: there are teachers up and down the country who are changing the world. The sheer, determined professionalism of many teachers is magnificent and rarely conveyed convincingly to the public. The responsibility to convey an accurate picture lies squarely with both the leaders of the profession and government and its agencies. Both should resist the temptation to gild lilies in order to put a given short-term case. There have, from time to time, been advertising campaigns designed to attract applicants to teaching. They have focused on the skills involved or the responsibility involved but, to my mind, they have never conveyed the vision of what teaching might become. The pundits tell us that most of us can expect to change job five or six times in a working lifetime. No doubt they are right. A person who takes up teaching in the 1990s can anticipate finding each of those five or six different jobs within the learning field. It has changed dramatically over the last ten years, but what has happened is nothing to what will happen in the next twenty. The teachers who enter the profession in the next five years will be the ones who lead the learning revolution across this society. They will be actors in the drama of professional reconstruction. Above all, they will be at the forefront of the creation of the learning society. These surely are the messages the public relations campaigns should be promoting. And the advertisements should be jointly sponsored by teaching organisations and government.

Any national campaign should be linked to local ones. In America, I once saw a billboard which read 'Greenfield Thanks Its Teachers'. Just that; a simple message of recognition and congratulation on one level but also – indirectly – a promotion of the profession and education as a whole. There is a moral here. Advertisements targeted at serving teachers may be more effective in the recruitment of the next cohort than a direct plea, thus serving a dual purpose.

Advertisements work best, the PR people will tell you, when they are linked to editorial coverage. Unless the government and teacher leaders promote the profession through their everyday comment in the press and media, the impact of any PR campaign will be limited. They would be assisted if the media was not so obsessed with conflict. When ministers praise teachers, their words vanish into the ether. Chris Woodhead's 1996 annual report not only identified 200 excellent or improving schools, but also pointed out that there were many excellent teachers and that the percentage of poor lessons that inspectors had seen in 1995–96 was less than in the previous year. The media reporting, overwhelmingly, was of the 15,000 failing teachers. Four per cent of the profession commanded 90 per cent of the reporting space. The extent of failure is, of course, news and is justifiably reported: but balance is important too. Beyond that, every individual teacher in her or his daily interactions whether in or out of school has responsibility for the morale, status and image of the teaching profession. Every now and then you hear teachers advising a young person not, on any account, to become a teacher. Each time they do so, they destroy another particle of their own credibility. Ultimately, cynicism is corrosive.

Becoming a Teacher

Most of the 10,000 new entrants to the profession each year arrive there having taken part in a course at a university and then a one-year PGCE course, two-thirds of which is spent in schools. A substantial minority, most of whom enter primary education, have done a four-year BEd or BA(Ed), generally at one of the new universities. They, too, will have spent a substantial amount of time in schools. Finally, there is a small minority of entrants who have joined the profession through a training course based solely in schools. Amazingly, the government, when it created this route into the profession, christened it SCITT, which stands for school-centred initial teacher training.

Until a few years ago, once a trainee had found a job in teaching they had to complete a probationary year. Depending on the school and the local authority involved, this was a more or less rigorous procedure. During the era of free-market Stalinism, this control on quality was abolished. If a school wanted to keep a teacher it would decide to do so, the thinking ran. If not, it would let them go. This missed the point. It is one thing to decide whether a particular teacher is right for a particular job or whether the school can afford them: it is another to decide whether that teacher is fit to be a member of a noble profession, regardless of the short-term pressures on the school concerned.

Once the probationary year had been abolished, there were no further controls on professional competence from the profession or anywhere else. This seems to me to border on the foolhardy. Successful completion of a one-year course of training – or a four-year degree course including training – can hardly be considered a sufficient guarantee of a teacher's ability to succeed throughout a career. I would like to see a complete rethink of entry into the teaching profession which would be simultaneously looser about course design and content, but tighter about outcome.

Modules in education and in teaching and learning (what German universities call *Pedagogik*) should be available to the vast majority of undergraduates and would be known as 'Standard Credits'. These might be attractive to students whether or not they were sure they wanted to become teachers. An understanding of education and teaching and learning will, after all, be central in many walks of life – certainly business, the professions and the civil service – in a learning society. Thus, in a three-year undergraduate degree in, say, English literature, a student might do two education-related modules out of a total of eighteen. Through this approach, our higher-education system would be preparing a pool of potential educators. Some of these would actually become school teachers, teachers in other sectors or managers with responsibility for promoting learning across a company. Others would, hopefully, apply their knowledge of education and learning in whatever career they chose. As the importance of learning in every workplace grows, this would become increasingly beneficial to the society as a whole.

Students who have successfully completed their degree, including the Standard Credits, and want a career in teaching, should join a three-year entry programme or apprenticeship, which could start or finish at any time of year. This would involve a combination of practical experience in more than one educational institution and the completion of a range of courses in educational and learning theory. The precise order in which those were undertaken could be left – within a broad framework – for the individual apprentice and the institution which employed them to decide. At the end of the three years, the performance of the apprentice would be assessed in three different ways: there would be a report from a mentor in the institution where the apprentice worked; there would be a report from an independent assessor (for example, a teacher from another school who had been trained for the role), who had watched the apprentice teach; and there would be both an extended dissertation and a written examination, which focused on educational and learning theory and was set by the university with which the apprentice was registered. Those apprentices who successfully completed each of these three assessments would become fully fledged teachers. Their salaries would rise modestly on completion of the programme.

After two more years in the profession, they would – like every other teacher – face the five-yearly MOT. The first MOT, however, should be considered a major step forward. The teacher would by then have completed not only a rigorous three-year apprenticeship, but also two years as a fully functioning teacher. Once the first MOT was completed, the beginning teacher would step on to the fully professional salary grade.

These proposals would have numerous advantages over the present arrangements. They would provide rigour and strengthen quality control. They would link theory and practice integrally from the outset. They would enable mature students to earn a living during their training and, crucially, they would provide the salary progression, after three and five years, that is so obviously missing at present.

Expert Teachers

One of the commonest complaints among teachers themselves at the moment is that they can gain promotion only by moving into management. They conclude, ironically, that the better you are at teaching, the less of it you do. On the other hand, teachers are strongly opposed to performance-related pay, fearing it would invidiously divide colleagues and encourage favouritism. Although the government has been keen to encourage performance-related pay for over a decade, so far it has had little impact. Teacher appraisal focuses on teachers' professional development and is not directly related to their pay. Since, following the 1988 Education Reform Act, schools have had full control of their own budgets for five years or so now, they have the option of awarding extra pay for classroom excellence. In fact, hardly any schools have chosen to do so because of the strong cultural resistance to it. On pragmatic grounds they are, in any case, probably right.

The research evidence on merit pay in general is mixed. In education worldwide it is largely negative. It appears to have worked only where three conditions have been met: where teachers are already well paid and the merit pay is a relatively small addition; where there are clear, published criteria on the level of performance required to gain the merit pay; and where everyone who meets those criteria receives the pay. These conditions do not exist in British schools. Teachers are modestly paid; there is no clarity about performance criteria; and, if there were, budgets are so constricted that only a handful of teachers at most could receive merit payment.

It was with these research findings in mind that, in 1991, I entered into an exchange of views about merit pay with Michael Fallon, then a minister of state at the Education Department, who was advocating merit pay in a meeting with leaders of the NUT. What did he think, I asked, would be the effects in a school of finding that sixty-three out of seventy teachers were excellent, but that only five could receive merit payments because of the state of the budget?

'I can't imagine a school with that many good teachers,' he replied, to which there was no answer.

If merit pay is unlikely to work, what could be done to reward excellent teachers who want and deserve promotion but do not want to become managers? There are schemes in other parts of the world that have solved this dilemma. Cincinnati School District has created, in agreement with the local union, a scheme of 'lead teachers'. New South Wales has developed the concept of the 'advanced skills teacher'. These are not merit-pay schemes in the traditional sense.

British schools could introduce similar schemes, if they wanted to, under the current regulations. To do so, they could advertise internally a 'lead teacher' post or more than one. They would set out in the job description what the holder of the post would be required to do. Presumably the responsibilities would include providing a lead and setting an example pedagogically, and perhaps mentoring or supporting other colleagues, especially newly appointed teachers. Then, any staff who felt capable of doing the job could apply, with the appointment involving classroom observation as well as the traditional interview. This would be an open, fair and worthwhile means of offering promotion within the classroom.

The Labour Party has promised to create an Advanced Skills Teacher grade to assist this process. The Teacher Training Agency, too, is developing proposals for an expert teacher. It appears that greater flexibility and opportunity for teachers may finally be about to arrive.

A Permeable Profession
Even if we had a more qualified, better-trained teaching force with greater opportunities, there would still be major constraints on its development. Given the bewildering pace of change and the explosion in the amount

of knowledge, it becomes increasingly difficult to see how teachers can possibly keep up throughout a career. The MOT concept, particularly if it required all teachers to do a term outside school every five years, would help, but it certainly would not solve the problem.

That requires an arrangement which, in addition to sending teachers out of school, also brings others in. It also requires encouraging teachers to develop the skills of working with adults in business and other walks of life. It was with this in mind that Tim Brighouse and I, a few years ago, urged the development of the notion of teaching associates, whom we saw as providing enrichment. We argued, in a pamphlet for the IPPR, that:

> schools would require from teaching associates a sustained participation in the learning experience of children. The one-off visit from an outsider will continue to have value, but will not bring about radical change. The teaching associate we propose will either make a regular contribution each week or so, over a considerable period of time, or participate fully in the life of a school over a shorter period. An industrialist on a half-day or day-release scheme; a PhD student who spends a morning a week in school; a business person given a six-month full-time secondment; a parent with appropriate qualifications who wishes to stay at home with a young child but spends two afternoons a week in a school providing a service; each of these would be examples of potential teaching associates . . .
>
> This kind of sustained participation from industrial or business employees will require commitment to the idea from private sector employers. While there has been a welcome development in recent years of education/business partnerships, all too often these have been unequal relationships. Many teachers have spent time in business to the benefit of both. Far fewer business people have spent time in schools. Implicit in the argument of many business people, that the cost of secondment to schools is too great, is the assumption that ultimately the business side of the partnership is more important. We reject this: we would like to see many more schemes built on the relatively few examples of good practice which already exist. Ford's 'Industrialists in Residence' scheme is a good example: so is the Danish 'guest teacher' programme.

We were keen to make clear that this kind of participation of outsiders would not in our view reflect badly on teachers. On the contrary, it would enhance their status and enable them to become more effective.

> The involvement of business people or PhD students or others in schools should not be seen as implying inadequacy among teachers. The challenges facing teachers are becoming steadily greater; the evidence of HMI reports demonstrates that, broadly, teachers are

successfully meeting them. Becoming successful managers of learning where teacher associates were a regular feature would be a further professional challenge. The benefits, however, could be considerable. In a time of rapid social and technological change, teachers cannot be expected to know everything which needs to be taught; they must, therefore, be empowered to manage the learning of children and young people by bringing community resources to bear.

This argument is consistent not only with the need to bring a much greater range of expertise into schools, but also with the broad communitarian agenda which has gathered such pace over the last two years, especially among the leaders of the new Labour Party. The teaching-associate concept may develop to some extent on the basis of mutual gain. To reap its full benefits, however, will require a new set of cultural attitudes which value, more than we have done in the last decade, the notion of making a commitment to the local community. Indeed, given technology, the community to which the commitment is made need not be all that local. Teaching associates would solve one of the problems constraining the development of the teaching profession. They would not solve the other.

Teachers give insufficient attention to the development and refinement of their own skills, partly because they are generous by nature and, given a choice, put their pupils' interest before their own, and partly because they simply do not find the time. Headteachers can address the first of these issues by emphasising the importance of continuous professional development and providing leadership which emphasises professional development. But the problem of time is more complicated than this. There is a relentlessness about so much of teachers' work that is unusual, if not unique. A primary teacher is faced, for almost the entire teaching week, with thirty or so children who make continual demands on them. Outside of the pupil contact time, there is the constant pressure to plan and to mark. A secondary teacher is likely to have slightly more 'non-contact' time, but will have relentless pressures of a different kind: he or she may teach, typically, six or seven different classes, each with up to thirty pupils: that means knowing, understanding and supporting the learning of around 200 pupils and marking their work. No wonder teachers find it so difficult to look beyond the immediate and raise their sights to the approaching learning revolution. From within, in the classroom of a primary or secondary school, such talk seems to border on lunacy; from that perspective the future appears dominated by the continuation forever of the demands of the present.

This set of circumstances demands change. It is simply no way to prepare a profession for the learning society. Timetables need to be freed up and made flexible. Pupils, especially in secondary schools, should spend more of the day learning but less of it in traditionally timetabled lessons. They need to be grouped flexibly according to purpose: sometimes according to ability, sometimes according to interest, and at other times according to the nature of the activity. If pupils are watching a film or a video, for example, there is no reason why the pupil:teacher ratio should not be 100:1.

This implies, for teachers, a more flexible contact in terms of the length of the teaching day: the gain would be in time for professional learning.

It would never work, however, unless the number of support staff in schools was increased. In the IPPR pamphlet, Tim Brighouse and I argued that, in addition to the teacher and the enrichment provided by the teaching associates, there needed to be support provided by teaching assistants.

> There is a tradition whereby our schools regularly employ people to assist in the process of teaching. Foreign students acting as language assistants in secondary schools, and classroom assistants and nursery nurses in nursery, primary and special schools are familiar examples of this point. The number of these types of people has grown and their tasks have diversified. For example, since the 1981 Education Act and the welcome move to the integration into mainstream schools of children with special educational needs, there has been a largely unremarked proliferation of adults employed in schools as 'one to one' personal care assistants to individual pupils. Elsewhere in the life of the school, the redefinition of teachers' duties has seen the widespread employment of lunchtime supervisors. What distinguishes these regular employees from other support staff in the school is that their job description (where they have one) necessarily requires them to have *regular contact* with children which is developmental in nature – as opposed to school, office and kitchen staff, caretakers and cleaners, who, of course, interact with pupils but for mainly simple and straightforward transactions. All support staff, whatever their duties, are vital to the successful school, but none more so than those regularly employed to work with pupils under the professional leadership of teachers. It is this group of people that we define as teaching assistants.

We suggested that this paraprofessional tier of educators should become more integral to the planning process of schools and should be entitled – just as teachers are – to regular appraisal, professional development and career counselling. We also suggested that courses should be developed not only to train these staff in their work, but also to offer them the option of ultimately becoming teachers if they chose to. Above all, we agreed that the balance between teaching posts and para-professional posts needed reconsidering. Since paraprofessionals cost less, and if the use of them were increased it would be possible to make major inroads into the pupil:adult ratios in schools, as a result greater flexibility would arise.

This, of course, will succeed only if there is a clear definition of which aspects of the work currently done by teachers demand a person with the full professional training expected of teachers and which could be done by paraprofessionals. Since the publication of that pamphlet, there has indeed been significant progress. It is even possible to detect an incipient, quiet revolution. The government has established successful training for specialist teaching assistants across the country. There is growing evidence of schools including their support staff within their staff development plans. Many examples of effective use of teaching assistants have been highlighted. It is worth pointing out that effective use of support staff depends to a large extent on the quality of the teachers with whom they work. Teaching assistants are least effective when they are being used to supplement an inadequate teacher. And the number of staff other than teachers in schools has grown rapidly over the last five years. Whereas in 1991 there were 120,000 of them (compared to 400,000 teachers) there are now over 160,000, and the numbers are still rising. At a headteachers' conference in 1994, I hazarded a guess that, by the end of the century, less than 50 per cent of the staff of a school would be fully qualified teachers. I thought this was bold, but a secondary head came to see me afterwards and explained that, in his school, that threshold had already been crossed.

Further support for teachers can be provided through the employment of more administrators. It makes obvious sense, for example, for much of the bureaucracy associated with recording assessments or, in secondary schools, doing exam entries to be done by professional administrators who are likely to be cheaper and more efficient than the deputy heads who have often carried out these tasks in the past.

This is potentially controversial territory, of course. Call administrators 'bureaucrats' or 'penpushers' and they are soon seen to be a 'drain on frontline provision'. Balance is everything. It makes no sense to reduce teacher numbers by funding an army of bureaucrats, but it is equally catastrophic so to burden teachers with administration that they are prevented from constantly developing their own skills and understanding.

A Third-Age Contribution

One of the most dramatic social developments of the last decade or so is the growth in the number of people, across a range of types of employment, who have retired early. Some of these have voluntarily stepped off the treadmill, others have retired under pressure. There is another group of people, some in their forties, who have been made redundant as businesses have either 'delayered' or buckled under the strain of recession, or both. Many of these people have outstanding management skills, and a wealth of experience in work and life, not to mention often outstanding educational qualifications.

Many, but not all, of these people would welcome the possibility of making a contribution to schools. Some would perhaps want to work part-time to supplement a pension. Others might seek full-time employment for a limited period of three or five years. Still others might be willing to make some kind of voluntary contribution. It is time those with responsibility for education policy began to think creatively about how best to attract this third-age and early-third-age group into schools. One way would be to offer those with relevant experience an accelerated route into the profession. Under the proposals outlined earlier in this chapter, they could start work in school with an experienced mentor and complete the standard credits and other assignments as they progressed. They might be able to complete the entry grade in two rather than three years but, in any case, could be paid a salary from day one.

It may also be necessary to design a specific 'conversion' credit aimed at this group. It would be important, for example, to hammer home the changes in the education system in the years since people of this age left school, although no doubt some would have had close contact with education as parents.

Another third-age group deserving further careful thought are those teachers who have spent twenty or thirty years in the profession before taking retirement in their early fifties. The number of early retirements has risen dramatically over the last five years or so, partly because of the inherent stresses of teaching, and partly because of the pressures the reform process has brought. In some cases, early retirement involving no further contact with schools is probably the best outcome for both schools and the individual. For many others, though, not only do they represent the loss of important experience to the system, they also have a continuing belief that they have a contribution to make. In any case, in terms of the use of scarce public resources, it seems incredible that we should be spending so much on enhancing people's pensions so that they can leave early, only to replace them immediately with younger teachers.

It would make sense to develop a system for schools that has been operating in universities for some time. Teachers taking early retirement would be offered a deal under which their contribution tapered out over three years rather than ended abruptly. During the three-year period, they could work part-time in the school. But, relieved of the burden of the daily grind, they could become involved, for example, in mentoring and supporting newly appointed young teachers rather than just tending children and young people. If they retained a sense of idealism, this could be a worthwhile and attractive role to many teachers in their early fifties who, though they no longer want the strain of full-time teaching, have something to contribute but currently no means of making a contribution. The world is full of people who would leap at the chance to pass on the accumulated wisdom of a lifetime if they were given the chance, a process which, if handled well, can bring a welcome element of continuity in a world characterised by discontinuity.

A Learning Profession

Seymour Sarason, the American guru, commented sharply on the crucial issue of teachers' learning in his brilliant study, *The Predictable Failure of Educational Reform* (Jossey Bass, 1990). Whereas it is assumed in universities that the faculty, as well as students, are there to learn, he points out that this is not the case in schools. Indeed, as he explains, it is perfectly possible to envisage a university without students, but a school without pupils is a contradiction in terms. It is not my intention to argue that schools should do anything other than put pupils first. On the contrary, my point is that, unless time and energy are freed up to enable teachers to learn and develop, they will be unable to put pupils first; they will become outdated, tired, ground down and demoralised. To quote another American guru, Roland Barth (not to be confused with the incomprehensible French philosopher, Roland Barthes), in *Improving Schools from Within* (Jossey Bass, 1990):

> It is interesting, in this context to consider the common instructions given by flight attendants to airline passengers:
>
>> For those of you travelling with small children, in the event of an oxygen failure, first place the oxygen mask on your own face and then . . . place the mask on your child's face.
>
> . . . In schools we spend a great deal of time placing oxygen masks on other people's faces while we ourselves are suffocating.

Teachers need to learn to keep up to date and to improve their performance in line with society's ever increasing expectations. They need to learn to implement government reforms and to make use of advances in technology. They need to learn to address the weaknesses they will identify from time to time in their performance. They need to learn to stay effective as society in general and the communities in which they work change. But most of all they need to learn because otherwise they will die professionally.

The previous section has explained, at least in part, how time can be found for teachers to learn. The MOT would ensure an expectation to learn from the profession as a whole as well as from the individual schools. One further reform is necessary, and it would involve a small but significant addition to public expenditure.

At present, a growing minority of teachers spend their own money on their professional development. They pay to attend conferences or, more likely, for a diploma or masters course. This is much to their credit but the funding of teachers' learning cannot rely on a voluntary approach or on the fluctuating financial circumstances of individual teachers and their families. Meanwhile, the government's investment in teacher development is designed to support either national reforms or school-level development. Important though these are, the result is a decline in the public funds available for individual teachers' development, unless they pay for their own. The idea of Individual Learning Accounts for employees across the workforce has been floated by a number of radical thinkers, including recently the Labour Party. They are advocated in the final chapter of this book as one element in the creation of a learning society. These accounts work on the old national insurance principle of the employer matching the contribution of the employee.

The point I want to make here is simply this: what better professional group among which to establish them first than teachers? They could be piloted on an entirely voluntary basis from the teachers' point of view. If a teacher chose to start one, the employer should be required to contribute. The accounts could, in addition, be given a boost through an initial contribution from government. The rate could be higher in areas of disadvantage as a way of rewarding teachers who choose to work in the country's most difficult schools.

Individual Learning Accounts among teachers would raise the status and profile of professional development and empower teachers to make their own decisions about how to develop their skills. They would make a significant contribution to ensuring that the professional growth which will be essential to the success of the education system in the future becomes, as it were, organic.

The Tight–Loose Profession

Teachers' work at present is defined largely by a set of assumed skills, a standard contract and the institution – the school – in which they work. There is only a loose sense of loyalty to a wider profession, though most teachers will also be members of one or other of the unions, if for no other reason than to insure themselves against injury or claims for damages.

The argument that I advance in this chapter, and even more so in the next, envisages a major diversification of the times and places in which teachers will work. They might work in a school, but increasingly schools will be open for longer hours, providing a much wider range of learning options. Teachers might work in an out-of-school study centre. They might provide individual tuition to pupils and their families.

It is possible to envisage still more radical options. Groups of teachers might work in the equivalent of consulting companies, and put together a portfolio of activities ranging from the design and development of courses and their delivery through distance learning techniques to school inspection and the provision of conferences. This has already begun to happen. It could be taken a stage further if, as part of restructuring, schools decided to put some of their provision out to tender or, to use the business jargon, to outsource it. A school might decide, for example, that while it wants to provide core subjects itself, it would welcome external involvement in some other subjects, such as history or technology. Teacher consultancies could bid to provide some or all of it for a five-year period. In a sense, this would only be an extension of what schools already do in, say, individual music tuition.

If the teaching profession diversifies or becomes looser in this or other ways – and a degree of diversification is both inevitable and desirable I think – it raises the question of what will hold the profession together. The current contract will not because, for many of the possible settings, it will be inappropriate. Even the salary arrangements, which are a great deal more flexible than they were five years ago, are unlikely to hold under the double pressure of diversification and the demand for more localised pay. Any government committed to improving education in disadvantaged areas, for example, would need to fund education institutions in those areas much better and allow them to pay higher salaries to attract the best teachers to the places where they are needed the most.

My argument, which should be obvious from all that I have written in this chapter, is that the glue that should hold all this together is commitment to a professional ethic. Relative to other professions, that unifying ethic has been weak in teaching. As we move towards a society in which learning increasingly takes centre stage, the need to define and gain commitment to a shared professional ethic has become overwhelming. Teachers need what Charles Handy calls 'a second citizenship', a sense of belonging not only to the place in which they work, but also to the profession as a whole. As Handy puts it: 'Modern organisations spend a lot of time working on that common cause (that second citizenship), establishing what it is, communicating it, reinforcing it. It can look like waffle, and it sometimes is. Properly done, it is not waffle but the glue of the enterprise.' The code of ethics should, of course, not be imposed, but instead emerge from professional ferment and debate. The outline of what it might include can, however, already be indicated.

It should include a commitment to the development of children and young people as self-confident learners who become increasingly independent; a commitment to foster learning and understanding of learning among parents and other adults; a commitment to refine and develop professional skills as an individual and to assist that process among other members of the profession; a commitment to the promotion of learning and education in the development of healthy communities and democratic society; and, finally, a commitment to the notion that learning has a part to play in the growth of global understanding and the sustenance of the planet.

If this sounds excessively ambitious, then reconsider for a moment the argument put in Chapter 1 of this book. Consider it this time in the terms of George Walker, Director-General of the International School in Geneva:

> Why should [students] worry about the 90 million annual increase in the world's population, the half million who sought asylum in Western Europe in 1991, the 19 million refugees supported today by the UN High Commission for Refugees, the 400 million unemployed in the 'South', the annual global per capita expenditure on the UN of $1.90 compared to an arms expenditure of $150, ozone depletion, drought, famine and poverty?
>
> There is, of course, one very obvious reason . . . Anyone . . . over the age of 50, given reasonably good luck, can expect life to go on much as it is now until we achieve our generous life expectancy. Those of you between 20 and 50 will need unusually good luck for that to happen, and anyone under 20 . . . has no chance at all. Something is going to have to change and this creates what a distinguished United States Ambassador to the UN in Geneva recently described as 'the culture of necessity'.

The culture of necessity: a chilling phrase. If the ethics of teachers do not promote world understanding, whose will? If teachers are not among the first to become, in effect, citizens of the world, who will?

It was thinking about these questions that led me to develop, for a conference of the International Confederation of Principals in Sydney in 1995, the notion of the educator's global paradox. I argued that:

> School leaders will need to see themselves increasingly as citizens of the world. If that sounds implausible, unrealistic or naive it is worth

noting that in the world financial markets and many areas of business it has already occurred. If the global marketplace is to operate within a framework of morality based on notions of democratic society and focused on solving the huge range of global challenges ahead, then the time left for schools and their leaders to catch up is limited. We need to develop and refine our own concept – as educators worldwide – of the global paradox . . . I would frame it thus:

> As the significance of education's smallest players – schools, teachers and learners – increases, adherence to a vision of global education and world citizenship will become ever more important.

The teaching profession cannot rebuild its sense of purpose and self-respect by hankering after the past. It needs – soon – to begin to think about the world that is coming and to prepare itself for the immense challenges ahead. The learning society cries out for the leadership of a learning profession.

9 · Creating a Learning Society 1: The Individual Learning Promise

Why, sometimes I've believed as many as six impossible things before breakfast.

Lewis Carroll

A Nation of Learners

This chapter begins by making three doubtful assumptions. Firstly, it assumes that, as a result of the reforms proposed in Chapter 5, there are no longer any failing schools. Instead, every school is either improving or successful, or both. Secondly, it assumes we are creating a Millennium Curriculum along the lines set out in Chapter 7. Thirdly, it assumes that, as a result of the reforms proposed in Chapter 8, we have a teaching profession which is bold, confident and ably supported by a range of teaching assistants and teaching associates.

Having made these three assumptions, it then asks this question: Would the successful implementation of those major reforms be sufficient to create the kind of education service which would meet the needs of the twenty-first century as set out in Chapter 1?

To this question, the answer must be negative, for however effective schools were and however skilled teachers were, the culture of this country, which has historically failed to give education sufficient priority, would still be inadequate. Moreover, true educational success depends not only on schools, but even more on parents. Yet, for a number of reasons, ranging from poverty and ignorance to the destabilising influences of a rapidly changing society, many parents and many families are not providing children with the upbringing they so desperately need. As a result, even the most effective schools in the world would find themselves swimming for much of the time against the flow of the social tide. In good schools, where they are not seeking to pass the buck, there is sometimes talk about the decline of parenting. Even parents talk about it. It not uncommon now for parents, especially of boys, to admit that they are unable to control their teenage children. I recently heard a devastating radio interview with a mother who – because she no longer knew what to do – wanted her fourteen-year-old boy to be 'locked up for his own good', as she put it.

Thus school improvement and a reconstruction of the teaching profession should be seen as necessary, but not sufficient, for the education revolution. There is another bridge to cross. Collectively, we will have to embark on the creation of a learning society.

It is inevitable now that the society of the twenty-first century will be 'a knowledge society' or 'an information society'. Indeed, it could be said to have already arrived. Nearly five million people in Britain alone have mobile telephones. The fax machine, the desk-top PC, the laptop computer and access to the Internet are spreading rapidly. Private and public sector organisations already know that the flow of knowledge and information is the key to success or failure. Politicians, too, recognise the importance of the information revolution. In his brilliant speech at Labour's 1995 conference, Tony Blair chose to give top billing to a deal he had done with British Telecom that would ensure that all schools, hospitals and libraries would be linked to the information superhighway under a Labour government. He also talked about providing laptops for every school child. Within days, Blairism was being described as 'laptop socialism'. Though the phrase was often used as a sneer, it is further evidence of this society's growing understanding that access to, and the flow of, information must be central concerns at every level.

Though an information society is a certainty, there remains enormous uncertainty about what benefits it will bring and to whom. For certain, only the well educated will be able to act effectively as citizens in an information society. If we continue to short-change a large minority of young people in educational terms, we will create something even worse than the disappointed, the disaffected and the disappeared. We will create the dispossessed: a group of people who live in our society but are not of it. By dint of our failure to educate them, they would be unable to act either as employees or as citizens or, increasingly, even as parents.

In an information society, the failure to provide education would be as serious as a failure to provide shelter, food and warmth. In many, perhaps most, cases those deprived of the one will in any case be deprived of some or all of the others too. The existence of a class of the dispossessed would be very dangerous. It would also be a gross injustice, an offence against humanity, made all the more repugnant by the fact that we have it within our power to choose to avoid it.

We can avoid it by setting out to create *a learning society*, in which everyone is able both to benefit from and to contribute to the flows of knowledge and information on which our future depends. In other words, a learning society is one in which every person is an active learner. Britain would cease to be a nation of shopkeepers and become instead a nation of learners. A learning society in this sense, unlike an information society, is not inevitable. We have to decide whether we want it and, if we do, we will have to create it. In short, it is a question of policy.

It might be argued that even attempting to create a learning society defined in this way is utopian nonsense. The idea of everyone learning, it could be argued, is absurd. I would admit that, as a goal, it is very ambitious. It is indeed a goal which has never been set for policy before, never mind achieved.

Critics, however, would need to provide a convincing alternative. The status quo is palpably inadequate. Among the tiger economies of the Far East, growth rates approach, and sometimes achieve, double figures, and education systems are far more cost-effective. Because education in those societies is highly prized, because parents as well as schools have high expectations of pupils, and because pupils work harder with more perseverance for longer, young people achieve higher standards at lower cost. In the Far East, class sizes of fifty are not unusual.

We can chase after them trying to do the same things they do better and better in an attempt to catch up. With our liberal traditions and diverse society (which contrast strongly with the authoritarian traditions of the Far East) and the many other pressing demands on public expenditure, it seems to me to be improbable that we could achieve it. It is probably also undesirable. If we attempt this, I predict that we will find ourselves left behind in what people are already beginning to call the Asian century.

Or we can attempt something different. We can try to encourage the development of a new, original learning culture which is consistent with western liberalism and social diversity and yet achieves standards of education which are much higher than those of the present or the past and which match those of the Pacific Rim. For this reason, I think the creation of a learning society is worth attempting. The rest of this chapter is an attempt to answer two questions: What policies would be required to make every person within the society an active learner? And, even if we could design policies that would achieve the goal, how could we possibly afford them?

Birth to Five

It has been known for many years that good-quality nursery provision builds a strong foundation for learning throughout school. Children who benefit from it are more likely to do well in national tests at seven and more likely to make good progress later in their school careers. The benefits are particularly noticeable among children from disadvantaged backgrounds. The American research on the Headstart programme also found that children with pre-school experience were less likely later in life to drop out of school or to engage in crime or drug abuse. It showed, in a dramatic finding, that for every dollar spent on pre-school education, the state would, in the long run, save seven dollars on dealing with the consequences of crime and disaffection. In spite of the strength of this evidence, and in spite of a continuing campaign among parents and teachers, the British government procrastinated throughout the 1980s. In its most blockheaded moments it even argued that nursery education was not important at all.

Then, finally – typically in a briefing to the *Daily Telegraph* – John Major admitted his conversion. This appeared to be a response to the report of the National Commission on Education, published in November of 1993. After eighteen months of further procrastination (and bickering behind the scenes), the government was ready to announce its proposals for nursery education. It seemed that, at last, a promise made by Margaret Thatcher when she was Education Secretary in the early 1970s was to be redeemed.

The truth was rather different. Certainly in the summer of 1995 the government promised to provide nursery education for every four-year-old whose parents wanted it, but not in the way Margaret Thatcher had envisaged a generation ago. It would do so, it said, by giving the parents of four-year-olds vouchers worth £1,100. These could be cashed in either at local authority nursery schools and nursery classes in primary schools, or at privately provided pre-school playgroups and other schemes.

The government found some new money, but most of the funding for the proposal was to be found by recycling money which is currently given to local authorities. Inevitably, this will threaten the existing nursery provision made by local authorities. Since most nursery education is provided by urban Labour authorities which cover the more disadvantaged areas of the country, this is disturbing for anyone who wants to promote education among disadvantaged groups. The government says that local authorities have nothing to worry about as long as the patterns of provision remain as they are now.

This is disingenuous, because it is obvious that patterns of provision will not remain the same. The voucher will go to *all* parents of four-year-olds, regardless of their wealth or whether they use local authority provision at present. As a result, the main beneficiaries will be those parents who currently pay for private pre-school provision and will now put their voucher towards it. In other words, the state will be funding many nursery places that were previously funded anyway by individual parents. Inevitably, therefore, less money will be available elsewhere in the system. This is what critics of voucher schemes call 'leakage' or 'dead weight', and it has often persuaded governments tempted by voucher options to turn their back on them. The problem is compounded by the fact that £1,100 barely covers half the cost of a place in a nursery class, whereas it might cover the cost of less educationally effective private child care, though one effect of the increased demand will no doubt be to force up prices here too.

A likely consequence of the voucher proposal is, therefore, that disadvantaged parents will lose out and parents who can currently afford to pay for pre-school provision will gain. In other words, it is regressive, the opposite of the Robin Hood approach, and the opposite of what is required to meet the educational challenges of the late 1990s.

There is no reason to be surprised about the use of the voucher idea. It has long fascinated the government's right-wing advisers, especially those gathered round No. 10 rather than the Secretary of State, Gillian Shephard. What is surprising is that the government has chosen to ignore the principles of its social security policy which, as Peter Lilley never tires of pointing out, is intended to reduce universal benefits and target social security expenditure at those who are most needy. The nursery vouchers scheme does precisely the opposite. It is a universal benefit whose only target is the short-term electoral gain of the Conservative Party.

Further undermining the credibility of the scheme is the absence of evidence that the supply of either places or teachers is there to meet the likely demand. The scheme appears to be a cheap pre-election stunt which sounds attractive, but will not have had time to fail before the election occurs. It seems to be a means of bribing the doubtful potential Tory voters in suburban and rural England. Far from achieving what Margaret Thatcher promised, it looks like a backward step. No wonder so few local authorities want to join the pilot phase. The government, yet again, has found itself depending on its three London musketeers – Westminster, Wandsworth and Kensington & Chelsea.

Meanwhile, Labour has made a commitment to provide nursery education not only for four-year-olds, but for three-year-olds too. It has established a group under MP Margaret Hodge to look at means of providing it, almost certainly through the local authorities. Its promise, however, is by no means straightforward either. It has not yet said how it will fund it and, privately, Labour's leaders are anxious about its implications for public expenditure. Before the 1992 election, Labour promised to redirect the resources currently spent on the Assisted Places Scheme to the provision of nursery education. In 1995, Tony Blair announced that this same pot would be used to reduce class sizes in infant schools. Both aims are worthy, but the same money cannot be spent twice. Given the determination of Labour's leaders, and especially Tony Blair and Gordon Brown, to avoid expenditure commitments which would enable them to be portrayed as a tax-and-spend party – as old Labour – the nursery education promise presents a demanding political challenge as well as an educational one.

Within the parameters of the nursery-education debate of the last generation, I doubt whether the problem is soluble. One of new Labour's virtues has been the courage it has shown in leaping beyond the parameters of traditional debates. As Tony Blair put it: 'new Labour attempts to go beyond the confines of the old left and the new right' (*Renewal*, October 1995). It will need to apply the same kind of radical thinking to the nursery-education debate. Firstly, government in the late 1990s will need to be much more ambitious than any of the ideas currently being debated. Nursery education for all three- and four-year-olds is not a radical idea. It is a 1970s promise which, as so often happens in British educational history, is about to be redeemed – shabbily and partially – a generation late. If the phrase 'too little, too late' ever applied anywhere, I doubt if it applied more appropriately than it does to the government's nursery-voucher scheme.

But it also applies to Labour's promise. Nursery education for all three- and four-year-olds would be not only expensive, but also inadequate. Increasingly, the research of people like David Farrington shows that the early months, never mind the early years, of a child's life are critical to their life chances. If this is the case, then if we are serious about the creation of a learning society, we need a policy not for nursery education, but for comprehensive birth-to-five education and health support. Ideally, before the end of the 1990s we would see the publication of a White Paper produced jointly by the Health and Education Departments entitled *The Foundation of Democracy: Education and the Family in the Twenty-first Century*.

What would it include? It would ensure that all prospective parents had access to both health and education advice while the mother was pregnant. The series of medical checks that almost all mothers attend would be part of a wider provision covering not only health during pregnancy, but also learning about a child's early learning. These sessions would build on provision made within compulsory schooling for learning about responsible parenting. Whereas, two generations ago, most prospective parents learnt parenting skills from the extended family, the combination of much greater social mobility and instability in the family as an institution now demands that alternative sources of this learning are made available.

Once the child is born, it is important that parents continue to learn how to educate it. Many health visitors already provide advice of this kind, but it needs to be made less haphazard and of higher status. Health visitors should have a wider brief, a new title and greater training and status. They might perhaps be linked to a primary school as well as to the health service.

Their work should be supported by the guarantee of educational advice provided through doctors' surgeries whenever the parents take the baby to be weighed and to have its health checked. These visits should also provide opportunities for parents to meet other parents. The loneliness of the long-distance parent, especially the single parent, needs to be broken down, and this is best done through informal networks. The role of the state agencies in these circumstances is not to provide, but to facilitate. There would, of course, also be a major role for the mass of voluntary organisations already operating in this field.

There is tremendous potential here for public–private partnership. Almost every parent, for example, has little option but to shop. Dragging round the supermarket through crowded aisles with a full trolley and a screaming child is, as any parent knows, one of the most soul-destroying experiences there is. If someone wanted to produce a half-hour documentary for Martians on late-twentieth-century life on earth, they would be remiss if they left it out. The combination of large numbers of people and extraordinary loneliness is excruciating.

Recently, and not before time, supermarkets have begun to acknowledge the damage their process has been doing. It has become hard to avoid the advertisements from Sainsbury's or Tesco telling us that children will be cared for and welcome. At last we have begun to move beyond the uncomfortable baby seat in the trolley. Over the same period of time, some leading educators have begun to recognise the potential of the supermarket as a route to parents. In 1989-90, Duncan Graham, the – extrovert first Chief Executive of the National Curriculum Council, produced leaflets on the National Curriculum, aimed at parents, to be distributed through these stores. It was a publicity stunt much mocked by the education establishment at the time, and whether or not it worked remains doubtful.

Nevertheless, the response to Graham's initiative was based more on a 'we know best' arrogance than on sensible reflection. I say this with all the more emphasis because I was as guilty of it as anyone else. A few years later, Tim Brighouse used the same means to promote his Birmingham Year of Literacy. This time we all welcomed the idea and it appeared more successful. Parents were now being asked to do something, rather than simply being informed. Tim Brighouse wanted them to 'bathe' their children in rhyme and song: to share 1,000 rhymes with them before they started school and to use the time in the supermarket to help enhance their language. He even argued that the catchy slogans and tunes churned out by advertisers provided a brilliant learning opportunity.

He is right, of course. Central to early learning of language is a sense of rhythm, rhyme and excitement. So, too, is having an avid listener close at hand. Surely there is potential for a private–public partnership which would link the incentive retail outlets have to attract parents of the young with a national strategy to educate, more effectively, children between birth and five. Could not supermarkets be persuaded to employ trainee nursery teachers and assistants to provide a range of educationally challenging opportunities rather than just a series of Disney cartoons? Supposing they employed, on a small stipend, students who were happy to spend some time supervising young children and some time working the till and learning the retail trade.

The key to creating the learning society is to seek the learning potential in everyday situations. The role of government should not, and could not, be to provide learning on the scale I am now envisaging. Instead, it must use its power and moral authority – as representative of the society as a whole – to encourage others to exploit the learning potential of these situations. In this way, we can invest a great deal more, as a society, in education than would ever be possible through traditional government funding.

Investment of this kind – social as well as financial – has immense potential for early learning, but its importance goes far beyond the under-fives. To create the learning society, we need to provide far greater learning opportunities for everyone. In the early 1980s, when Tony Benn was at the height of his influence, I heard him give a brilliant speech at Hackney Town Hall. In the front row, watching him mesmerised, was an elderly pensioner. Tony Benn characteristically struck up a rapport with him. During one of his cascading passages about education, he urged that 'the school leaving age should be raised to . . .' He paused, and looked warmly at his new pensioner friend, then continued: '. . . be raised to eighty-five.'

Through public–private partnership and the vision of the learning society, we can now make this happen, though perhaps not in the way the old socialist would himself have envisaged.

The Limits of School Improvement, the Potential of Re-engineering

Early learning is, in two senses, only the beginning. It has been neglected for a century and a half, and must now be given status and priority. Education in the compulsory school years – five to sixteen – by contrast has been a major political priority for at least a decade. It has been the subject of public debate for a generation now and of fierce controversy since the mid-1980s. It is, in short, news. And, as we have seen, progress has been made. The priority given to school improvement is important, it is shared by leading politicians in both parties, it has the air of a movement, of a revivalist religion among heads and teachers, and it is making a difference. More and more schools are adopting the lessons of research about how best to improve themselves. It is really beginning to work. The majority of schools are improving, some of them rapidly.

Yet, for all that, something is missing. It is, I think, a question of focus. The education reforms of the last decade have made the school the focus of change. Whereas, before the 1980s, the local authority was seen as the vehicle of change, now the school has taken centre stage. Its governing body has control of the budget and the powers of an employer. Heads are being trained better than ever before, though there is still much for them to learn. In return for this new autonomy, the school is held accountable through regular inspection, through published league tables and through the power of parents to express a preference. Under the present arrangements, the ultimate determinant of a school's success is whether it recruits pupils.

All this has contributed, crudely perhaps, to encouraging schools to improve themselves. It has certainly led to a growing acceptance of the view that school improvement is a task for schools. The impact of the policy has already been examined in Chapter 5. The question is, however, whether this focus on school improvement, though a necessary step forward, will ever be sufficient. In my view, it is deficient as a model of educational salvation in four respects. Firstly, even in improving schools, there are significant numbers of pupils who slip through the net of educational success. Secondly, though many improving schools work hard at relations with parents, the focus on *school* improvement casts the parents in the role of (perhaps supportive, perhaps not) bystander. It does not put them in the spotlight as co-educators. Put more bluntly, it lets them off the hook. Thirdly, the implicit assumption behind school improvement is that all the educational aspirations of every learner can be met within one school. As society becomes more diverse, the pace of change more rapid, the range of opportunities more bewildering and the extent of learning provision outside school more extensive, this assumption becomes increasingly questionable and perhaps even absurd. Fourthly, the school-improvement movement, with its important focus on making schools responsible, also fails to address sufficiently the overall inadequacy of British cultural attitudes to education and learning. It is not, and can never be, an alternative to changing the culture, though certainly it is a precondition of it.

For these four reasons, though it cannot be proved, I believe that the welcome shift of emphasis towards school improvement among politicians of all parties will not be sufficient to enable this western democracy of ours to achieve the levels of educational success that are being achieved in the countries of the Pacific Rim. There, the cultural value attached to education, much higher expectations, the extent of cultural homogeneity and of respect for authority combine to enable the success of formal, traditional approaches to education. It is tempting – and one sees this in the rhetoric of right-wingers here, such as Her Majesty's Chief Inspector, Chris Woodhead – to believe that our salvation lies in attempting to emulate these achievements. But in my view, though our children are evidently no less talented, we would not be able to create the cultural conditions that enable children in large classes in Korea, for example, to succeed where children here in much smaller classes fail. In any case, as I pointed out at the start of the chapter, it is questionable whether a liberal pluralist democracy such as ours would see the cultural attitudes of Korea, Singapore or Taiwan as desirable. It would involve sacrificing notions of liberty which stretch back at least to the eighteenth century, if not to the Magna Carta.

For these reasons, I believe we should not attempt to emulate the educational achievements of the Pacific Rim by adopting their approaches to education. To achieve standards comparable to or in advance of theirs, however, we do have to do something. If school improvement is unlikely to be sufficient, where do we turn? We will need to go beyond school reform. Finding our own path to educational success demands that we seek to reconstruct our entire approach to education. We need to redesign the whole process of learning. Doing so will not be easy, but it would certainly be easier than imposing Pacific Rim cultural attitudes, and would be more consistent with our liberal aspirations. It may make the last ten years of educational reform – which are said to have exhausted everyone involved – look like a tea party, but if we keep our eyes on the prize it should prove a great deal more rewarding.

In any case, the lessons of re-engineering in business will help us to find the way. In their fascinating study of the business revolution, *Re-engineering the Corporation* (Nicholas Brearley Publishing, 1995), Michael Hammer and James Champy provide an informal definition of re-engineering: 'Re-engineering a company means tossing aside old systems and starting over. It involves going back to the beginning and inventing a better way of doing work.' This, precisely, is the argument I have been making about educational reform: we need to reinvent the learning process. Most business books are bigger on hype than analysis, but in this case the coincidence inspired me to read on. Over the page they provide a more formal definition: 'Re-engineering is the fundamental re-thinking and radical redesign of business processes to achieve dramatic improvements in critical, contemporary measures of performance such as cost, quality, service and speed.' They argue that this definition has four key words. Firstly, 'fundamental': they are not interested in tinkering, they want to question the basic assumptions. In the case of education, they might argue, it is not sufficient to reform schools – the role of school itself in the learning process should be questioned too.

Secondly, 'radical': this demands, they argue, 'inventing completely new ways of accomplishing work. Re-engineering is about business re-invention – not business improvement, business enhancement, or business modification.' To take an educational parallel again, they might argue that the debate over whether all schools should be grant-maintained or part of local authorities is an issue of modification – the radical question is whether all learning should take place in school. Could we reinvent the learning process?

Thirdly, 'dramatic': they are not interested in 5 or 10 per cent improvements in performance, but in much more substantial shifts. They provide instances. IBM Credit, for example, 'slashed its seven-day turnaround [of credit applications] to four hours. It did so without an increase in head count.' Educational reform in the last decade has brought steady marginal improvements in performance as measured in GCSE or A Level achievement, but few would argue that the shifts are dramatic. Yet if we are to have the successful economy and society to which we aspire, dramatic shifts are what we require and we need to achieve them without massive injections of additional public money. In short, we need ambition.

Fourthly, 'processes': 'Most businesspeople,' they argue, 'are focused on tasks, on jobs, on people, on structures, but not on processes.' In a book about education, it should be added that this is not a question of process as opposed to product outcomes, it is a question of both. Hammer and Champy go on to argue that: 'Under the influence of Adam Smith's notion of breaking work into its simplest tasks ... modern companies and their managers focus on the individual tasks in this process ... and tend to lose sight of the larger objective ...' Just as, one might add, schools and school reform tend to focus on an aspect of education and lose sight of the learning process, particularly as it is experienced by individual learners. Is it sensible, for example, for secondary school pupils to charge round buildings, carrying their bags and jostling their peers as they dash from forty-five minutes of one subject to forty-five minutes of another? This bizarre dance governed by the insistent ringing of bells could not be created by anyone who started from the beginning – the learner – and focused on the learning process.

Hammer and Champy identify three sets of circumstances in which companies have embarked on re-engineering. 'First are companies in deep trouble. They have no choice ... Second are companies that are not yet in trouble, but whose management has the foresight to see trouble coming ... The third type of company ... are those that are in peak condition. They have no discernible difficulties ... but their managements are ambitious ... Companies in this third category see re-engineering as an opportunity to further their lead over their competitors.' This country's educational predicament means that it is certainly not in the third category. It is, at best, in the second and, at worst, somewhere between the second and the first. The time to begin re-engineering is certainly now.

In examining some case studies, Hammer and Champy draw out three further themes, each of which again is strikingly relevant to the prospects for education in this country. Firstly, they emphasise that, in each of their case studies, the decision-makers were deliberately ambitious. No doubt there were cynics who told them 'it's pie-in-the-sky', 'it'll never happen', 'it's not possible' – all phrases which are familiar in the education reform debate – but in each case they achieved their objectives, or something close to them. The same cynicism will certainly be thrown at anyone who attempts to promote re-engineering in education. Even now there are plenty of cynics who would like to turn the clock back to the mid-1970s when 'partnership' operated, decisions took forever, and over 40 per cent of all young people in this country left school with nothing to show for it but a bruised ego. Still they snipe away at proposals for change, still they find support among those who fear change or find it exhausting. Still they delude themselves that one day the calm mediocrity of the past will return. These are the people who say you cannot really measure quality in education – 'it's all relative' – and that therefore the concept of a failing school is meaningless. This nonsense is comforting to the cynics and to their fearful and tired allies. Unfortunately, it is not much help to the thousands of pupils whose life chances are being ruined by the failure of their school. No job? No self-esteem? No prospect of further learning? Don't worry, it's only relative.

All of which is a way of saying that any government that embarks on re-engineering in education will not succeed if it lacks courage or determination or ambition.

Secondly, Hammer and Champy point out that those who succeed in re-engineering deliberately broke traditional rules. Assumptions which had governed the way they worked for generations were deliberately challenged and overturned. Education in this country is full of traditional assumptions of this kind. The reforms of the last decade have questioned some of these, but not most of them. To its credit, the present government has listened carefully to researchers telling them that it takes seven years to turn a school round: and, having listened, it has ignored them. It has insisted on real progress within two years, and has been proved right in many cases. This is a good example of an assumption being challenged because politicians, aware of the bigger picture, simply cannot contemplate the researchers being right. Ultimately, it is an example of what politics is for.

Yet other, more fundamental assumptions remain completely unchallenged. Pupils in our schools, for example, are grouped according to their age, but why? Learning is assumed to take place best when groups of around thirty pupils are put in one room with one teacher, but why? In spite of the explosion of learning opportunities, we still assume that a school – any school – can provide all the learning opportunities that any young person might seek, but why? And we could extend the list almost endlessly. If we seek to re-engineer education, these and other assumptions will have to be questioned and perhaps overturned. Rules are there to be broken.

Thirdly, each of their case studies involved 'the creative use of information technology'. As they argue in relation to two of their cases: 'Ford's changes would have been impossible without modern information technology – which is likewise true for the re-engineering effort at IBM Credit. The new processes at both companies are not simply the old processes with new wrinkles. They are entirely new processes that could not exist without today's information technology.'

Although educators are increasingly conscious of the potential of information technology to contribute to education, so far its impact has been extremely limited. It has made a significant contribution to improving school management. It has become an attractive add-on to the curriculum. In this capacity, it has – the research suggests – helped to motivate young people and to encourage them to become more independent learners. All of this progress, however positive, remains peripheral. Most teachers are shy of, and anxious about, the use of information technology, not least because the government, while it has invested in hardware and sometimes software, has neglected to invest in teachers' ability to use either. Even among those teachers who have become confident in the use of the new technologies, few have used it to reinvent their approach to teaching and learning. Hammer and Champy point out that, in their case studies, 'The agent that enabled these companies to break their old rules and create new process models was modern information technology. Information technology acts as an enabler that allows organisations to do work in radically different ways.'

This has barely occurred anywhere in the educational firmament. This is partly a question of investment but, much more importantly, it results from a failure to ask the fundamental questions. If we assume the present learning process is adequate, it is hardly surprising that we have not sought to use information technology as an 'enabler' in its redesign.

In what follows, I have attempted to sketch – at least in outline – a re-engineering of education. In order to focus on the learning process and to ensure that old assumptions, explicit or implicit, are questioned, I have begun with the learner and her or his experience of learning. I make three new assumptions: one is that every learner matters. Though we have paid lip-service to this for years, the reality as opposed to the rhetoric is that we have consistently written off a significant minority of young people. The second is that a young person's learning depends upon both the parent and the school, and that therefore parental responsibility for a child's learning ought not to be seen as a helpful optional extra, but as essential and central. The third is that no school, however good, can provide all the learning opportunities that all its learners might need or want and we should stop pretending that this is the case. The result of these assumptions is what I have called the Individual Learning Promise.

The Individual Learning Promise

The Individual Learning Promise is a proposal which should be at the heart of the re-engineering process. It is a commitment to learning agreed between a school, a learner and the learner's parents. It is the key which could unlock a revolution. At present, parents have a statutory duty, under the 1944 Education Act, to ensure that their children turn up at school or are provided with an alternative education. Parents then have a number of rights in relation to choice of school, to make complaints and to receive information. These are set out in the Parents Charter. In other words, parents have many rights and few responsibilities.

This imbalance needs to be corrected. Parents should be expected to meet their child's teacher once every six months to discuss her/his progress and to plan the next steps. The question of whether this expectation is statutory or not is of relatively minor significance: what matters is that it happens. The discussion would result in an agreed plan for that child's education over the following six months. It would set out targets for the child's achievement, identify the necessary resources and specify the responsibilities of the school, those of any other educational agencies outside the school that might be involved and – crucially – those of the parent too. Increasingly, as the child got older, he/she would also become directly involved in the process of both agreeing and achieving the targets.

The notion of an ILP, if implemented nationally, would revolutionise the provision of education. It would ensure that parents took their responsibility for the education of their child seriously. It would recognise, in policy terms, the reality that the education of a child is not solely the responsibility of the school. It would recognise and establish the role of parent as co-educator. More dramatically, it would shift the focus from institutions to individuals and from teachers to learners. The notion of schools meeting the needs of individuals is not new, but it has been more evident in the rhetoric than in reality. Indeed, the phrase has often been linked with a series of soft and sometimes fashionable statements about education, such as the idea of 'pupils working at their own level' and 'achieving their full potential'.

The reality has been quite different. It has meant, sometimes, pupils sinking to their own level as expectations fall; it has meant perceiving 'mixed-ability teaching' as a means, not an end, and it has led to the widely held view that each child has a 'full potential' and that somehow teachers know what this is. This seems to me to deny one of the central characteristics of humanity, which is that people often surprise you. They turn out to have qualities, talents and skills that no one, not even they themselves, believed they had. When Christy Brown drew a letter 'A' in the ashes on the hearth at the age of four, he revealed a potential that, until then, only his mother had believed in. And his extraordinary talents as a writer were developed only because she was there looking for the unexpected when it happened. When I hear the phrase 'full potential' in relation to a child, I shudder at the arrogance it implies.

With an ILP in place, each school would be required to concentrate on the needs of each individual. Every six months, in discussion with the parents, they would need to review that child's work and carefully plan a programme for the next six months. The ILP would be a mechanism for ensuring that each pupil was given serious attention and had a learning programme based on evidence about her/his performance. That performance would be properly monitored, and targets for improvement regularly set and reviewed. The aim would be to ensure that each pupil was always improving against her or his previous best. In short, neither the school nor the parent could give up on the child. The tragedy of wasted talent which has been a central strand of British educational history could be brought to an end, for at its core has been a broadly shared assumption that – in reality as opposed to rhetoric – not every individual does matter and that some are bound to fail.

There will, no doubt, be many objections to the proposal for each child to have an Individual Learning Promise. Before looking at how it would work and seeking to deal with the objections, it is worth first examining a few examples of the impact it might make on children. First, consider the startling fact that up to a third of children at the end of primary school are either very poor readers or not readers at all. Consider, too, the fact that the evidence suggests that reading standards are at best static, and at worst falling significantly. No one seriously believes that all those who are poor readers at eleven are so because of an innate lack of ability or because of their home background. The evidence shows incontrovertibly that some primary schools are far more successful than others with a similar intake.

So how does it happen? A child falls behind in reading. The teacher either does not pick it up at first or does so and attempts to do something about it. The teacher, however, has many pressures on her, and may or may not crack the problem before the end of the year when, most likely, the pupil moves to another class. Though schools are much better at assessing and recording progress than they were, there is no guarantee that the next teacher will have examined the record of that pupil. I was once told, at a parents' evening, when my daughter appeared to have made little progress in mathematics in the autumn term, that it was because the new class teacher had underestimated her ability for the first month or two of the term. Surely there should have been records of what she had done the previous year, which presumably should have been consulted.

So the new teacher works on the child who has fallen behind again and, of course, some succeed at this stage. Others don't. And, as their peers move on, now able to access all sorts of other information through their literacy, our child is likely to be perceived as 'not very bright' and quite possibly a behaviour problem. At which point the focus may well shift from the cause to the symptoms. And the drift continues.

Take another child who succeeds reasonably early in grasping the mechanics of reading. This child, however, does not come from a house full of books and many of her classmates are struggling with reading. The busy teacher, naturally enough, leaves her reading to her, since those who cannot read need more attention than she does, and the teacher cannot do everything. And so this child never moves on from being a functional reader to one who wants to read for pleasure, who sees the potential of reading for unlocking the world of reality beyond the school and for exciting the imagination.

Take a third child, who moves to secondary school already behind in literacy terms. By the second year of secondary school, this boy is becoming increasingly troublesome in school, more likely to disrupt others and less likely than ever to hand work in on time. When finally he gets concentrated attention, it is within a behaviour and discipline frame of reference. Even now, the underlying literacy problem which caused the traumas may not be addressed. Indeed, by now, the literacy problem may be explained as resulting from the boy's failure to hand in work and concentrate in class. In many cases, only now is the parent summoned to the school to take part in decisions about the boy. The parent, having been at best tolerated or at worst patronised for several years, arrives at the school feeling, perhaps, ashamed and, very likely, defensive because the boy has got himself into trouble. How different the conversation might have been had there been serious discussions in the past in which the boy's educational difficulties had been explained and, hopefully, addressed.

And a fourth child. This one has been a good citizen of the primary school and revealed an interest in music. Prompted by who knows what – a friend, a television programme, a passing remark from a teacher – she has a passionate desire to learn the trombone. The school does not have a trombone teacher and the parent, sound and unimaginative, thinks the daughter's passion can only be a passing fad. The child buries the passion and when the possibility of learning the trombone arises at secondary school, all that is left is a residual resentment.

Four cases: each of them realistic. Each of the failures described would have been avoided had a system of Individual Learning Promises been in place.

Rethinking the Provision of Learning

The Individual Learning Promise could make a real difference only if we begin to think differently about how we provide learning opportunities for young people. Over the last century or so, the basic premise of policy has been that better education will result from providing more schooling. First, between 1870 and 1918, the state provided elementary schools for those not provided for by the Churches. Then, between 1918 and 1944, elementary education was extended to cover everyone to the age of fourteen. Between 1944 and now, secondary school for everyone was provided, first to age fifteen then, from 1972, to age sixteen.

The reforms of the late 1980s changed the power relations between central and local government, between local government and schools, and between teachers and parents. They prompted, or at least coincided with, a growing and welcome debate about the *quality* of schooling, but the underlying assumption that schooling and education were, practically speaking, synonymous, remained unchanged.

One of the few areas of agreement between the government and its most vociferous critics is that the reforms of the late 1980s brought market forces into the provision of education. This is certainly true, but it is in fact a very crude model of market forces. While parents, on behalf of their children, are entitled to express a preference for a particular school on the basis of more published information than ever before, this is a far cry from other sorts of market. It is as if a state monopoly in the provision of supermarkets were to be broken down by telling consumers that, from now on, they could choose which supermarket they shopped at; but once they had made their choice – assuming the supermarket was not over-subscribed and too full to be able to accept their custom – they would have to do all their shopping there.

Ironically, this extremely limited market model has been implemented during a time when, apparently unnoticed, there has been an enormous proliferation in the range of learning opportunities available to young people both in formal settings outside of school and at home. The employment of private tutors is booming. There are tremendous opportunities available to young people outside of school: from music, dance, every imaginable sport, brilliant museums and science parks and outward-bound-type adventure opportunities to theme parks, live music, film and other entertainment. The boundaries between education and entertainment have become difficult to identify, but the extension of opportunity is unmistakable.

The most striking feature of these opportunities, however, is their uneven distribution. In some parts of the country, they are more obviously available than in others. Most disturbing, though, is that these opportunities benefit only those young people whose parents have both the will and the means to exploit them. Most of them cost; some cost a great deal. Even where they are relatively cheap (and a young person can still learn pottery for two hours a week for £1 an hour in central Hackney), it still depends on a parent taking and collecting, researching and finding out and, above all, making the time available. Thus, for a large number of children, this proliferation of provision is an irrelevance since they have no access to it. Data on this area is sketchy – it is largely unresearched – but it can probably be conservatively concluded that over a third of young people benefit from it hardly at all.

If this is true, it is profoundly worrying. However much schools improve, inspiration and motivation to learn are much more likely to come to children who benefit from involvement in these out-of-school activities as well as formal schooling. Schools themselves are aware of this, and many make sterling efforts to open the eyes of children and parents to this extended vision of education. They provide museum visits, theatre visits, outings and a range of residential visits. They know the benefits in terms of building relationships as well as education. Teachers will often give up extraordinary amounts of time for such out-of-school activity because of their generosity and the professional satisfaction it brings. In Birmingham, the primary schools have signed up to a 'guarantee' to every parent which promises, among other things, to make a residential experience available to every child because they recognise its educational benefits.

This whole area – crucial to a young person's education – is notable for the absence of policy surrounding it. Occasionally it has been cut across by government writing unworkable guidelines on charging for school activities or by concerns about the safety of adventure centres, but these isolated debates have not resulted in policy-makers thinking coherently and systematically about learning out of school as a policy issue. Ironically, as a result of government neglect, it is an area of education where a true market operates: there is choice, price is fixed by demand, and those with limited resources or interest do not participate.

Much the same applies to learning at home. The opportunities to learn at home are multiplying rapidly through the availability of CD-ROMs such as the Microsoft *Encarta* Multimedia Encyclopedia, and access, increasingly, to the Internet. Also influencing this trend is the growth in the number of children whose parents are graduates – the children of the Robbins generation – and who are therefore more likely to have a confident attitude to learning, shelves full of books and the encouragement to study at home. The case of a mother who wanted her child to attend school half the time and learn at home the other half may be a straw in the wind. Although the importance of learning at home is universally recognised, here again there is an absence of policy to influence it. Of course, secondary schools and some primary schools set homework, but there is no government guidance on it. It is recognised that, for some young people, it is much more difficult actually to do any homework because of circumstances at home. In the past – and occasionally still in the present – some teachers concluded from this observation that, in order to be fair, it would be better not to set homework at all. This was classic levelling-down of the worst sort.

A more positive response is the effort increasing numbers of schools have made to ensure that the library or other study centres are open during lunch hour and/or after school. Some schools even open early in the morning: the growing number of breakfast clubs, especially in urban schools, is an encouraging sign. Even so, provision to encourage learning at home, or to make alternatives available, is patchy, and so far government has left this area to the vagaries of the market. Its official position is that policy on homework is a matter for each individual school.

David Blunkett, Opposition Education Spokesperson, has been more forthright. He has argued that a Labour government would establish minimum expectations for the amount of homework students of different ages should do each evening. Needless to say, his proposals created controversy. He was accused of creating excessive work for teachers, of interfering unnecessarily in the affairs of schools, and of entering into territory where a government could not possibly enforce its will. In fact, his announcement anticipates what will become a centrally important question of policy: learning at home is such an important part of educational success that governments are bound to take an increasing interest in it. In any case, the enforcement issue is a red herring. It is legitimate for government to attempt to influence popular expectations; it is for parents and governors at school level, not government, to check whether these expectations are being met by any given school.

The problem with David Blunkett's expectation is that, for a significant minority of children, doing homework is no easy matter. Home can be crowded, poor, unhappy, unstable or violent. If the expectation is to become a reality, then policy must make the necessary learning opportunities available to all. There will need to be learning centres, either in schools or elsewhere, available to every disadvantaged young person. It may also be necessary to find a means of making learning resources, particularly the extraordinary information sources that technology can already offer, available in every home.

Until now, education policy has been developed on the assumption that school is what matters and that everything else can be left to chance. If we are to create a true learning society, this will need to change. Policy-makers will need to begin to think of education as having three strands:

- learning at school;
- learning in organised out-of-school locations; and
- learning at home.

They will need to consider how to make all three strands of learning available to every young person, not just those whose parents have the will and the means. And they will need to think about the balance of provision among the three strands. At the moment, the emphasis is very much on the first in terms of focus and resources: but is this right? Is it even sensible? And what would the consequences of the introduction of a system of Individual Learning Promises be for this balance? The next section examines these questions.

A New Role for Schools

The new emphasis in the 1990s on school improvement has led to consideration of the length of the school day. John Patten, in one of a number of absurd decisions, suggested that the school performance tables should include information on how many hours of teaching a school provided. If he wanted a longer school day, why not legislate? After all, he did for almost everything else. Kenneth Baker suggested recently in an interview that he had considered legislating to extend the school day by 'one full period' per day in order to fit in the National Curriculum as he conceived it. Instead, John Patten asked the Office for Standards in Education to see if it could find any association between performance and the length of the school day. Not surprisingly, it could not: what matters overwhelmingly is the quality of the education provided, not the length of the day – within reason of course.

However, once we begin to think about the three strands of learning, it becomes obvious that, rather than lengthening the traditional school day, we should shorten it. This would then provide an opportunity to expand dramatically that range of formal after-school learning opportunities. These could, I think, be the key to motivating the disappointed and the disaffected and to attracting back to education the disappeared.

In short, we should be aiming to shorten the formal school day and lengthen the learning day. During the shorter formal school day, the school would have a clearly defined role. It would be required to guarantee every child the basics of the twenty-first century: literacy, numeracy and technological competence. Note the term 'guarantee'. It is not enough for the school to offer these things. There would be no question of giving up on a pupil or the pupil moving on to another class teacher and starting all over again. They would continue to be taught until they learnt. Unless this is the expectation, the term 'basics' is meaningless: if basics are those things which are essential to further learning, then it is a matter of definition that they be mastered before a pupil moves on to other things.

Especially in primary schools, teaching the basics must be the overriding goal. Secondary schools, by contrast, should be able to broaden and deepen children's understanding and expand their horizons. It *could* be argued that, currently, our education system is upside down: we expect primary schools to fire the imagination and secondary schools to get down to the serious business of education, when the reverse would be preferable. Of course it is not that simple: exciting the minds and imaginations of children is important at all levels, and motivating them to learn more is a central issue. Nevertheless, the mastery of the basics is so important that it cannot be left to the whim of the child: there is a need for them to have the disciplined environment which expects nothing other than – however unenthusiastic they appear to be – that they will succeed in learning to read well and in the central challenges of numeracy.

For this reason, I think this country should set itself a new national target, to be achieved by early in the next century: that every child should be able to read as well as the average eleven-year-old can now. In effect, this means demanding that every eleven-year-old reaches at least Level 4 of the National Curriculum, a level reached in 1995 by only 48 per cent of eleven-year-olds. The Literary Task Force established by David Blunkett in May 1996 will explore in depth whether and if so how this can be done. A similar target should be set for numeracy. Since the evidence suggests that as many as four out of ten eleven-year-olds in England's metropolitan areas have a reading age of nine or less when they transfer to secondary school, this would represent a considerable challenge. The first reaction of teachers and their leaders to such a challenge would probably be one of horror: it cannot be done, they might say. Alternatively, they might argue that it could only be done with the expenditure of additional sums of public money, beyond the means of any imaginable government.

Before responding in this way, however, it would be wise to give the proposal further consideration. First of all, international comparisons suggest that in mathematics, where comparisons are easiest to make (because cultural factors have least impact and the influence of home is less significant), eleven-year-olds in this country fall some distance behind continental and Far Eastern competitors. It is true that the methodology of each study can be questioned, but the results are so consistent across studies with different methodologies that we would be living in a fool's paradise if we chose to ignore the results. (One study, for example, showed that whereas Swiss eleven-year-olds do most simple calculations in their heads, British pupils are still counting on their fingers.) If we accept them, then we can either conclude that British eleven-year-olds are innately less good at mathematics than, say, Swiss or Korean eleven-year-olds – which seems improbable – or that there are things about our education system and/or culture which are in need of change.

This analysis can be confirmed by solely British evidence. Studies have demonstrated that some primary schools are much more effective than others with a similar intake. Secondary headteachers whose schools receive pupils from a number of different primary schools are confident that children from some of them will be able to read well and that some of those from others can be expected to struggle. If all primary schools were as effective as the best, we would meet the targets I have proposed.

Add to these facts the growing body of evidence that we have about how best to teach reading, and the conditions are in place for the necessary transformation. There are important analyses of reading approaches going on at the moment – one funded by the Teacher Training Agency, for example, and others by the Reading Recovery team at London's Institute of Education – which can make a major contribution to this understanding. Gillian Shephard's decision to establish twenty-five reading and numeracy study centres across the country could provide the infrastructure which translates research knowledge into real change in classrooms, though it will need to be associated with investment in teachers' skills since some are still hung up on failed ideologies and others, more numerous, are desperate to improve their ability to help children learn.

The power of the ambitious targets would be much greater than this, however. It would provide a real opportunity to generate excitement and enthusiasm across society; everyone would have a part to play in creating a truly literate and numerate nation. Parents, especially, could benefit from being better informed, both through schools and through the media, about the part they could play in raising reading standards. Perhaps primary teachers, instead of feeling beleaguered and isolated, as they have so often in the last decade, might begin to believe they were at the heart of a social transformation. And, of course, if that happened, then the funding for primary education that successive reports in the 1990s have said is necessary would be much more likely to be forthcoming.

While clearly vital, the basics should not be the only concern of schools. They would also be responsible for developing in children a profound understanding of the moral codes of a democratic and environmentally conscious society. This is a task for both primary and secondary schools. Here it is important to point out that the social organisation called 'school' is essential to the achievement of these goals. Those who would de-school entirely in the attempt to re-engineer miss this crucially important socialising function of school. We require school to ensure that children learn, for example, how to solve their disagreements without resorting to violence and to respect other points of view or religious beliefs. Amitai Etzioni, in *The Spirit of Community*, explains it this way:

> two requirements loom over all others, indeed are at the foundation of most other needs: to develop the basic personality traits that characterise effective individuals and to acquire core values ... both are sometimes referred to as 'developing character'. We mean by character the psychological muscles that allow a person to control impulses and defer gratification, which is essential for achievement, performance and moral conduct. The core values [include] hard work pays even in an unfair world; treat others with the same basic dignity with which you wish to be treated (or face the consequences); you feel better when you do what is right than when you evade your moral precepts.

There is a somewhat puritanical tone about these prescriptions, but maybe that is precisely the right tone for the situation we find ourselves in.

School would have another important role too. It would be the source of information, advice and guidance to parents and young people on their educational progress and on the extraordinary range of learning opportunities that would be available. What learning approaches would most suit that child? What combination of learning packages would best enable her or him to progress towards a given career or target? What could be accessed through home computer links and what should the balance be between learning out of school in formal settings and learning at school or at home? How should this balance vary as the child grows up?

An important aspect of this role would be the school's part in securing for pupils the resources necessary to achieve both their essential goals and their desired goals. In short, the school, and a specific member of staff within it, would need to act as a champion of the pupil. Though the analogy is by no means exact, this role is similar to that of a GP. A GP provides the first port of call for an individual's healthcare needs: he/she is also able to meet the bulk of patients' basic needs. However, when a need arises which the practice cannot meet, the GP's role changes. He/she offers advice and guidance; he/she also takes responsibility for identifying the necessary expertise and can command the resources necessary to make them available. The champion in the school would do the same for the child. He/she would be responsible for ensuring that a child's Individual Learning Promise became a reality.

This new role for the school, though no less important than the present role, represents a radical change and would, of course, have major implications for their staffing and organisation. These will be examined shortly, but it ought to be emphasised that it also makes the role of the school much more manageable. For a century or more, we have been piling more and more responsibilities on to schools and teachers: extra subjects, new exams and tests, integration of pupils with special needs, training prospective teachers, identification of child abuse, drugs education, alcohol education, a daily act of collective worship, self-management, and so the list goes on. No wonder they feel overburdened and under-respected, overworked and underpaid. It is one of the ironies of the last decade that the same government which has consistently criticised schools and teachers has also given them more and more responsibility. This double pressure, perhaps more than anything else, explains why the system has appeared, sometimes, to have reached breaking point. At some stage, the creaking system will collapse altogether unless the burdens which schools are currently being asked to carry are shared. Schools cannot do everything, and we should stop pretending they can. Teachers cannot do everything, and they should stop pretending they can. Instead, we need to give greater responsibilities to those who provide learning out of school and to parents, and make the role of schools both more manageable and more satisfying.

It is hard to imagine the precise consequences of this re-engineering for the staffing of a school. It would certainly need to be very differently staffed from schools at present and would imply the need for the changes along the lines of those set out in Chapter 8. Since much specialist learning, certainly at secondary level, would take place out of the formal school day, schools would require fewer teachers than at present on their core staff. Those they had would need much greater expertise in the processes of teaching and learning than at present. They would also need to be much better supported, both by administrators who would relieve teachers of the administrative chores, and by trained paraprofessionals who would be able to make a direct contribution to the learning process. This would be necessary to provide the flexibility that is so obviously lacking, especially in primary education, at present. In order to be able to vary group size, provide individual tuition in reading (for example), find time for detailed six-monthly consultations with all parents and command learning resources across a locality, a school would have to have more adults. Not all of these, however, need be trained teachers. Thus it is possible to imagine extensive use of paraprofessionals – for example in the management of small groups, in following up with individuals the themes of lessons taught to the whole class, and in helping to manage pupils who are involved in seeking or analysing information through computers.

Central to the whole re-engineering would be the idea of enabling teachers to do what they're good at: teaching. They should become experts in learning, pedagogical wizards or, in Tim Brighouse's evocative phrase, 'alchemists of the mind'. In other words, we should aim to free the frontline workers to do their job. Just as we want police on the beat and doctors to diagnose (rather than fill in forms), so we want teachers to teach. The goal should be that the additional support will enable them, individually and collectively, to teach better than ever before. This would demand that they took responsibility for continuously refining and updating their own teaching skills. The reconstruction of the profession set out in Chapter 8 would be crucial to enabling this to occur across the education service.

An additional group of staff who should be involved in school and in the provision of education, would be the teaching associates also discussed in Chapter 8. As was suggested, these associates might come from a range of backgrounds. They could be businesspeople, PhD students, retired people or adults working at home but keen to make a contribution to their community. Their roles in school would vary, too, from supporting teachers to accepting students on placements, from working with groups to supporting individuals, from providing expertise otherwise not available in school to acting as a mentor to a student at risk. Some may be paid, others would be volunteers. All should be trained. It is common to assert that it would be wrong to require those who volunteer for community service to be trained. In fact, the provision of training as a requirement may well make volunteering more attractive. It often affords generic skills and the status which would not otherwise be likely. In another field, the example of RELATE, the marriage guidance charity, is instructive. The skilled nature of the work demands that the volunteer counsellors be trained to a high degree. They make a contribution towards the cost of their training and they do the counselling – should they succeed in the training – because of the intrinsic interest of the work. RELATE became anxious at one stage that too many people undertook the training because of its merit and reputation and then did not become counsellors. They now require those who participate in the training to commit themselves to taking on a certain number of cases. There is no reason why a similar approach would not work with teaching associates.

The point is that the provision of worthwhile training would make the role more attractive, not less.

If the proposed re-engineering would alter the staffing of schools, it would also alter the way time was used within them. Rather than, as at present, dividing the day into a number of periods designed to 'cover' the National Curriculum (as in secondary schools) or plonking thirty children in one room with one teacher for a whole day (as in primary schools), we could imagine a much more flexible approach to the use of time and human resources. We might imagine a school designed around the objectives set in the ILPs of the pupils. In other words, the organisation would be built around the learning process, rather than the other way round.

If we entered such a school on any given day, we might find a variety of activities in progress. In a primary school, we would expect to find many of the pupils working on literacy. We might find the more able working on extensions of their literacy skills in a large group with a teacher; we might find those who were having more difficulty with reading being tutored in small groups by assistants or associates working under the direction of a teacher. We might find a range of individual pupils engaged in work with information technology. Some of them would be using integrated learning systems to supplement their learning of literacy and numeracy; others would be using the computer to seek information or to analyse and organise it. If we came at another time, we might find very large groups – up to fifty or even a hundred – listening to a teacher engaged in direct teaching: demonstrating a method, issuing instructions or supervising assessments. Certainly, once a week, if we entered the school, we would find teachers, through information technology, examining the progress made by the children they were responsible for and planning the next steps towards realising their Promises.

In a secondary school, we would find a similar range of activities and group sizes. There would, of course, be traditionally taught classes here as in the primary school, not least because the evidence shows that direct teaching can be remarkably effective. However, one might imagine a range of adults in the school, assisting with the learning process: a businessperson contributing to a small group undertaking a cost-benefit analysis; a chemistry PhD student, under a teacher's supervision, contributing to a science lesson on the structure of atoms and drawing on their own research to do so (thus, incidentally, enabling the teacher as well as the pupils to learn); or business and community mentors spending time counselling individual students.

Students might be in formal lessons, in small groups or in the large extended library or learning resources centre, drawing on a range of information sources accessed through both traditional and technological means. Some of them might be in touch, directly through the use of technology, with recognised experts in different fields – GPs, researchers, historians, lawyers, even estate agents – who have volunteered to be on the school's list of associates. Elsewhere, a group of over a hundred students might be in a traditional lecture relevant to many of them.

These are brief glimpses, begging many questions, I know. The point is to begin to visualise schools that are not as they have always been. If we are to create the future, we must attempt to imagine it first. It will almost certainly not turn out as we imagined it, but unless we attempt that leap we will continue to be restricted by the narrow idea of school that permeates society at present.

A further point needs making. A school is not a building. It is a community of people, of learners. I have taught fifty Zimbabwean pupils in a brick shell of a room on a building site. Others have taught students under the open sky. These are as much schools as those primary schools with the most solid-looking Victorian buildings in Britain's large cities. The school I am describing includes the pupils, the teachers, the parents, the support staff and those who are loosely associated with the organisation. The corollary is true, too. The building which houses the school during the shorter school day will also be available to house a range of activities during the rest of the twenty-four learning hours in the day, for the pupils, for adults and for community organisations. This is important to bear in mind throughout the next section, which considers learning out of school.

Organised Learning Out of School

Many thousands of children and young people participate in organised learning out of school. They take part in the Cubs and the Brownies, the Scouts and the Guides. They attend dance lessons and music lessons. They ride horses or go swimming. They join football clubs and brass bands. Some go to Sunday schools, others attend supplementary schools designed to promote learning among particular social groups, and there are those with private tutors, too. The children and young people who benefit from this range of activities only do so because their parents have both the will and the means. They seek out the opportunities, they commit the time and energy and, where it is required, they stump up the necessary cash.

These parents, the ones who make the effort and, if they have it, provide the funding, are good parents. The benefits their children reap are incalculable. These activities are educationally wonderful. They provide another social setting – different from school and from the family circle – in which to learn about getting on with people. They provide a wide range of activities in which young people can discover their talents and find success. They provide opportunities for praise, the key to so much progress. They broaden horizons and excite imaginations. And, since they are largely voluntary, they provide regular evidence of the benefits of choosing to learn and to achieve. All this is in addition to whatever discipline or set of skills are being taught. These kinds of opportunities are, therefore, extremely important to young people's all-round competence and profile of intelligences and to their self-esteem. Also, because in general they link enthusiastic expert teachers to enthusiastic pupils, they can be vital in developing among young people the motivation to learn and to continue learning for its own sake. In terms of addressing the stark issues of poor motivation set out in Chapter 3, they have a decisive role to play.

Yet provision at the moment is haphazard and depends upon the whim of individual parents. A crucial aspect of the growth and development of young people is simply left to chance. If we are to create the learning society, we will have to become much more systematic and thoughtful than this about learning out of school. The Individual Learning Promise is, as we have seen, part of the solution. It will provide a means of ensuring that the young person's wider learning needs and wants are identified. It will ensure that parents and teachers become aware of them. It will set out the responsibilities of both school and parents for ensuring that these learning needs are met, either from inside or from outside the school. In short, it solves the demand side of the problem. Children whose parents show no interest in broadening their horizons will, through the ILP, at last have the opportunities they have been denied.

The supply side of the problem has two aspects to it. Means have to be found of making available, on the ground, the opportunities that children and young people seek, especially for those whose parents are unable to afford them. It is, therefore, a funding issue as well as an organisational one. The second aspect of the problem is finding a means not only of providing these learning opportunities, but also of formally recognising them. This is a question of accreditation: out-of-school learning needs to be brought within a national framework of qualifications.

Part of the supply problem will be solved through the market mechanism. The ILP will bring more funding into out-of-school education, partly because it will release some money for out-of-school provision that is currently tied up in school provision, and partly because it will encourage those parents who can afford it to spend more than they do currently on their child's education. This will be true both of good parents, who will find the ILP pushes education up their list of spending priorities, and for less good parents, who, having spent little or nothing on their children's education in the past, now spend more. The ILP notion may, too, bring resources currently spent on private education into the state sector. By ensuring that an individual child's learning needs, including the opportunity to accelerate ahead where the motivation and ability is there, may well persuade parents who have chosen private education back into the state fold. It would, in any case, provide a bridge between the two sectors, since there would be no reason why a young person at a state school could not access some learning opportunities in the private sector.

The greater demand thus unlocked would encourage teachers and others to provide out-of-school learning opportunities. If, in the next few years, all parties continue to promote the development of specialist schools, then they will be contributing to the creation of the diverse resources necessary to make the proposals in this section work successfully. The availability of well-resourced school buildings and other community-learning locations would enable provision to be made at a relatively economic price. Private schools would no doubt be attracted, like other providers, into the growing market.

None of this, however, solves the problems of children from disadvantaged backgrounds whose parents – however good, however committed – could not afford even low-cost learning opportunities, although their learning development and success must surely be of the highest possible priority. For this reason, it is essential that government provides both an infrastructure and the necessary funding to encourage the development of a range of out-of-school learning opportunities in disadvantaged locations. Local government would have a crucial role in ensuring the provision of a colourful tapestry, especially in disadvantaged areas.

Fortunately, the thinking about how this could be provided has already been done. Furthermore, there is sufficient, properly evaluated experience to know that it would work. Over the last five years, especially (but not solely) in disadvantaged urban locations, we have seen the development of study-support centres, which are open in the evening or at weekends and are usually aimed at young people of secondary school age.

At this early stage in the development of the idea, there is a variety of practice. Some of the centres are based in community locations – libraries, shopping centres, youth clubs and so on – others are on school sites. Primary schools are rarely used for this purpose but, given that they are often a focus for the community, they might in many cases be an ideal location. Their opening hours vary, too. Some are open straight after school, others later in the evenings. Some are open at weekends and in the school holidays as well as on weekdays. A few are open at breakfast time. In choosing opening hours and location, the organisers are rightly taking careful account of the community they serve.

There is also a variety of types of provision in the centres. Some are homework clubs: a warm, welcoming place to do homework with the support and supervision of some adults. Others are more ambitious, providing supplementary tuition in a range of subjects and even providing a base from which to organise a range of other learning experiences including museum visits and residential opportunities. The evidence suggests these centres are successful. They are popular with both young people and their parents. More importantly, young people who attend them regularly achieve more educationally.

Realising the vision in this chapter demands that a national network of these study-support centres is created. There is no reason why any community so minded could not make provision for one. Increasingly, this is precisely what is happening. The government, however, should ensure that centres are provided in the 1,000 most disadvantaged locations in the country. In creating such centres, it should be ambitious. It should set out to provide the best learning centres in the most disadvantaged areas, partly as a matter of equity and partly to set an example for other communities to follow. They should be provided with the best information technology available, including access to the Internet, CD-ROMs and ISDN lines offering young people a huge range of sources of information and expertise. The centres should be well staffed by a combination of professionals and volunteers. An effective way of ensuring they were well staffed at low cost would be to train university students to work there for two sessions a week in return for spending three days being trained and a stipend of £1,000 per annum – a significant contribution, incidentally, to student support. In Israel, a scheme of this kind is already functioning well. One in every five Israeli university students contributes to school-level education. The employment of university students would not only enable a very favourable adult:pupil ratio because they would be economical to employ, but would also provide excellent role models for the users of the centres and help to change peer group attitudes to the importance of education.

In order to support the IT network, to provide the necessary students and to research and evaluate the development, it would make sense to link the study-support centres to a university. Any given university could be linked to around forty centres. The universities would maintain and continually update the IT network; they would recruit and organise the undergraduate students employed in the centres. They would evaluate the development and, above all, share best practice among their network of centres. They should be a source of information, inspiration and leadership to the whole network. Through the universities, the local networks would be linked nationally. The Prince's Trust put a proposal to the Millennium Commission to establish a national study-support network which has not yet been supported. If it were successful, it would provide the necessary catalyst.

It is important to recognise the benefits of this kind of development, not just to young people who attend them, but to the system as a whole. Of course, the whole country would benefit if more young people achieve more, but the potential significance of the centres is much greater. They would provide an opportunity for educational innovation, experimentation and development that is currently unavailable. We would have established part of the educational infrastructure which was not burdened with the weight of tradition. Furthermore, for a school, any major innovation in pedagogy always involves very high stakes. There is thus an understandable pressure for caution from both teachers and parents. If we had both schools and a national network of study centres, innovation could be more confidently contemplated without necessarily risking the entire education of a given group of young people. Moreover, innovation through the study-support network would not run into the conservatism of the vested interests which play such a major part in the politics of education. Thus, the study-support network would provide a relatively low-risk means of encouraging radical change.

This gain should not be underestimated. Indeed, it would not be an exaggeration to say that a major priority for the next five to ten years is the development of radically different approaches to teaching and learning. The public debate about pedagogy is shallow in the extreme. It focuses on whether children should be taught in whole classes or small groups. Important though this is, it is only one dimension of a multidimensional issue. We might describe the challenge as the invention of the new pedagogy. It will not be easy to develop this solely in schools, which are hidebound with tradition and still locked in debates of yesteryear. Study-support centres, on the other hand, could be created with the invention of the new pedagogy high on their agenda.

The strands of the new pedagogy can already be identified: making full use of the new understandings of the brain and its learning processes; understanding the importance of questions and dialogue in classrooms; the integration of information and communications technology into the heart of the educative process; encouraging independent learning;

improving the diagnosis of learning needs and their identification; further thought about how high expectations and high pupil self-esteem can be promoted simultaneously; and rethinking the praise:blame ratio in teaching and learning.

This last point is worth extending a little, even though it involves a slight digression. The praise:blame ratio has long been implicitly or otherwise at the heart of education. In a book entitled *The School Master*, published in 1570, Sir Roger Ascham asserted: 'I said . . . how, and why, young children were sooner allured by love, than driven by beating, to attain good learning.' To reinforce his case, he made the same point through a different metaphor: 'There is no such whetstone, to sharpen a good wit and encourage a will to learning, as is praise.' Recent evidence supports Sir Roger Ascham. Interestingly, for example, Research Machines' *Successmaker*, an integrated learning system designed to help people learn basic literacy and numeracy, has built into the software the assumption that, for every time the learner fails at something, he or she should succeed at least three times. Research into participation in voluntary adult education has shown that people whose success:fail or praise:blame ratio falls below 3:1 tend to drop out.

Yet schools, though in terms of rhetoric committed to encouragement, have often, through their processes, emphasised the blame not the praise: work handed back with only critical comments, letters home to parents about individuals only when they are in trouble with the school authorities, teachers pressured into overdoing the criticism of individuals and classes even though the theory tells them to do otherwise.

Praise, as Sir Roger Ascham pointed out, is crucial. This does not mean that teachers should praise shoddy work or poor behaviour. This simply leads to a lowering of standards and expectations which can ultimately be fatal, as we discovered in Hackney Downs School. It is this that makes the praise:blame ratio such a challenge pedagogically. Many good schools have demonstrated it can be done. They actively seek actions to praise, events and achievements to celebrate; they encourage teachers to hone and refine their questioning skills so that pupils at all levels are able to answer some. They reward and recognise a wide range of contributions and achievements so that there are repeated opportunities to shine. And they find means, sometimes of truly Biblical proportions, of forgiving sinners, wiping the slate clean, so that young people who have dug themselves into holes can climb out and start again.

In relation to study-support centres, the first point is this: attendance is voluntary – they need to attract young people to them: unless they get the praise:blame ratio right, no one will come. The second point is that they can provide the place to develop the praise:blame strategies that work. The universities to which they are networked can evaluate their practice, refine it and disseminate it. In relation to this aspect of the new pedagogy – and all its other aspects – the study-support centres can become the seedbed of innovation and change.

Someone will read this and think: sounds fine, the rhetoric's OK, but where would the money come from? No doubt any politician, however impressed with the idea, would ask that question, and rightly so. There is tremendous pressure on public funds, and taxes cannot easily be raised: public tolerance of high taxation levels has long since dissipated.

Fortunately, for this aspect of the proposals in this chapter, the detailed costings have been done. The capital cost of providing study-support centres of outstanding quality, and equipped with the best technology available, in 1,000 locations around Britain, would be under £150 million. The cost of running them, including the provision of a national co-ordinating centre to oversee implementation of the plans and to co-ordinate and represent them thereafter, would be around £60-70 million per annum. This amount would also, crucially, cover the cost of constantly updating the technology and of providing day study visits and an annual residential experience for all users.

This sum sounds large, but it ought to be put into perspective. It is less than half of 1 per cent of total government expenditure on education in this country. It is roughly the same as the running cost of twenty-five average-size comprehensive schools. It is equivalent to one-sixth of what the government spends annually on teachers' professional development. It is no more than a drop in the ocean. Yet the gains would be immense. It is hard to think of a social-policy proposal that would represent better value for money. The centres alone would be worth the money, but their value would be doubled or trebled because they would inspire and inform countless community initiatives along the same lines. In the next section, which examines learning at home, a proposal is made for finding even this small sum as part of a wider redistribution of social expenditure.

Learning at Home

Every household with teenage children knows all about learning at home. It is the focus of family arrangements; it is a challenge to parents who thought they knew a bit of maths, but 'it wasn't like this in the old days'; and it puts pressure on parents to turn off *Neighbours* and send their reluctant teenager upstairs to do their work.

It is important. Anthea Millett, Chief Executive of the Teacher Training Agency, suggests, on the basis of research evidence, that where a school has a rigorous, well-planned homework policy it is equivalent to adding a whole day to the school week; in other words, it represents a 20 per cent gain. Some schools argue that the effect is even greater: the equivalent of a fourth term in the school year. It has become even more important with the rise of coursework assessment. This is sometimes associated with the introduction of GCSE in 1988, though its origins go back much further. Even in O Levels – still remembered with longing by traditionalists – there were increasing numbers of coursework-based examinations. I taught a history O Level in the early 1980s, for example, which was 50 per cent coursework-based. In that O Level, as in other coursework assessments, working at home was crucial. The better projects, which were first-rate, simply could not have been completed to that standard in class time alone. Classes became, in effect, consultation sessions among pupils and between pupils and teachers on work done at home.

In this context, the importance of home circumstances can hardly be exaggerated. A pupil who is able to work hard at home, who has the space, the resources and the encouragement to study, will achieve far more. In the private sector, even at primary and preparatory level, this is appreciated. Eight-year-olds bob home and do thirty minutes to an hour of homework four nights a week. In the state sector, practice is more varied. While coursework is much favoured at GCSE level and beyond, in the lower part of secondary school homework practices are patchy and, at primary level, homework is often not set at all. In a report published in 1995, OFSTED had this to say:

> Most schools set homework. Where staff, pupils and parents treat it seriously, it has the potential to raise standards ... The majority of secondary schools and a quarter of primary schools ... had a policy statement [on homework, but] there was little systematic and regular monitoring of the implementation of homework policies ... and consequently there was little knowledge of their impact or effectiveness.

This hardly amounts to a ringing endorsement.

Schools in disadvantaged circumstances often point out in defence of their not setting homework that many pupils' home circumstances would prevent them from doing it anyway. On the face of it, this sounds plausible, but it is in fact a profoundly damaging attitude. In effect, it is saying that these pupils, compared to their peers, are disadvantaged already; why don't we disadvantage them some more?

If there are pupils whose home circumstances prevent them from doing homework – and there are – the answer is not to stop homework, but to find policy solutions. The provision of study-support centres is an example of a possible solution. As mentioned above, some schools have taken the initiative themselves. They have staffed breakfast clubs, lunchtime homework sessions and after-school provision. Instead of bowing before the social pressures that undoubtedly affect many students, these schools are rising to the challenge they present. The heroism of some schools in the face of enormous disadvantage is magnificent and ought to be celebrated.

At the moment, however, from the point of view of the individual pupil, this is a lottery: will he or she attend a school that is heroic or a school that has given up or one that is in between? If we are serious about creating a learning society, we will have to do better than this. The network of study-support centres proposed in the last section would be a major step forward, but I doubt whether it would be enough. I think that, in addition to study-support centres, we need to think about equipping homes with educational resources.

Technology has developed to a stage where this has become a realistic proposition. We are just waiting for realistic politics to catch up. Consider the fact that, within the foreseeable future, every home in this country will be linked to the fibre-optic network. Consider also the fact that the price of software and hardware is falling steadily and, in relative terms, rapidly. Finally, consider the fact that the *Encyclopedia Britannica* is now available on CD-ROM. Suddenly it becomes possible to imagine a conversation between teacher and pupil that goes like this:

Pupil to teacher: 'I couldn't do the homework, sir. We don't have any books at home.'

Teacher to pupil: 'Yes you do, you've got the Encyclopedia Britannica.'

Not long afterwards, the teacher's reply can be bolder still: 'Yes you do, you've got the Library of Congress.'

These developments make learning at home potentially more productive than ever before. Through the ILP mechanism, parents will be encouraged to equip their homes as places of learning. There will, however, still be significant numbers of parents who either won't or can't do so.

Those who could, but decide not to, would still come under pressure through the ILP process, but there is no point deceiving ourselves. There will still be parents in the next millennium who don't care about their children; there will still be parents who beat and abuse their children; and there will still be parents who create such emotional trauma in the home that study becomes virtually impossible. Education policy alone cannot solve these problems, though it can help to mitigate them. For example, a mentor from business or the community should be appointed for every child whose parents take no interest in their ILP, and family mentors for parents who want to help but are not sure how to. Schemes along these lines are already springing up in places and making a difference, though of course no amount of policy can fully replace the benefits of a loving, supportive home.

Fortunately, parents who are actively destructive are a tiny minority. There is a much bigger group of parents who want to help and support their children, but do not have the means to. These parents will attend the ILP meetings with the best will in the world; they will want to do what they can for their children. The limits of their income will, however, prevent them from providing the kinds of educational resources that a home should have. To meet this circumstance, the possibility of introducing a Pupil Learning Resources Credit (PLRC) should be considered. These would be credits, held by the school, which could be spent only on learning resources for the home to benefit the particular child concerned: books, CD-ROMs, other educational software and, sometimes perhaps, extra individual tuition. The credits could be spent only after a formal agreement between the parent and teacher about what should be purchased. These agreements would be part of the ILP process. The credits would empower the parent in the ILP discussions and sharpen the quality of debate.

The PLRCs should be a targeted, not universal, benefit. They should be aimed at the parents of the poorest four million children. The level of the credit should be related to parents' income. In case, even with these restrictions, it sounds prohibitively expensive, consider the figures. Credits worth £250 per annum per child could be paid to the parents of the poorest four million children at a cost of £1 billion. Child benefit costs over £6 billion per year. If it were taxed – not phased out, but taxed at the standard rate – enough money would be raised to pay for that number of credits and for the study-support centres described in the last section. In fact, providing credits for four million children is erring very much on the generous side. Help to the poorest two million would make a major impact and cost only £500 million. More fortunate parents would be expected to spend at least that amount on their child each year and could, if they chose, do so by paying that sum to the school to be held as a credit for their child. In other words, through the expenditure of £1 billion of public money, government could unlock two or three times that amount for spending directly on the learning needs of children and young people. If a government did not want to tamper with child benefit it is worth bearing in mind, as Claus Moser has pointed out, that if we raised the percentage of national income we spend on education to the level of the mid-1970s it would raise not

£1 billion but £3 billion. If this additional expenditure were linked to a progressive redistribution of overall education expenditure in favour of schools in disadvantaged areas it would help to transform standards.

The learning society cannot be funded by government alone. Government needs constantly to seek means of targeting public money in order to unlock private funds. How a democratic society spends its public money is a statement of its priorities. Retargeting under £1 billion pounds in the way I have described would be a powerful statement from ours that we were serious about creating a learning society. We would be saying loudly and clearly that learning in a learning society – as I argued above – is as important as food, clothing and shelter.

Guaranteeing Standards

Woolly, sentimental, child-centred nonsense: I can hear the right-wing critique of what I have described already. It is a serious point. Child-centred education in the past had its positive side, but overall, and without doubt, it failed.

Some of the differences between that 1970s philosophy and what I have described in this chapter are almost too obvious to need pointing out. I will, nevertheless, identify the most important one: the Individual Learning Promise would ensure that each individual was indeed engaged in trying always to improve against previous best performance. Both parent and teacher would be signed up to it. In any case, child-centred education in the past was, in fact, nothing of the sort. It insisted, for social-engineering reasons, that all children should be grouped according to their age and taught in mixed-ability groups. In this sense, what I have proposed is much more child-centred than the child-centred approaches of the past ever were.

But all this is to recap. There is a new and important point that needs to be made explicit, which is that, in another sense, nothing could be less child-centred than what I have proposed. At the core of the old child-centred approach was the notion that the child shaped her or his own curriculum: the child learnt by discovery. The metaphors involved flowers unfolding and learning as a journey, not a destination, with the child rather than the teacher (and certainly not the state) choosing the route. As a result, some children learnt – they travelled far – others, lacking motivation or inspiration, barely travelled at all.

What I am proposing explicitly rejects all of that. The basics taught in the formal school day would be laid down in the statutory National Curriculum, described in Chapter 7, whose standards were based on comparisons with the most advanced education systems in the world. Children's progress in them would be assessed regularly; the results of these assessments would be reported to parents through the ILP meetings; a school's performance as a whole in these basics would form a major element of its public accountability.

Improvement against previous best would be measured against these nationally established standards. The rigour absolutely essential to any successful education system would thus be integral to the whole approach. Furthermore, although the proposals here offer far more choice to parents and pupils than any existing or previous education system, the basics – the National Curriculum -would be compulsory. It would be the non-negotiable core: the learning that this society maintains is essential for anyone who is to become a citizen in the fullest sense of the term. This combination of a compulsory curriculum, regular national assessment and individual targets for every learner makes these proposals not only infinitely more rigorous than the old child-centredness, but also much more rigorous than present arrangements.

This leaves open an important question about how to accredit the learning that young people do, whether in the basics of the National Curriculum or in that wide range of other activity in which they will become progressively more involved. The portfolio idea – piloted in education in the 1980s under the title 'Records of Achievement' – has much to commend it. Indeed, the concept has gained currency across the business sector as a way of demonstrating a person's worth.

Records of Achievement in their experimental phase involved much more than just a record of marks gained. They covered the full range of achievement, including arts, music, sport and contribution to the school community. They also involved an element of self-assessment by the learner and included examples of the learner's work. Sir Ron Dearing's 1996 report on examinations for the sixteen-to-nineteen age group makes a welcome proposal to revive and renew Records of Achievement.

A number of developments since the 1980s ought to make it possible to build upon this experience a twenty-first-century accreditation framework. One step forward is the possibility of using information technology not only to mark assessments, but also to gather and analyse results of individuals and groups. In 1994, I had a fascinating conversation about this with a senior official at the then Department for Education. He had seen what he considered to be very imaginative use of IT in the assessment of five-year-olds in Solihull. I described to him some research we were then engaged in at Keele University which involved producing educationally sound activities – based on the National Curriculum – which young people could do using computers. There are, of course, thousands of pieces of software of this kind. What made ours different was that the computer would assess the student's work in accordance with the National Curriculum guidelines.

This, I pointed out, had important implications for the fierce dispute about national testing. After all, the heart of that debate was that tests which had educational credibility and were valid and reliable tended to require a lot of marking and, therefore, excessive workload. On the other hand, short, sharp tests which generated little workload tended to be educationally questionable. The teaching profession was split on whether it wanted sound tests or little workload. It could unite only on the impossible dream of having no tests and no workload. This, of course, would not be acceptable either to government or to the public. With IT-based assessment, such as we were developing at Keele and such as my friend the official had seen in Solihull, the dilemma disappeared. Educationally valid tests which create no workload have been developed and could form the basis of the national assessment system.

'It would, of course, be very expensive to do,' commented the official, resorting to the last bastion of the hard-pressed civil servant.

'Yes,' I said, 'but less expensive by far than the £30 million per annum you have already committed to provide external markers for this year's tests.'

He shook his head ruefully: he realised it was true. With information technology, as long as we use it to re-engineer, not simply to do the same tasks slightly differently, we can radically improve assessment and indeed education in general. Imagine a situation where, at any moment, a parent could go to a school and the headteacher could call up on the computer the child's record across all aspects of education so that it provided a sound basis for informed discussion. Why imagine it? It already happens in some schools.

Imagine, too, that instead of rigidly assessing pupils at given ages, we assess them – as proposed in Chapter 7 – when we think they are ready. Without this step, it would be hard to envisage the ILP notion functioning effectively. It is central to the whole idea that it enables the talented, hard-working pupil to race ahead and to reach for the sky. The danger with the model comes if the teacher has low expectations and allows the student to drift along. The combination of the ILP and rigorous national assessment would prevent this from occurring. Again, some schools are already working in this direction. In Birmingham in 1995, some eleven-year-olds who had progressed rapidly in maths successfully took GCSE, designed for sixteen-year-olds.

In the computerised world we are moving into, regular – perhaps weekly, certainly monthly – updating of pupils' assessment records in the basics and other areas of learning should certainly be possible. Then imagine that, for public accountability purposes, but for no other, we maintained public reporting of results at the ages of seven, eleven and fourteen. Imagine too that, again for this sole purpose, we have national assessments in the basics of literacy and numeracy, as proposed in Chapter 7. These measures would ensure that we had a clear picture of national standards and how they were changing over time. They would also enable us to analyse and compare the results of different schools, different localities and different groups of pupils within the population as a whole.

The national tests would clearly need to be marked according to national standards. To ensure their objectivity, no teacher should be involved in marking the tests of pupils from her or his own school. These, however, would be relatively short, standardised tests that would virtually mark themselves. Their workload implications, and indeed their cost, would be negligible.

Much more important would be to find an effective means of ensuring the consistency and validity of the assessments pupils were taking as they progressed. Here I think the schools of the future should take their cue from the universities of the present. Assessments in a given field, say history, should be undertaken by the teachers of the pupils being assessed, but samples of them should be checked by external examiners – teachers from other schools – just as happens in universities. This arrangement would not only provide a check on the school's standards, it would also help to spread awareness of standards among schools. It would be a highly effective means of promoting the professional development of teachers.

However, to give the assessment framework greater public credibility than the external examiner system would do, the national inspection system should have a double function. In addition to reporting in general on the quality of a given school, it should also have the specific task of examining the school's policy and practice in relation to assessment of pupils' work. If these are found to be sound, then the school would become an approved assessment centre and left, broadly speaking, to get on with the job, subject only to the possibility of random inspection, similar to those of restaurants by public health inspectors. If the school's assessment approach was flawed, then an external consultant would be appointed to check assessments over a period while the flaws were corrected. It is possible to imagine that a school's assessment policy was either so corrupt or so inadequate that it should be discontinued. Government should certainly have the power to take this step *in extremis* but, given the overall education policy described here, any such profound flaw would be very rare indeed, since a slide in quality ought to be detected long before this state of affairs was reached.

One of the features of the education service I have described is that a great deal of learning would take place outside the formal school day. The assessment framework described so far covers only learning in school. The first point to make in relation to learning elsewhere is that the school would retain general responsibility for pupils' well-being and educational progress, even when much of their learning takes place elsewhere. The school, after all, would have a statutory responsibility for each pupil's ILP. The school would thus have a first-line responsibility – along with parents – for seeing that whatever learning a pupil was engaged in, whether in school, out of school or at home, was of appropriate quality. However, where a pupil was undertaking, say, music with a private tutor or a history module provided by a museum, the school could not be expected to assess their work. This would be a task for the provider of that learning experience. A national framework of assessment of learning out of school would therefore be necessary. In Birmingham, important work is currently being undertaken to develop the idea of a University of the First Age (UFA), which would have responsibility for encouraging the development of out-of-school learning opportunities and for finding means of accrediting them. This is precisely what is required: the exact features will no doubt emerge over time, but they would certainly involve any provider of education in being evaluated before becoming registered with the UFA and therefore being publicly declared fit to assess. They would also, no doubt, involve random inspection of providers and, of course, a requirement for them to report regularly on individuals' progress to the appropriate school. This would be necessary to ensure that the pupil's record of progress was up to date and complete.

All of this seems a long way from the education system at present. When I sketched out this vision at the North of England Conference in Gateshead in January 1996, the reactions were mixed. Both parents' and teachers' leaders described it as 'fantasy' or 'fairyland'. Paradoxically, the other chief criticism was that much of it was happening already. Both lines can't be true. Perhaps it is dreaming. Dreaming is, in my view, the first step to radical change. I would argue that it can be done if we want to do it. This is not simply an assertion: much of what I have described is in pockets or beginning to happen. I have shown how it can be done at reasonable cost. Two things are still missing: the drive to achieve it across society and the key at micro-level to make it happen. The growing concern of politicians, especially Tony Blair, about the need for radical improvement in the country's educational performance will provide the former: the Individual Learning Promise the latter. It can happen.

Lifetime Learning

This book is chiefly about children, young people and their learning, but it is also about the creation of a learning society. In this section, I want to indicate how the school reforms described in the earlier parts of this chapter might articulate with education in adult life.

It is essential that the notion of a school-leaving age should become a quaint anachronism: it has no relevance to a society in which everyone learns. Already 70 per cent of young people stay on in full-time education after the age of sixteen, and over 80 per cent are in full- or part-time education. Over 30 per cent of each age cohort now proceeds to higher education. Though, in 1996, these statistics have stabilised after a decade of rapid growth, they are likely to move upwards again, particularly if Ron Dearing, in his review of higher education, is able to solve the problems of funding.

Certainly if the learning society is to become a reality it is essential that all young people between the ages of sixteen and twenty-one are in full-time or part-time education. If they enter the employment market, their employers should certainly be providing time and investing resources in their continued education. For most of this century, British employers have had a dismal track record in terms of investing in the education of their employees. In the last decade this has begun to change, though there is still a long way to go. The recession of the early 1990s was the first in which business disproportionately protected, rather than cut, expenditure on training. In 1996, at the North of England Conference, Sir Geoffrey Holland, former Permanent Secretary at both the Employment and Education Departments, pointed out that the amount business spent on education and training was £35 billion; since government spends only £27 billion this is a startling statistic. Less than half of what this society invests in education comes from government: I doubt whether psychologically we have come to terms with this changed state of affairs or with the fact that, over time, the proportion of expenditure on education spent by government will inevitably fall further.

On the whole, big business is rather better at providing for education of employees than small business. This is hardly surprising, given the multiple pressures on small businesses in recent years. Ron Dearing's review of higher education may need to reflect not just on what we traditionally think of as higher education, but also on the wider question of the funding of education after the age of eighteen. If, as seems likely, we move towards some form of graduate tax, for example, then we will have established a principle with wider acceptability. We would be saying it is acceptable, in effect, for an individual to borrow money for education now, to be paid back through higher taxation rates in the future. If we had sufficiently compelling evidence of the value, and guarantees of the quality, of some education and training outside university, why not apply the principle to those cases too? This approach might help people with good employment prospects to fund substantial structured education early in their careers: after all, a higher rate of tax for many years to come is only worth taking on if it buys the prospect of substantially better earnings – albeit with an element of risk – for many years to come.

It is not an approach that would fund continuous learning opportunities for a person in employment. Nor would it pay for the short course or the occasional inspirational conference. Some of these opportunities will no doubt remain funded as they are now: through the training budget of the employer and a process of more or less *ad hoc* negotiation with the employee. Increasingly, too, private individuals will simply choose to spend disposable income on education, perhaps because it enhances their competence or opportunities in employment, or because they find it intrinsically worthwhile. The typical student at the Institute of Education, a postgraduate college of the University of London, is a thirty-seven-year-old woman who works full- or part-time and is paying for her own Diploma or MA course. A similar pattern can be found across large swathes of postgraduate education and, as the increased number of graduates emerges following the expansion of higher education in the last decade, growing numbers can be expected to opt for learning on these grounds.

To promote active learning among those with less motivation or less financial security, to support learning across society and to encourage employers to take their responsibilities seriously, the idea of Individual Learning Accounts has been proposed by a range of people and organisations, including Sir Geoffrey Holland and, more recently, the Labour Party. These would work on the original national insurance principle. If the employee chose to make a monthly contribution to her or his individual learning account, the employer would be required to pay in a matching amount. The total would then be available to spend on education and training. Labour's trade union allies were said, in the press, to be dismayed that Labour had chosen to support this approach and to drop the idea of a training levy under which employers who did not spend a certain percentage on training would be taxed. This seems an odd response to me. The Individual Learning Account empowers employees and gives them the opportunity to set their own training agenda in a way that the old levy would never do. It also provides a classic opportunity for trade unions to use their representational skills to publicise the schemes and to pressurise employers to take them seriously.

The idea of every adult building up an Individual Learning Account could surely make a powerful contribution to the creation of a learning society. People would not only be in a position to think about constantly, and realise from time to time, their learning needs; they would also have some means of funding further learning – if necessary – during the periods of unemployment which many people, however highly skilled, will find they have to go through. Much detail needs to be worked out. What are the limits on where or how the ILA is spent? Presumably a one-day conference on a theme related to a person's work could count, and a day out at Alton Towers would not? Or could it only be spent on accredited courses? And, in any case, how would all that be policed?

These are practical details which are being solved by careful thought and experimentation. More fundamental is whether the state should contribute financially, or whether it should simply legislate to bring a scheme into being. Beyond that, there is the question of whether the scheme should be statutory at all. Some would no doubt argue that if it is such a good idea it will happen voluntarily. In my view, there should be a statutory basis for ILAs. Good employers who choose to invest in training are not the problem. It is the reluctant ones who need encouragement, who need, like everyone else, a combination of pressure and support. The statutory obligation should be on the employer to match an employee's contribution if the employee chooses to make one. Furthermore, if a learning society is to be created, then government must play a part in changing cultural attitudes. To do so, some major legislative steps, which are both practical and symbolic, are essential. This would be a prime example.

Whether or not central government should contribute is another issue. It could do so by making tax concessions to both employers and employees. It might also consider providing incentives to employees to build up their accounts by offering to make a contribution after two or three years where people have kept up their payments. It seems clear that, given the constraints on public expenditure, any central government contribution would be limited and therefore would require careful targeting.

Plans for guaranteed training for all unemployed people should be linked coherently to the idea of Individual Learning Accounts. Clearly, the notion of a learning society would break down if there was a substantial minority who were effectively abandoned to unemployment. If the education reform programmes described in this chapter had been implemented and proved successful – two big ifs – there should be many fewer people emerging into adulthood with no skills and a sense only of powerlessness and dispossession. Nevertheless, certainly in the short term and, to a more limited extent, even in the longer term, there will be some. The critical issue, then, is the relationship between the benefits system and the education and training system. Both the incentives to train and the supply of opportunities need to be in place to make it happen. Too often in the last decade, either the incentives have been undermined by a poverty trap, or the supply has been uneven and of doubtful quality. The experience of that decade should have provided us with the lessons we need to do better in future.

Though, increasingly, politicians of all parties – at least superficially – take lifetime learning seriously, occasionally a policy issue reveals how far there is still to go to change thinking. Take, for example, Labour's advocacy of a minimum wage. Ever since it became part of the political agenda, the minimum wage has been at the centre of not one controversy, but two. The first is between Blair's new Labour leadership on the one hand and the trade unions on the other. It is about the level at which the minimum wage should be fixed. Some major trade unions, including the Transport and General Workers Union, believe, absurdly, that it should have been fixed in 1995 at slightly over £4.00, even though the date of the election was unknown and the rate of inflation unpredictable. New Labour argues, by contrast, that it cannot be fixed until after an election, and only then after a commission of employers and trade unions has investigated the economic state of affairs thoroughly.

The second controversy is between Labour and the Conservatives over whether a minimum wage is a good idea at all, whatever level it is set at. Labour claims it is, and that its effect on the economy will be positive because it will boost earnings among the lower paid, who will then spend more on mainly British goods and thus help to set in motion a virtuous Keynesian circle. The Conservatives reply that a minimum wage will destroy jobs because common sense tells us that if you push up wages for each employee, then employers can afford to employ fewer of them.

These two disputes will, no doubt, form a major factor in the political conflicts of the next two years. What disturbs me is that all of the protagonists have missed the central issue if we are serious about a learning society. It is this: a minimum wage is not enough. In a learning society, everyone, regardless of status, should have the opportunity to learn as well as earn. We should be promoting not just a minimum wage, but a minimum condition too. The right to the establishment of an Individual Learning Account would provide this step.

Ten Objections, Ten Rebuttals

I have tested out the ideas in this chapter so far on one or two audiences in addition to the 1996 North of England Conference. I therefore have a keen sense of the likely objections to them. Although, in making my case, I have already dealt with some potential objections, I thought it would help the reader to summarise both the likely attack on the proposals and my defence.

Objection 1
You will never be able to make parents play their part in the ILP process.

Most parents, if encouraged by school, government and peer pressure, will play their part as a matter of course. Some schools, including schools in disadvantaged areas, have already successfully established processes similar to the one I propose. In the few cases where the parents really will not play a part, the essential priority is to put the interests of the child first. If a parent repeatedly refused to take any interest in their child's education, a community or business mentor would be appointed to take care of the child's interests and perhaps to help change attitudes in the family. Where the parents were actively destructive in relation to their child, the ILP process would make it more, not less, likely that social agencies would take action.

At Greenwood Junior School in inner city Nottingham they introduced structured homework planning, home-school contracts and an expectation that parents would meet their child's class teacher three times a year. The school is in a disadvantaged community with over 50 per cent of the families on income support. Yet every parent is now committed to the scheme. At Fair Furlong School in Bristol in similar circumstances 99 per cent of parents attend on parents' evenings.

No one is pretending it would be easy to do this across the system but these examples prove it could be done. In any case, the issue is whether children and learning would be better served under the ILP process or the present haphazard state of affairs. On this issue there is surely no contest.

Objection 2
We're already doing it.

Amazingly, some of the people who put Objection 1 have also put Objection 2. It palpably isn't happening already, though some schools have moved towards what I have described. Where schools have successfully brought about advanced attitudes and processes for the involvement of parents, however, it does suggest that the proposals I have made are more realistic than some cynics have suggested.

Take the example of Burntwood Girls' School in Wandsworth described in a government report published in 1996:

> A written agreement, signed by every new entrant, her parents and the principal is a formal expression of the rights and responsibilities of each of these parties. A firm belief in student entitlement and the notion of 'services to students' underpins the agreement. Unusually, both staff and students declare formally their expectations of each other. Such is the climate in the school, with its thinking, self-critical, open approach to planning and development, that students have been trusted to make explicit their expectations of staff. While initial reactions were understandably cautious from a number of staff to what was regarded as a 'high risk' strategy, the effects have been positive. The school's expectations policy is clearly understood by both sides, gives guidance on what should happen if either students or staff do not meet expectations and helps to reinforce students' confidence in the general quality of teaching in the school.
>
> Parents' involvement is focused on their daughters' academic progress and development. Every student in the school is set targets, twice yearly in Years 7 to 11 and on a termly basis in Years 12 and 13. Each girl is fully involved in the collation of her end-of-year report. She helps draw up the targets in each subject; she shares the completion of a 'tutorial assessment' section showing National Curriculum levels attained; and she knows that she must discuss the general tenor of the report with her parents, who at this stage do not receive the report but are given early notice of the date and time of the 'Student Academic Counselling Day' at the beginning of the autumn term. Students and their parents are expected to attend this key event in the school's calendar to discuss and together agree the targets. Parents attend one hour before the appointed discussion time. This allows them time and space in comfortable surroundings, with refreshments provided, to receive the report and study it jointly with their daughters. Staff regard this as the most successful element of the target-setting approach; parents value the direct involvement and personal feedback they receive on their daughters' progress and feel they have a clearer understanding of how they can support the students' learning at home.

However, parents appeared to benefit too. They
appreciate being given a detailed 'curriculum guide' for each year, a homework timetable and a note of which member of staff to contact to answer specific queries about progress towards targets. The time and attention spent planning and organising the reporting process is considerable but worthwhile. Staff have given careful attention to organisational details in order to ensure maximum parental involvement in the process. They personally contact the small number of parents who do not attend to make sure they are drawn into the learning agreement in other ways. That learning and achievement are valued in this school cannot escape parents' attention since the importance of academic achievement is constantly reinforced and communicated to parents in a variety of ways. Parental involvement in the formal, signed agreement about targets strengthens the commitment to progress.

The inclusion of out-of-school activities within the purview of policy remains to be achieved, but the problems it presents are already being thought through in, for example, Birmingham's University of the First Age and the Prince's Trust Millennium Fund bid.

Objection 3
Schools are not organised to do what you propose.

True: the whole point is to change their role, to re-engineer. Some schools, however, are already moving in the direction set out in my proposals. There are schools with learning plans for every child, with focused parental involvement, with flexible grouping of pupils, with innovative timetables, with integral information technology, and with advanced use of support staff and community resources. The challenge is to combine these innovative features into a strategy for re-engineering.

Objection 4
The infrastructure of learning outside school is not in place.

True: at least it is not yet sufficiently developed to deliver what I propose. Nevertheless, it is expanding: museums, science parks, London Zoo and countless other organisations are rethinking how they provide education and relate what they do to the formal education system. Out-of-school study support is also growing rapidly. Computer technology in homes is still far behind what I describe, but it is developing at a great pace. Indeed, Britain leads the world in ownership of home computers.

Furthermore, the infrastructure – in terms of fibre-optic cable – is speedily being put in place. Look how quickly video players became, in effect, basics.

Objection 5
Teachers are not trained to do what you suggest.

It is true that any implementation of radical change in education will require a major retraining programme. There is no escape for government from enhancing its investment in teachers' skills. I have outlined in Chapter 8 a vision of a reconstructed teaching profession which would be capable of driving the re-engineering of education. My proposals are intended to be cost-effective, but I do not pretend they are cheap. Bear in mind, too, that a strong thrust of the proposal is that teachers should help lead change, not just respond to it. There is no doubt that this presents a challenge to all teachers, but surely an exciting and motivating one.

Objection 6
The whole package is prohibitively expensive.

Certainly it would cost more, but it is not unrealistic. I have shown where the money could be found. I do believe that small but steady growth in education expenditure is necessary. Some must come from government, some from the private sector and some from individuals. There is a need to redistribute investment in education too. For people in disadvantaged circumstances, reaching the same high standards does, on average, cost more. It is to everyone's advantage that we should make this investment. As American bumper stickers put it: 'If you think education is expensive, try ignorance.'

Objection 7
Some pupils or students will be unimpressed and won't play ball.

No doubt, but the question is whether the number of such students will be greater or smaller than at present. For many reasons, set out in this chapter, I am confident that the number will be far smaller, not least because individual learning needs, improvement against previous best and motivation are at the heart of the programme.

Objection 8

The movement of pupils of secondary age from school to other places of learning on a regular basis will waste their time and make it hard to monitor what they are doing: there will, in short, be leakage.

There is a great deal of leakage now. Remember the 5 per cent who 'disappear' now and the 15 per cent who truant regularly now. The question is whether my proposals would reduce 'leakage'. There is, it is true, an added risk if there is large-scale movement around, but information technology is important in this context. It will help keep much better records; indeed it already does in places. And it will enable a huge variety of learning experiences to be provided down the line, as it were. To do what I propose at the end of the century will involve much less movement than it would have done in 1990. Also bear in mind that, although I imagine a shorter formal school day, much of the formal learning out of school will in fact take place on the school campus.

Some movement will be an attraction to young people who are well motivated. If ILPs and new approaches to teaching and learning don't significantly improve motivation, the whole plan fails. The research evidence suggests that they will.

Objection 9

We had child-centredness before and it was a disaster. It has been a major contributory factor of the problems we face now.

My proposals bear no relation to the notion of child-centredness you are referring to. See the section of this chapter entitled 'Guaranteeing Standards' and come back with a serious objection, if you can.

Objection 10

It is an infringement of civil liberties to make it a statutory requirement that parents attend meetings at schools at least twice a year.

Hardly. There are already numerous laws governing parents' rights and responsibilities, including a statutory requirement to ensure that a child is educated. This would only be a modest extension of that obligation. In any case, whether it is statutory is not the central issue. Much more important is to find a means of changing social expectations so that parents do attend meetings at school because they see it as a basic responsibility of parenthood. The state of affairs at present is manifestly inadequate: statutory change should be considered only in so far as it promotes positive change in the behaviour of parents and teachers. If voluntary activity can bring about the necessary change, so much the better. But not changing should not be an option.

10 · Creating a Learning Society 2: Changing the Culture

> If a nation expects to be ignorant and free, in a state of
> civilisation, it expects what never was and never will be.
>
> Thomas Jefferson

The Leadership of Government

Much of what I have advocated in this book demands a government which puts education at the heart of its work and is prepared to create a new legislative, administrative and economic framework fit for a learning society. The revolution which I have outlined would require, undoubtedly, visionary and assertive leadership. In this section, I want to examine the leadership role of government, its role as an agent, not just of legislative change, but also of cultural change.

For most of the post-war era, education has not been high on the agenda of prime ministers. Mostly, they appointed ministers on their way up, or on their way out, for brief periods of tenure in reshuffles in which the focus was on other jobs – the Treasury, Home Office or Foreign Office – which were considered the plums. Sometimes the Education Minister did not even have Cabinet rank. Prime ministers thought about the amount of public money education absorbed, but otherwise they assumed that the education service, local authorities and teachers could be left to get on with it. Harold Wilson, for example, who was Prime Minister during the early phases of comprehensivisation in the 1960s, was sufficiently distant from it all to happily send his sons to an independent school in north London, a decision which, for a Labour prime minister, seems unthinkable now.

All that changed with James Callaghan's speech at Ruskin College on 18 October 1976 already quoted in Chapter 2. It is worth emphasising in this context his comment on the relatively limited role his predecessors had played: 'The Labour movement has always cherished education . . .

There is nothing wrong with non-educationalists, even a Prime Minister, talking about it now and again.' He made it clear, too, that he considered prime-ministerial interest in the outcomes of education legitimate and likely, at least while he was in office. Kenneth Baker, interviewed in 1996, acknowledged the importance of Callaghan's gesture:

> [Callaghan] questioned the quality of state education because he was getting lots of complaints . . . from parents and from businesses . . . he expressed this view very strongly and the education establishment, as it were, sandbagged him. It was not the job of prime ministers to make speeches like this. The job of the Prime Minister was to announce the creation of new universities or open schools . . .

For much of Margaret Thatcher's first two governments, there was a reversion to the pre-Callaghan type. Then, during the long teachers' pay dispute, her patience snapped. In May 1986, she appointed Kenneth Baker as Secretary of State for Education, with a mission to do something – although, according to him, she was not sure what: 'I think Margaret appointed me to that job to do things . . . the things she wanted were very inchoate in her own mind but she . . . felt something had to be done.' By 1987, Margaret Thatcher had put education at the centre of her priorities and at the centre of her speech to an adulatory party conference of that year: 'Our most important task in this Parliament is to raise the quality of education . . . We want education to be part of the answer to Britain's problems, not part of the cause.' Behind the scenes, her involvement was active too. Kenneth Baker described her role vividly in his interview:

> Margaret did not mind ministers who argued with her . . . as long as they argued sensibly and from knowledge. Those who argued with her from sentiment . . . she would grind into the ground . . . you had to be robust and stand up for your corner. And I did this, constantly. She would be very rude to me at times, as only she could be. The handbag went and, you know, it can be quite a nasty process in front of colleagues.

Ever since the handbagging days, prime ministers have maintained a close interest in education policy. They have recognised its growing significance, economically and politically. John Major has made a succession of important speeches on education, beginning with the infamous one at the Café Royal in 1991. He has also chosen to associate himself with major education announcements such as the 1991 White Paper on further and higher education. In 1995 and 1996, when education became a key pre-election battleground, the Prime Minister's interest was sharpened further.

From Baker's time on, partly as a result of this growing prime-ministerial interest, there have been tensions between No. 10 and the Department for Education. These have heightened as the political significance of education has grown. A series of speeches and press briefings from the No. 10 policy unit in 1995 and 1996 appeared at times to destabilise Gillian Shephard's careful and steady emphasis on school improvement. The nursery-vouchers scheme, the extension of the Assisted Places Scheme, and the renewed emphasis on reviving selection schools, all owed their origins to No. 10 rather than the Education Department. As the election has approached, the search for clear blue water has seemed to outweigh the considerations of the impact on announcements on the education service. Prime-ministerial interest in education is therefore a mixed blessing, given its propensity to destabilise. It is, nevertheless, desirable. A prime minister who invests a substantial degree of personal capital in education is, after all, more likely to support pleas for education expenditure, even when the constraints are great. The extra £770 million for education in the 1995 budget – at a time when Tory backbenchers were baying for tax cuts – illustrates the point.

Moreover, if there is to be a learning society it is necessary too. All the evidence suggests that, whatever happens in elections, the Prime Minister will want to keep a close interest in education. John Major says education is top of his domestic priorities. Tony Blair claims he has 'a passion for education' and has highlighted its importance in a series of speeches which began during his campaign for the leadership of the party. The press has claimed from time to time that he and his Shadow Education Spokesperson, David Blunkett, suffer from the same strained relationship that plagues John Major and Gillian Shephard. In fact, the two have a close bond based on mutual respect and a shared agenda. Such is Tony Blair's single-mindedness, his determination to lead and his personal commitment to educational change that, in any Labour government, the Education Minister will have to be prepared to follow his lead.

Since the days before Callaghan's speech, therefore, the landscape has changed dramatically. It has become almost impossible to imagine a prime minister who does not take education seriously. On the other hand, the role of prime minister in a learning society – what one might call 'a learning prime minister' – remains to be delineated. It is time to attempt to sketch out that role and to establish what might be thought of as the performance indicators for a learning prime minister. Given that both party leaders claim to give education top billing, establishing performance indicators seems a sensible way of judging the extent to which their actions match their rhetoric.

Presumably, the first indicator of a learning prime minister would be a series of significant speeches on the theme, perhaps three or four a year. Other major speeches and set-piece television interviews should also be laced through with references to, and evidence of an understanding of, education. A learning prime minister should be at the head of a crusade to transform cultural attitudes to learning and education. Whereas in 1976 a prime-ministerial speech on education was a rarity, by 2006 it should be the norm. Secondly, a learning prime minister should spend time visiting learning institutions – schools, colleges, universities, but also businesses, training centres, libraries and other centres of community education. He or she might consider establishing a personal award for innovative approaches to learning in all its varied locations.

So far, the indicators are important symbolically but peripheral in terms of real practical action. Of much more significance is what the Prime Minister chooses to do with the Department for Education and Employment itself. Historically, its predecessor departments have been seen as a low-status backwater. One President of the Board of Education in the 1930s described it, without much exaggeration, as an outpost of the Treasury. Mrs Thatcher, after her spell there as a minister in the early 1970s, described it as 'an awful place'. Kenneth Baker said that moving there from the Department of the Environment in 1986 was 'like moving from the manager's job at Arsenal to Charlton. You crossed the river and moved down two divisions.' Though most of us would see any move away from Arsenal as a promotion, Baker clearly had a different view.

As long as the department had such low status, it could hardly play the role required of it in the creation of a learning society. A combination of factors has meant that, already, it has moved up the league table of departments. The reforms from 1988 onwards gave it tremendous powers and thus – potentially at any rate – influence. The review of its functioning in the second half of 1993, undertaken by Coopers and Lybrand, gave it a new sense of direction and helped it to put behind it the isolation of the brief but disastrous era (1992–93) when policy-making fell apart. Finally, in the summer of 1995, John Major boldly merged the Departments of Education and Employment to create a new power in the land. The new department now has responsibility for all of education and training, as well as the employment service and labour relations. As it stands, therefore, it is a much more attractive proposition for an ambitious or talented minister and, now that its internal reorganisation is complete, for ambitious civil servants too. As if to enhance the freshness of its image, its first Permanent Secretary, Michael Bichard, is unique among his peers in having served most of his career outside the Civil Service.

John Major's merger has, therefore, given the DfEE much of the status and the powers over lifelong learning that it would need to help build a learning society. It remains to be seen what an incoming Labour government would make of the new Leviathan. There is a powerful and traditional Labour attachment to the old Employment Department. Trade union leaders remember a close working relationship with it that stretches back to Ernest Bevin and the old Ministry of Labour. They particularly remember the legislative programme of workers' rights that Michael Foot took through Parliament when he was Employment Minister in the mid-1970s. There is likely to be a substantial lobby in the party to persuade Tony Blair to separate the two departments again.

The unease over this did not affect Blair's Shadow Cabinet allocations following Major's merger in 1995. Harriet Harman and David Blunkett were the two incumbents at Employment and Education. David Blunkett had no need to fear a Harman takeover of his portfolio: new Labour could surely never put Education in the control of a prime minister and minister both of whom sent their children to the same west London grant-maintained school. In the end, Harman took on Health, Blunkett Education and Employment. In the 1996 Shadow Cabinet reshuffle David Blunkett's responsibility for the merged portfolio was affirmed. This seemed to indicate that the possibility of separating the two departments was receding. In addition to the idea of separating the old departments – which would certainly be a retrograde step – a number of kites are being flown. One is not to undo the merger, but to take away labour relations from the new department and merge it with all or part of the Department of Trade and Industry, leaving the DfEE in control of all of education and training. This would still leave the DfEE as a major power in the land.

A more radical kite – apparently flown by Gordon Brown – is that there should be three new ministries: of the First Age, covering school education; the Second Age, covering what might be called sixteen to sixty; and the Third Age, covering the burgeoning population of over-sixties. These would include not just Education and Employment, but also Social Security and Health. This is certainly a radical proposal, but it has substantial defects. In the short term, it would throw Whitehall into confusion. That is not a problem in principle, but an incoming governing party, after seventeen years in the wilderness, would presumably want to make an impact out in the country rather than in Whitehall, where turmoil could hamper its best efforts.

More problematic in principle is that it slices up responsibility for learning just when we seemed to be on the brink of putting it all together.

A break between ministries at sixteen could, for example, cause grave difficulties in bringing about the coherent fourteen-to-nineteen curriculum which we have been edging painfully towards in the 1990s. Similarly, at the other end of the age spectrum, the notion of retirement at sixty or sixty-five is becoming increasingly obsolete, as many take early retirement but in fact carry on in a variety of forms of employment, while others seem barely to retire at all.

Out of all this ferment, what ought to matter most, in my view, to a learning prime minister is that there should be a powerful Whitehall department responsible for promoting learning across society. This department should be a great office of state on a par with the Foreign Office or the Home Office. If the learning society is to be a reality, nothing else will do. I would want to see the DfEE remain one department, but to change its name – symbolically but importantly – to the Department of Lifelong Learning. It could even be called DOLLY for short. Goodbye DfEE, as it were, Hello . . .

The status of the department responsible for education is a key indicator of a learning prime minister's performance, but it is not enough. There is also the sensitive matter of the ministers he or she puts at the head of it. The enhanced status of the department should help to ensure that more successful politicians go there, but it is no guarantee. Look at Michael Howard's tenure at the Home Office, for example. There is also the question of the length of tenure of ministers in a given post. At Education, the average tenure of a minister since the war is somewhere between eighteen months and two years. This is disastrous in many respects: it means the ministers barely have time to understand the brief before moving on. It also means that they are all too easily outmanoeuvred in the Cabinet's spending round, as Gillian Shephard was in her first year in office, with almost disastrous consequences for her own strategy. It is much to her credit that she showed the political acumen to recover from the blow in the ensuing twelve months.

The preferred ministerial model for a Department of Lifelong Learning – the one we should surely recommend to a learning prime minister – is the Foreign Office model. Here, the tendency has been to appoint widely respected, obviously competent ministers and leave them in post for several years. John Major need only stand by Gillian Shephard. If Tony Blair is looking for a Minister of Lifelong Learning who would fit this bill, he need look no further than David Blunkett, who has already proved himself the most formidable Opposition Spokesperson on Education for a generation and has been one of the most effective members of the Shadow Cabinet.

The performance indicators so far are either symbolic or administrat-

ive. The next two are what, before the BSE scare, we might have called
the red meat of our demands. The Prime Minister needs to establish
effective working relationships with those involved in learning, which is
to say, ultimately, with everyone. Of course, no prime minister can or
should set out to please everyone. What he or she can do is bring to the
policy-making process clarity and openness. It is absolutely right in a
democracy for there to be certain broad policy thrusts which are non-
negotiable: otherwise the concept of election on the basis of a manifesto
falls apart. When I interviewed Kenneth Baker about the implementation
of the National Curriculum immediately following the 1987 election, the
exchange revealed this very clearly:

> MB: You must have learnt . . . that the vast bulk of what was coming
>   [in response to the National Curriculum] was opposed to the
>   idea.
> KB: They were opposed to the whole idea of the curriculum . . . this
>   was . . . the system fighting back and saying 'lay off, this is our
>   territory'.
> MB: And did you just say, well, that is simply a defence of the status
>   quo and we are elected to get on with this . . . ?
> KB: To some extent, yes. I used the mandate.

The issue for a learning prime minister is more subtle than this: it is
– non-negotiable or not – that policy needs to be implemented in a way
which enables it to work. To create a society in which everyone is an
active learner depends not only on enthusing the million or so people
whose job it is to provide learning at various levels, but also on motivating
many millions, some of whom did not enjoy learning in the past, to
choose to take it up again. This is a formidable challenge, and any return
to free-market Stalinism or variants of it would destroy it.

Finally, a learning prime minister will have to put his or her money
where his or her mouth is. The creation of a learning society depends
upon the society as a whole spending more than it has ever done on
learning. The trends show that, albeit slowly, this is happening. At the
level of the business or the individual, more and more private money is
being spent on learning, and the trend needs to continue.

This investment needs to be in addition to, not instead of, increased
resources from government; otherwise the result will be still greater
inequality in the distribution of learning outcomes. Given the inevitable
constraints on public expenditure – from the low tolerance of taxation
to the pressures of an ageing population – it is hard to envisage massive
extra growth. Slow but steady growth over the lifetime of one Parliament,
if not two, ought to be achievable. Incidentally, there are many in the

education system who would sacrifice a little growth to gain the steadiness. The fluctuations of expenditure from year to year which have characterised education funding disrupt improvement strategies.

And, of course, the growth should be directed to the areas of most dire need: nursery provision, the literacy campaign at primary level, provision of learning resources in disadvantaged homes and communities. A small but significant investment in the encouragement of school level innovation would also be essential. Government could negotiate and then monitor and evaluate innovation contracts with individual schools. The proposals set out in the previous chapter envisage the most radical shift of learning resources to disadvantaged communities since the war. They are achievable within existing levels of taxation, with the exception of taxing child benefit. They may not be perfect – I do not claim to be a tax expert – but I shall be looking to see whether prime ministers who claim to recognise the importance of education stand by their rhetoric in each annual spending round. If they do not, the title of 'Learning Prime Minister' should justifiably be withheld.

Robbie Fowler and the Learning Culture

Ajax Amsterdam won the European Cup in 1995 with a young and brilliant team that was not assembled at a cost of millions. In 1996, in spite of a spate of serious injuries to key players, they reached the final and lost only in a penalty shoot-out. In August 1996, even after the Dutch national side's defeat by England, they defeated the otherwise all-conquering Manchester United. They recruit the best young footballers in Holland at a very young age and coach them, focusing, until their mid- or late teens, on developing their skills. The club also insists that their young recruits take school learning seriously. Their progress as footballers is indeed associated with their willingness to take their school work seriously. The club coach does not insist on this for altruistic reasons. He argues that a player who is clever off the field is more likely to be clever on it. If, as so often happens in modern football, the opposition changes its tactics part way through the match, he argues, the clever Ajax team should be better placed to adapt than other teams would be.

Soon after I read about Ajax, I also read what Robbie Fowler, the young Liverpool goal-scoring wizard, said to *The Times* on 9 March 1996 about his prospects of playing for England. He based his argument on a comparison with young Patrick Kluivert of Ajax, who has already made an impact on the Dutch national side. If he can do it at that age, Fowler implied, why can't I? Why not indeed? The boy is brilliant. He scores instinctively with both feet and his head. Ian Rush, his mentor, believes he will outdo his own legendary feats in the game. If a forty-year-old is allowed to admit to having footballing heroes, Robbie Fowler is mine. The difference between Fowler and Kluivert, however, may be less a question of footballing skill and more one of whether they have joined the learning society. Kluivert, brought up at Ajax, is of course a fully paid-up member. Fowler, however, had this to say to *The Times*: 'I have bought a new house and moved my mum in with me. She does the washing, ironing and cooking. I haven't really got a clue about anything but football and scoring goals. I wasn't totally stupid at school, but near enough.'

This is the man whose football is so good that his dressing-room nickname is God! This quotation from my hero sends questions reeling across my brain. Did his school know about Howard Gardner and the seven intelligences? Did he see success as something to be achieved through school or in spite of it? What is Liverpool football club doing to educate the boy now? Money, after all, is not a problem, and Fowler will be lucky if he can keep scoring goals for a decade and a half. Then what? Above all, what do we still need to do to create a learning culture? And will a British club ever win the European Cup again? A learning culture must, after all, mean finding learning in the most unlikely places, even at Liverpool Football Club or even, *in extremis*, at Arsenal. At present, while Ajax has anticipated the learning society, and indeed created it in microcosm, Liverpool for all the beauty of their football in 1996, appear locked in the twentieth century. England's evident improvement in Euro '96 notwithstanding, every football club, indeed every organisation in Britain needs to think again.

There is no doubt that a radical culture shift is necessary if the challenges set out in Chapter 1 are to be met, for in a chaotic and rapidly changing world in which the limits of government have been so starkly revealed the chief distinction between success and failure in a society is likely to be culture – the context within which decisions are made – rather than politics. Francis Fukuyama, the historian and social scientist who, at the start of the 1990s, declared that, to all intents and purposes, history had ended because the clash of political ideologies which had characterised the twentieth century had been settled by the Cold War, has now changed his ground. The political arguments are essentially over, he still maintains, but success and failure depend upon more than politics.

> We all know we are going to be living in liberal democracies and capitalist systems plugged into the global economy. The real ground of interest is going to shift elsewhere. It's not going to be things like ideology and institutions. It's going to be . . . civil society and culture because those have not converged around the world to the same degree and in many ways I don't think they are going to converge either.

Nations will succeed, Fukuyama argues, if they are 'sociable' and able
to achieve the ethical consensus which underpins competitiveness (*The
Times*, 2 October 1995). There is an interesting similarity between this
point and Will Hutton's forceful argument in *The State We're In*. It is
not sufficient to rely on individual firms being effective, it is also necessary
to create the institutional and cultural context which makes it more likely
that they will thrive. My argument is that this applies – perhaps even
more strongly – to our educational success and to our efforts to give
birth to the learning society.

As a means of concluding my argument, I want to give three examples
of simple, no- or low-cost changes which could help to change that cultural
context. I do not pretend for a moment that the three are sufficient: rather
they are meant to suggest a new way of looking at the world.

The first relates to the almost unimaginably dull subject of company
annual reports. They should be required to include a substantial and
detailed section on what the company has done that year to promote the
creation of the learning society. There should be two broad aspects to
what they describe. Companies' prime responsibility is to learning among
their own workforce: the annual report should be required to report who
has learnt what and why; how many have learnt how much and what
for; what the annual expenditure on education per employee is; and what
the plans are to extend learning in the future. Almost as important
is the responsibility companies have to promote learning more generally
in the community. The accounting firm KPMG, for example, is promoting a marvellous scheme which links headteachers to senior consultants
in a mentoring partnership. Many firms take young people on work
experience, others sponsor schools or particular activities within them,
some provide mentors for young people who are considered at risk.
These are just a handful of examples of a burgeoning area of activity.
Annual reports should tell us all about this beneficial activity. The companies that whinge about educational standards and make no contribution
should be shamed into having something to report. Perhaps we should
have league tables of performance in this field.

These changes in annual reports might be brought about through statutory regulation. Ideally, however, they would come about as a result of a
code of practice drawn up by industry itself. Some companies already
report effectively on both aspects of promoting learning. Boots the Chem-
ist, for example, includes a five-page section in its annual report for 1995
on 'Employees, Community and the Environment'. It tells us that: 'Some
£25 million per year is invested in training, plus the cost of the time of
those being trained . . . [we] have 11,000 staff registered for the National
Vocational Qualification Retail Certificate . . .' It also tells us that Boots is

an 'Investor in People'. Under the sub-heading 'Community' it goes on to explain that it is 'ethical and socially responsible'. It contributes to education through donations as well as through support for some local educational initiatives such as the Nottinghamshire Childcare Forum.

Reckitt and Colman does rather less well in its annual report for the same year. It has a good line in rhetoric: 'Reckitt and Colman is committed to the recruitment and development of outstanding people through empowerment, teamwork, training and competitive reward systems within an environment which is committed to excellence and extraordinary success . . .' It tells us little or nothing about its practical achievements in pursuit of these noble objectives. The section of its report on 'Cash Flow and Borrowings' is much longer than its section on 'Employees', which suggests a doubt about its true priorities.

Whatever the nature of Reckitt and Colman's priorities, the point remains clear. If the learning society is to become a reality, companies must tell us in some depth what they have done to extend learning among their employees and the community, two of their major stakeholders. Companies can currently seek, through the Training and Enterprise Councils, the 'Investors in People' award as recognition of their good practice in human resource management. It is not perfect, and some companies beat the system. I know of one Investor in People, for example, which employs illegal immigrants, pays them cash so there is no tax involved, and sacks them if they step out of line. Even so, the scheme has been beneficial and has highlighted the importance of comprehensive plans for promoting learning among employees. Perhaps it is time we developed a new award – a step beyond investing in people – for Investors in the Community.

The second change I want to propose is to the role of the media. Do the media make enough of a contribution to learning in this society? They clearly play a vitally important role in providing information and education, whether through news reporting and analysis or documentaries and drama. This is not in dispute, but I want to focus more narrowly. What are the media doing consciously to promote the creation of a learning society? The answer to this is more doubtful. Do they do enough to promote it or create it? Could they do more? The answer to this, surely, is clear. They could do much more.

Two examples of how should suffice. One is with regard to children's programming. There are problems with it at present. Children are served up a great deal of what can only be called pap. It is enough to attract their attention – just – and serves well in a child-minding capacity. It does little to promote learning and, in terms of its impact on attention spans and opportunity cost, is probably negative. There are some

examples of excellent children's television and the BBC has recently
expanded its provision of children's drama, such as the brilliant *Agent
Z and the Penguin from Mars*. The problem is that children are much
more likely to watch adult television than they are to watch the children's
television that is programmed for them. The six programmes that drew
the biggest audiences in the four to fourteen age group in early 1996 were
Gladiators, *Neighbours*, *Casualty*, the *National Lottery Live*, *Eastenders* and
Coronation Street. Furthermore, as Nicholas Tucker pointed out in a
powerful article in the *Sunday Times* on 7 April 1996, in the old days,
'childhood was partially defined by ignorance . . . about much that went
on in the adult world . . . [now] under-11s watching grown-up as well
as children's programmes have access to adult preoccupations and secrets
as never before'.

It is impossible to turn the clock back, but surely it should be possible
to alter the market forces that create the current tawdry state of affairs,
so that children are better served. Tucker suggests government intervention. A crude approach would be unlikely to succeed, but government
could influence the state of affairs by encouraging the expenditure of
lottery money to promote better children's programming and, more significantly, by changing the criteria for the ITV franchises when they are
next up for renewal. In addition to price and quality in general, a strong
emphasis on worthwhile programming for children could be written in.
Similar criteria could be applied to the BBC when its Charter is due for
renewal.

This kind of approach to regulation could also be used to encourage
direct promotion of the learning society. I avidly watch BBC2's *Video
Nation* shorts. These brief, one-minute slots from the Community Programmes Unit provide fleeting insights into the lives and obsessions of
ordinary people. What if a proportion of them actively promoted learning? A mother or father hearing a child read, for example, and describing
the pleasure it can bring? An adult who has recovered self-confidence
through returning to learning? There are so many possibilities. And
suppose they were shown not at 10.29 pm, just before *Newsnight*, but at
7.29 pm, just before *Eastenders*? In April 1996 at the launch of his
ambitious 'Campaign for Learning', Sir Christopher Ball proposed that
companies should sometimes vary their advertisements to encourage
learning. Imagine, he suggested, Bob Hoskins saying at the end of the
BT advertisement, 'It's good to learn.' This is precisely the kind of
thinking that is necessary.

The BBC already makes an important educational contribution. The
OU . . . the Learning Zone . . . educational themes in the storylines of
its soap operas . . . Surely, however, it could do more. It was with this

thought in mind that I went to see some staff from its education department in November 1995. They were sceptical about my thinking. They thought – probably rightly – that I was ignorant and they were expert. They were worried that unsubtle promotion of learning might lose them viewers and perhaps even undermine positive attitudes to education. They also worried about trying to shape the culture: that is not our job, they said. I heard them out, and still I disagree. Promotion of learning is, technically, no different from the promotion of hamburgers or soap powder. Advertisers spend millions promoting these things, more or less subtly, because they know it works. Why should it not work for learning?

As for not shaping the culture, that is not an option. A broadcasting organisation such as the BBC has no choice but to shape the culture. The only issue is whether it does so consciously or unconsciously. Given the overwhelming need this society has to raise educational standards and improve attitudes to learning across it, it seems to me only sensible to encourage public service broadcasting to play a part in doing so. The public service in public service broadcasting ought to be explicit – simply surviving in the cut-throat broadcasting market is not enough. If survival is all, then the plug should be pulled. If the BBC is to be drawn into simply competing with commercial broadcasting and doing similar things, then it has no distinct role and might just as well become fully commercial. If public service broadcasting has a future at all, surely it must lie, at least in part, in mixing entertainment and information with the promotion of positive attitudes to education and learning. Fortunately, the BBC is conscious of this challenge. The broadcasting industry is about to be turned on its head as cable, satellite and computer technology combine. The BBC's plans for the digital revolution, published in May 1996, involve an ambitious science, arts and education channel. It also plans 'tele-schools' offering remote control learning to homes and schools. Ideally, these services need to relate integrally to its mainstream services. The BBC's market share may well be expected to fall, perhaps dramatically. Nevertheless, it clearly has a major role, at least into the first decade of the next century, and it could make an immense impact before then. If it succeeds in the short term, it should be better placed to survive and thrive in the topsy-turvy broadcasting world of the twenty-first century. The alternative, is to give up now, in which case I for one will begin to resent paying a licence fee.

The third change I want to propose is in everyday conversation, and at this point in my argument I must make reference to *USA* (1930–36), the panoramic trilogy by the great American author, John Dos Passos. His novel describes, better than any other work, how a nineteenth-century agrarian society became a twentieth-century industrial power. You need ambition and a summer holiday to read all of its 1,000 pages and to follow the lives of its array of characters. The preface by contrast is short enough to read during half-time at a rugby match. There Dos Passos tries to capture the essence of his great work. 'USA is the slice of a continent. USA is a group of holding companies, some aggregations of trade unions . . . a chain of moving picture theatres . . . USA is a set of bigmouthed officials with too many bank accounts. USA is a lot of men buried in their uniforms in Arlington cemetery . . . But mostly USA is the speech of the people.'

We are living through a similar period of transformation as we attempt – fumbling painfully – to create a learning society from the ashes of industrialism. The policy agenda of the learning society is beginning to form: standards must rise, schools must improve, lifelong learning must become more than an aspiration; and increased investment in education from government, business and individuals is becoming essential. Yet none of these answer the Dos Passos challenge. How will this social transformation be reflected in 'the speech of the people'?

In industrial Britain, once the pleasantries were over, for people at an Islington dinner party or on the terraces at Highbury, the most likely question was: 'What do you do?' Its meaning was narrower still. It meant: what paid work do you do? And by the 1980s it had become the only question. What, in a learning society, will be the equivalent question? We could wait and see. No doubt fifteen years from now some megasociological study will be able to tell us how the pattern of language has changed. But this is the passive approach. It underestimates the power of language. Language does not change simply to reflect the changes in society. On the contrary through changing the language people can change society. Advertisers have known this for years. Educators have just woken up to the fact. In one school I know you can ask any pupil what the headteacher's favourite word is and I guarantee the reply will be 'achievement'. Over the past five years its exam results have risen dramatically: the power of language.

If this is so, why don't we decide to change the language in order to help create the learning society? For the only question that people used to ask is certainly obsolete. After all, people's work is now likely to change several times during a lifetime. Many of us will experience temporary (but hopefully brief) periods of unemployment and, as more people create the portfolio lives that Charles Handy advocates, asking what paid work people do will be far too narrow a question to generate really interesting conversation.

So in order to help create the learning society what should we ask? Isn't it obvious? The question has to be: 'What did you learn today?' I took my courage in both hands recently and tried this out at a social gathering. The effect was electrifying. I had more fun and learnt more than at any other event I can remember. One person told me in graphic detail that she had learnt how to prune hypericum. Another person told me that he had learnt how you replace a smashed windscreen on a car, a useful thing to know in our part of north London. Then two people told me what they had learnt at a presentation by a leading Labour politician about the principles underpinning the 'new Labour' project.

All this was in one evening. Even now I don't know whether these people were doctors or panel-beaters, accountants or lion-tamers, and the important thing is I don't care. I learnt something. In fact, I thought of starting a club for people who have stopped asking 'What do you do?' and ask instead 'What did you learn today?' Members could receive a certificate saying 'Learning? I asked for it.' The real reward, however, is the satisfaction of fascinating conversations.

More importantly still, each time someone asks the question they play a small part in raising the priority society gives to learning, in pushing education up the cultural agenda, in building the social and political momentum, which will assist in the creation of a learning society. In this creative process, it is clear that both government and those involved in providing education – teachers and others – have roles of daunting significance to play. Employers and a range of social agencies have major roles too. Ultimately, though, the transformation I envisage depends on everyone playing their part. Most of all, the learning society, like the United States, is the speech of the people. The time has come for everyone, even Robbie Fowler, to join the learning game.

Bibliography

Alexander, R., Rose, J., Woodhead, C., 'Curriculum Organisation and Classroom Practice in Primary Schools', a discussion paper (The Three Wise Men) (DES, London, 1992)

Auld, R., *The William Tyndale Junior and Infants' School*, Report of the Public Inquiry (ILEA, London, 1976)

Baker, K., *Turbulent Years: My Life in Politics* (Faber, London, 1993)

Barber, M., *The Making of the 1944 Education Act* (Cassell, London, 1994)

——*Parents and their Attitudes to Secondary Schools*, interim report of a research project in the Centre for Successful Schools, Keele University (Keele University, Keele, 1994)

—— *Young People and their Attitudes to School*, interim report of a research project in the Centre for Successful Schools, Keele University (Keele University, Keele, 1994)

——*The Curriculum, the Minister, His Boss and Her Hairdresser* (Curriculum Association, London, 1996)

Barber, M., Brighouse, T., *Partners in Change: Enhancing the Teaching Profession* (IPPR, London, 1992)

Barber, M., Carr, D., Carter, M., 'Haywood High School' in National Commission on Education, *Success Against the Odds: Effective Schools in Disadvantaged Areas*, pp. 175–199 (Routledge, London, 1996)

Barth, R.S., *Improving Schools from Within: Teachers, Parents and Principals Can Make the Difference* (Jossey-Bass, San Francisco, 1990)

Bierhoff, H., *Laying the Foundations of Numeracy: A Comparison of Primary School Textbooks in Britain, Germany and Switzerland* (NIESR, London, 1996)

Bloom, A., *The Closing of the American Mind* (Penguin, London, 1987)

Board of Education, *Report of the Consultative Committee of the Board of Education on the Education of the Adolescent* (Hadow Report) (HMSO, London, 1926)

Board of Education, *Report of the Consultative Committee of the Secondary Schools Examination Council on Curriculum and Examinations in Secondary Schools* (Norwood Report) (HMSO, London, 1943)

Brooks, G., Pugh, A.K., Shagen, I., *Reading Performance at Nine* (NFER, Slough, 1996)

Burghes, D., Blum, W., 'The Exeter Kassel Comparative Project: A Review

308   *Bibliography*

of Year 1 and Year 2 Results', in *Proceedings of a Seminar on Mathematics Education* (Gatsby Foundation, London, 1995)

Burghes, D., 'State Schools as They Should Be Organised', *Sunday Times*, 18 Feb. 1996

Bynner, J., Steedman, J., *Difficulties with Basic Skills: A Report on the Analysis of Data Collected in the 21 Year Sub-sample Survey of the 1970 British Cohort Study* (Basic Skills Agency, London, 1995)

Callaghan, J., Speech at Ruskin College, Oxford, *TES*, 22 Oct. 1976, pp.1–3. Extracts also appear in: Moon, B., Murphy, P., Rayner, J. (eds.) *Policies for the Curriculum*, Appendix 1, pp. 271–276 (Hodder & Stoughton in association with the Open University, London, 1989)

CASE, *Better Learning: A Report from the CASE Project* (King's College, University of London, 1990)

Davies, N., *The Thief of Brixton, Guardian*, 31 Aug. 1994

Dearing, R., *The National Curriculum and Its Assessment: Interim Report* (SCAA, London, 1993)

—— *The National Curriculum and Its Assessment: Final Report* (SCAA, London, 1993)

—— *Review of Qualifications for 16-19 Year Olds* (DFEE, London, 1996)

DES, *Report of the Committee of Inquiry into the Teaching of English Language* (Kingman Report) (HMSO, London, 1988)

DES, Welsh Office, *English for Ages 5 to 16* (Cox Report) (HMSO, London, 1989)

DfEE, Cabinet Office, *The Skills Audit: A Report from an Interdepartmental Group*, (DfEE, Cabinet Office, London, 1996)

DfEE, OFSTED, 'The Improvement of Failing Schools: UK Policy and Practice 1993-1995', a paper prepared for the Seminar on Combating Failure at School, OECD, Nov. 1995 (DfEE, OFSTED, London, 1995)

DfEE, Welsh Office, *Choice and Diversity: A New Framework for Schools* CM2021 (HMSO, London, 1992)

DfEE, Welsh Office, *Self-government for Schools*, CM 3315 (HMSO, London, 1996)

DTI, *Competitiveness: Helping Business to Win* (White Paper) CM 2563 (HMSO, London, 1994)

DTI, *Competitiveness: Forging Ahead* (White Paper) CM 2867 (HMSO, London, 1996)

Education Act 1993, Ch.35 (HMSO, London, 1993)

Education (Schools) Act 1992, Ch.38 (HMSO, London, 1992)

Education Reform Act 1988, Ch.40 (HMSO, London, 1988)

EOC, OFSTED, *The Gender Divide: Performance Differences Between Boys and Girls at School* (HMSO, London, 1996)

Etzioni, A., *The Spirit of Community* (Fontana, London, 1995)

Francis, A., 'Improving the UK's Industrial Competitiveness', *RSA Journal* No. 5463, Oct. 1995, pp.25–39

Fukuyama, F., *The End of History and the Last Man* (Penguin, London, 1992)

Fukuyama, F., *Trust: The Social Virtues and the Creation of Prosperity* (Hamish Hamilton, London, 1995)

Fullan, M., Stiegelbauer, S., *The New Meaning of Educational Change* (Cassell, London, 1991)

Further and Higher Education Act 1992, Ch.13 (HMSO, London, 1992)

Galbraith, J.K., *Affluent Society*, 4th edn. (Deutsch, London, 1985)

Gardner, H., *Frames of Mind: The Theory of Multiple Intelligences*, (Fontana, London, 1993)

—— *The Unschooled Mind* (Fontana, London, 1993)

Gleick, T., *Chaos* (Abacus, London, 1987)

Gould, R., *Chalk Up the Memory: An Autobiography of Sir Ronald Gould* (George Philip Alexander, Birmingham, 1976)

Graham, D., Tytler, D., *A Lesson for us All: The Making of the National Curriculum* (Routledge, London, 1992)

Hammer, M., Champy, J., *Re-engineering the Corporation: Manifesto for a Business Revolution* (Brearley Publishing, London, 1993)

Handy, C.R., *The Empty Raincoat: Making Sense of the Future* (Hutchinson, London, 1994)

Hofkins, D., 'Half the 11-Year-Olds Below Standard', *TES*, 19 Jan. 1996, p.1

Hutton, W., 'Educated Guesses Are Wide of Mark', *Guardian*, 8 Jan. 1996

Hutton, W., *The State We're In* (Vintage, London, 1996)

Hymas, C., Cohen, J., 'The Trouble with Boys', *Sunday Times*, 19 June 1994

Johannsen, R. (ed.), *The Lincoln Douglas Debates of 1858* (OUP, Oxford, 1965)

Judd, J., 'Parents Pleased with Schools', *Independent*, 22 July 1994

Labour Party, *Excellence for Everyone: Labour's Crusade to Raise Standards* (Labour Party, London, 1996)

Lankester, T., 'National Challenge That We Can Be Proud Of'. *TES* School Effectiveness Supplement, 6 Oct. 1995, p.ii

Lawlor, S., *Teachers Mistaught: Training in Theories or Education in Subjects* (CPS, London, 1990)

Major, J., *Education – All Our Futures*, text of speech to CPS, Café Royal, London, 3 July (Prime Minister's Press Office, London, 1991)

Mortimore, P., Little, V. (eds.) *Living Education: Festschrift for John Tomlinson* (Paul Chapman, London, not yet published)

Mortimore, P., Sammons, P., Stoll, L., Lewis, D., Ecob, R., *School Matters: The Junior Years* (Open Books, Wells, 1988)

National Commission on Education, *Learning to Succeed* (Heinemann, London, 1993)

National Commission on Education, *Success Against the Odds: Effective Schools in Disadvantaged Areas* (Routledge, London, 1996)

North East London Education Association, *The Future of Hackney Downs School: Report to the Secretary of State for Education and Employment* (NELEA, London, 1995)

OFSTED, *Boys and English, 1988–1991* (OFSTED, London, 1993)

OFSTED, *Access and Achievement in Urban Education: Papers and Report of the Conference Held on 2–3 Nov. 1994* (OFSTED, London, 1994)

OFSTED, *Homework in Primary and Secondary Schools* (HMSO, London, 1995)

OFSTED, *Standards and Quality in Education 1994/95: The Annual Report of Her Majesty's Chief Inspector of Schools* (HMSO, London, 1996)

OFSTED, *The Teaching of Reading in 45 Inner London Primary Schools*, Ref: HMR/27/96/DS (OFSTED, London, 1996)

OFSTED, DfEE, *Setting Targets to Raise Standards: A Survey of Good Practice* (OFSTED, DfEE, London, 1996)

Patten, J. 'There is a Choice: Good or Evil', *Spectator*, 18 April, pp.9–10

Reynolds, D., *Making Good Schools: Linking School Effectiveness and Improvement* (Routledge, London, 1996)

Reynolds, D., Cuttance, P. (eds.) *School Effectiveness: Research, Policy and Practice* (Cassell, London, 1992)

Reynolds, D. et al, *Advances in School Effectiveness Research and Practice* (Pergamon, Oxford, 1994)

Reynolds, D., Farrell, S., *Worlds Apart? A Review of International Surveys of Educational Achievement Involving England* (HMSO, London, 1996)

Richardson, S., *Inspection Under Section 9 of the Education (Schools) Act 1992: Hackney Downs School* (OFSTED, London, 1994)

Sammons, P., Hillman, J., Mortimore, P., *Key Characteristics of Effective Schools: A Review of School Effectiveness Research, International School Effectiveness & Improvement Centre, Institute of Education, University of London for OFSTED* (OFSTED; Institute of Education, University of London, London, 1995)

Sammons, P., Thomas, S., Mortimore, P., 'Accounting for Variations in Academic Effectiveness Between Schools and Departments', paper presented at the ECER/BERA Annual Conference, Bath, Sept. 1995 (Institute of Education, University of London, London, 1995)

Sarason, S.B., *The Predictable Failure of Educational Reform: Can We Change Course Before It's Too Late?* (Jossey-Bass, San Francisco, 1990)

Satterthwaite (alias M. Barber), 'Head Aches', *Education*, 9 July 1993, p.36

Schama, S., *Citizens: Chronicle of the French Revolution*, (Penguin, London, 1990)

Secondary Heads Association, *SHA Survey of Intake Tests in Secondary Schools* (SHA, Leicester, 1996)

Taylor, A.J.P., *The Origins of the Second World War* (Penguin, London, 1961)

Taylor, C., *Raising Educational Standards* (CPS, London, 1990)

Index